To Kathleen.
Happy Christmas 1981.
Michael, Pat, Nicola & David.

PORTRAIT OF THE SHAKESPEARE COUNTRY

THE *PORTRAIT* SERIES

Portrait of the Broads
J. Wentworth Day
Portrait of the Burns Country
Hugh Douglas
Portrait of Cambridge
C. R. Benstead
Portrait of the Channel Islands
Raoul Lempriere
Portrait of the Chilterns
Annan Dickson
Portrait of the Clyde
Jack House
Portrait of Cornwall
Claude Berry
Portrait of the Cotswolds
Edith Brill
Portrait of Dartmoor
Vian Smith
Portrait of Devon
D. St. Leger-Gordon
Portrait of Dorset
Ralph Wightman
Portrait of County Durham
Peter A. White
Portrait of Edinburgh
Ian Nimmo
Portrait of Gloucestershire
T. A. Ryder
Portrait of the Highlands
W. Douglas Simpson
Portrait of the Isle of Man
E. H. Stenning
Portrait of the Isle of Wight
Lawrence Wilson
Portrait of the Isles of Scilly
Clive Mumford
Portrait of the Lakes
Norman Nicholson

Portrait of Lancashire
Jessica Lofthouse
Portrait of London River
Basil E. Cracknell
Portrait of the New Forest
Brian Vesey-Fitzgerald
Portrait of Northumberland
Nancy Ridley
Portrait of Peakland
Crichton Porteous
Portrait of the Pennines
Roger A. Redfern
Portrait of the Quantocks
Vincent Waite
Portrait of the Severn
J. H. B. Peel
Portrait of the Scott Country
Marion Lochhead
Portrait of the Shakespeare Country
J. C. Trewin
Portrait of the Shires
Bernard Newman
Portrait of Skye and the Outer Hebrides
W. Douglas Simpson
Portrait of Snowdonia
Cledwyn Hughes
Portrait of Somerset
Bryan Little
Portrait of Surrey
Basil E. Cracknell
Portrait of the Thames
J. H. B. Peel
Portrait of the Trent
Peter Lord
Portrait of the Wye Valley
H. L. V. Fletcher
Portrait of Yorkshire
Harry J. Scott

Portrait of
THE SHAKESPEARE COUNTRY

J. C. TREWIN

**ILLUSTRATED
AND WITH MAPS**

ROBERT HALE · LONDON

J. C. Trewin 1970
First published in Great Britain 1970

SBN 7091 1342 0

Robert Hale & Company
63 Old Brompton Road
London S.W.7

PRINTED IN GREAT BRITAIN
BY EBENEZER BAYLIS AND SON, LIMITED
THE TRINITY PRESS, WORCESTER, AND LONDON

CONTENTS

ILLUSTRATIONS

AUTHOR'S NOTE

Shaped roughly like a diamond, Warwickshire is England's central county. Stratford-upon-Avon, where William Shakespeare was born, is in the south-west, by the river that separates what used to be the woodland of Arden, to the north and west, from the smaller pastoral Feldon, William Camden's "plain champaign country . . . rich in corn and green grass", to south and east. The outer boundary of the Shakespeare Country, for the purpose of this book, runs clockwise through Kenilworth, where the castle is built in the red Keuper sandstone; Leamington, on an Avon tributary and very close to the hill-town of Warwick; the ridge of Edgehill, with the brown marlstones of the Middle Lias; the Rollright circle, just across the Oxfordshire border; Long Compton, in the extreme south of Warwickshire; Chipping Campden, which is Cotswold; Evesham, in the market-gardening valley of the Avon; Alcester, and Henley-in-Arden (the former forest lies upon the red soil of the Keuper marls).

The Rollright circle is 18 miles from Stratford; Evesham, 14 miles; Henley-in-Arden, 8; Kenilworth, 13½.

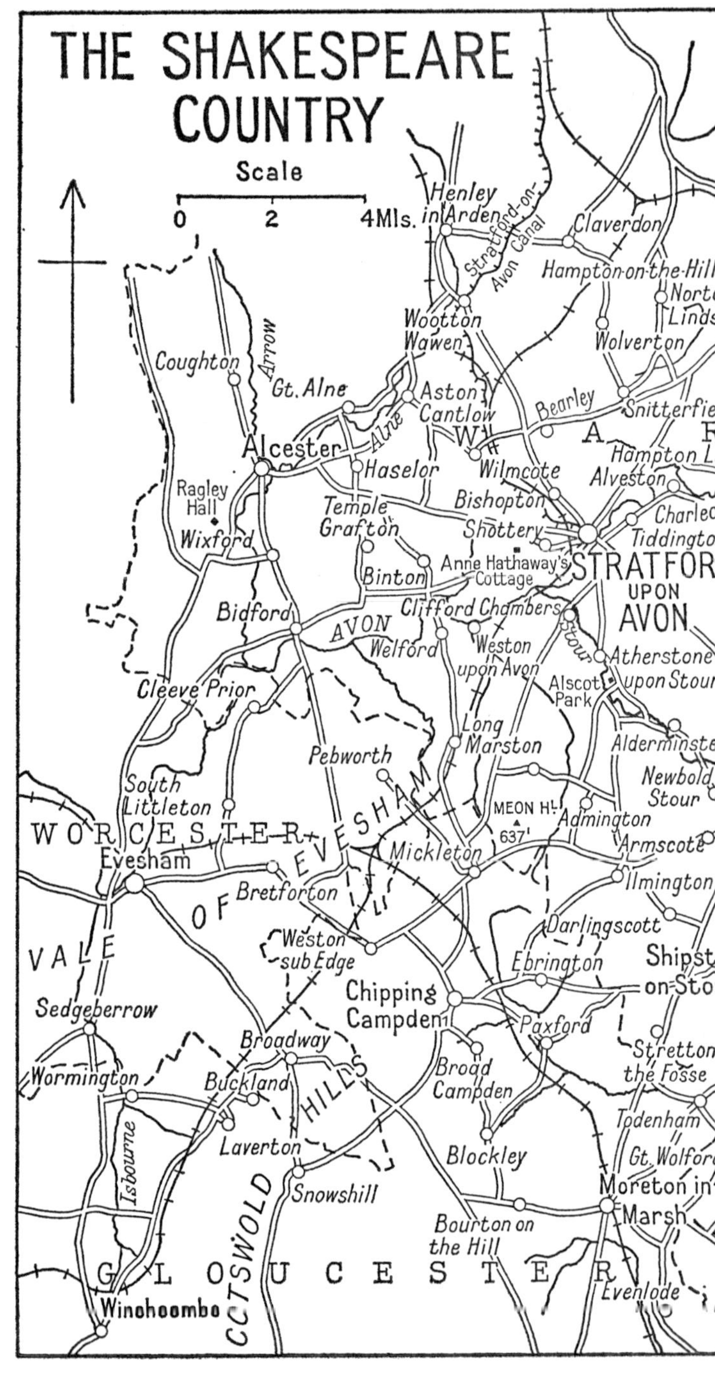

THE SHAKESPEARE COUNTRY
Scale
0   2   4 Mls.
Henley in Arden
Claverdon
Hampton-on-the-Hill
Nort
Linds
Wolverton
Stratford-on-Avon Canal
Wootton Wawen
Bearley
Snitterfie
WAR
Coughton
Gt. Alne
Aston Cantlow
Arrow
Alne
Hampton L.
Alveston
Alcester
Haselor
Wilmcote
Bishopton
Charlec
Shottery
Tiddingto
STRATFOR
UPON
AVON
Ragley Hall
Temple Grafton
Anne Hathaway's Cottage
Wixford
Binton
Clifford Chambers
Stour
Atherstone
upon Stour
Bidford
AVON
Welford
Weston upon Avon
Alscot Park
Cleeve Prior
Long Marston
Alderminste
Pebworth
Newbold Stour
South Littleton
MEON H!
637'
Admington
Armscote
WORCESTER
EVESHAM
Mickleton
Ilmington
Evesham
OF
Bretforton
Li
Darlingscott
VALE
Weston sub Edge
Ebrington
Shipst
on-Sto
Sedgeberrow
Chipping Campden
Paxford
Broadway
Stretton the Fosse
Wormington
Buckland
HILLS
Broad Campden
Isbourne
Laverton
Blockley
Todenham
Gt. Wolfor
Snowshill
Moreton in
Marsh
COTSWOLD
Bourton on the Hill
GLOUCESTER
Evenlode
Winchcombe

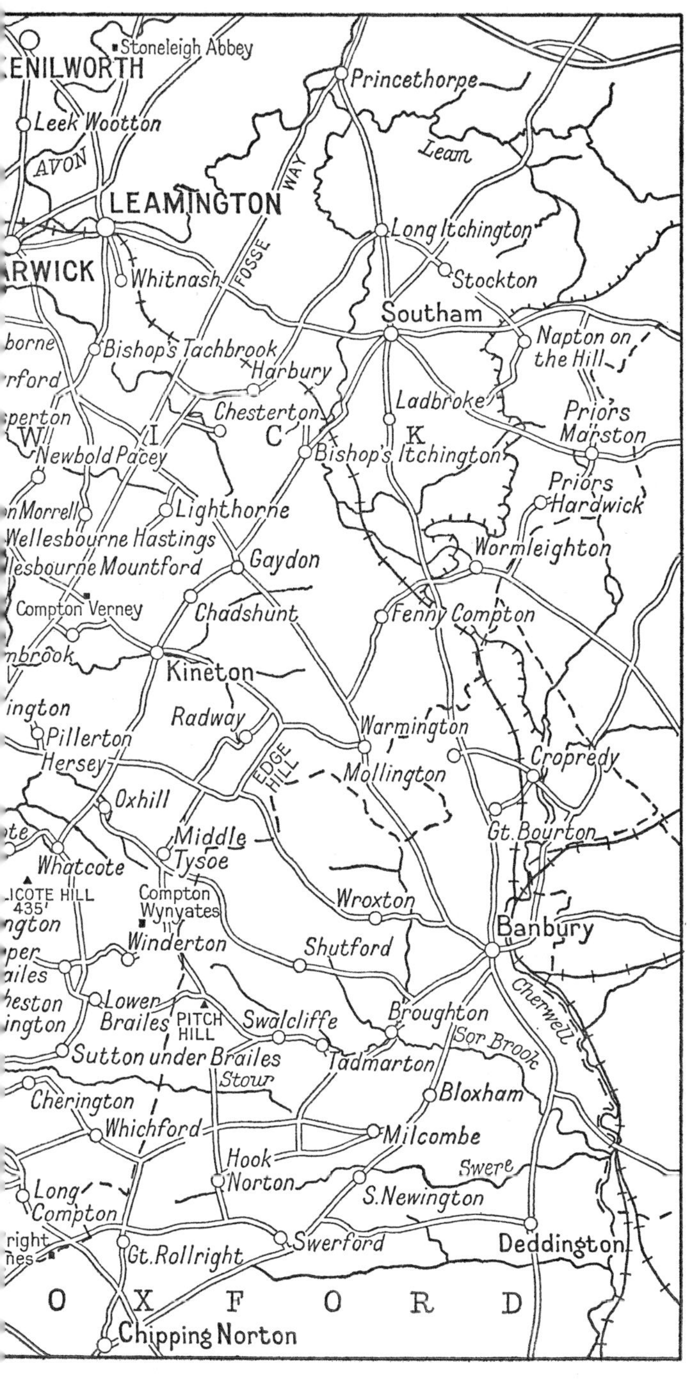

Stoneleigh Abbey
ENILWORTH
Leek Wootton
AVON
LEAMINGTON
Princethorpe
Leam
Long Itchington
ARWICK
Whitnash
FOSSE WAY
Stockton
Southam
borne
Bishop's Tachbrook
Napton on the Hill
rford
Harbury
Ladbroke
Priors Marston
perton
Chesterton
W
I
C
K
Newbold Pacey
Bishop's Itchington
Priors Hardwick
n Morrell
Lighthorne
Wellesbourne Hastings
Wormleighton
lesbourne Mountford
Gaydon
Compton Verney
Chadshunt
Fenny Compton
mbrook
Kineton
Radway
Warmington
ington
Cropredy
Pillerton Hersey
EDGE HILL
Mollington
Oxhill
Gt. Bourton
te
Middle Tysoe
Whatcote
ICOTE HILL
435'
Wroxton
Banbury
ngton
Compton Wynyates
per
Winderton
Shutford
ailes
Cherwell
heston
Lower Brailes
Broughton
ington
PITCH HILL
Swalcliffe
Sor Brook
Sutton under Brailes
Tadmarton
Stour
Cherington
Bloxham
Whichford
Milcombe
Hook Norton
Swere
Long Compton
S. Newington
right
Gt. Rollright
Swerford
Deddington
nes
O   X   F   O   R   D
Chipping Norton

For
WENDY
"Who ever loved that loved not at first sight?"

INTRODUCTION

This is a personal impression of the area, mostly in South Warwickshire, that we know as Shakespeare's country:

> A ripple of land . . .
> And open pastures, where you scarcely tell
> White daisies from white dew; at intervals
> The mythic oaks and elm-trees. . . .

Shakespeare's wider country is mapped in the plays. Because his theatre stands in Stratford-upon-Avon, I have discussed its record more amply than other writers have done. But I make no further claims: the book is an affectionate portrait, not a formal guide. After a chapter on the aspect of Shakespeare and his region, we begin in Stratford, move round the streets, remember Jubilee and Tercentenary, pause at the theatre, go out to the towns, wander among the villages east and west of Avon, and return—after edging three times across the county frontier—to the base which must always be Stratford and Shakespeare. If it were a play, it would be called an episodic sequence. Shakespeare heads the cast; and there are good parts as well for such people—unchronologically—as Richard Beauchamp, David Garrick, Frank Benson, Edward and Charles Flower, John Jordan, Samuel Phelps, Marie Corelli, John Coleman, the Hon. Mrs. Skewton, Richard Jago, Walter Scott, Prince Rupert, W. Bridges-Adams, and Mr. W. Field of Leamington, who is one of the historical commentators—with Leland and Camden and Celia Fiennes—and who, in the late Regency, could write in this way when he felt like it:

[*Garrick Jubilee*] A story which we ardently wish, for the credit of [Stratford], could be blotted out of the pages of its history. Where honour was sincerely and even devoutly intended, never surely was the memory of a sublime genius so dishonoured as by the low pageantry of that day! An exception may, indeed, be made in favour of the *Ode* of GARRICK which contains some fine passages; but the oration was hardly worth either the speaker or the subject. . . . And the rest of the whole train of ceremony was scarcely superior to the meanest pantomime that was ever exhibited in the most degenerate time of his own theatre! We tremble to hear the hint thrown out of another intended jubilee! He must be a bold man who hopes to succeed where GARRICK has failed!

It is lucky that Field is not here to pass judgment on a selective and discursive text. Though I have acknowledged special debts, the general reader will hardly need a bristle of references; as it is, an appendix lists many valuable books, Field's own included.

I am grateful to many people: in particular, to my publishers who have borne patiently with a teasing delay; to Herbert van Thal for his wise encouragement; to my friend across the years, J. H. B. Peel; to Ion and Simon Trewin, who were with me at Edgehill; to Denis Carey and Raymond Marriott, who were at the Rollright Stones; to Charles Landstone, who was at Brailes; to Mrs. D. L. Mackay and Mrs. Valerie Day for so closely transcribing my first manuscript; to Wendy, my wife, whose book this is, who has been everywhere, put up with much, and improved more; and, if I may, to the shade of William Shakespeare about whom Jago observes charmingly, "Ev'n Royalty, arrayed by thee, moves more majestic."

ONE

SEEKING THE FACE

I

He was "William Shakespeare of Stratford-upon-Avon in the county of Warwick, gentlemen". Today a man of the world, he still belongs to Stratford. Here, in the pastoral south-west of Warwickshire, he was born on presumably 23rd April 1564; he was baptised on 26th April, as the parish register proclaims: "Gulielmus filius Johannes Shakspere". In Elizabethan times the spelling of your name was at every man's mercy, and often you would use the form that occurred to you first. Stratford, a small and prosperous market-town, Camden's "proper little mercate town" (1586), built of brick and timber, with only a few major streets, lay remote among its water-meadows. Some 2,000 people lived in it; there are now nine times as many. Half a million more come annually for Shakespeare's sake, to the festival or to the town's "memorials and things of fame". Stratford is still among elms and willowed, rushy meadows; still within the smooth curve of the Avon reach; the central ground-plan of those "very lardge streets" (John Leland's term) little altered; its river spanned by the Clopton bridge of grey stone with fourteen of its arches visible—others have long been hidden on the town side—and under the last arch on the east the backward eddy Shakespeare put into his poem of *Lucrece*.

Inevitably, it must be Shakespeare-upon-Avon. On the Birthday—for in Stratford this word receives its capital letter—his lovers take their violets, lilies and daffodils (the hues of sovereignty), their rosemary and laurel, from the Henley Street house where he was born, to the riverside church where he and his children were christened. There in April 1616 "Will Shakspere, gent" was buried in the chancel. On the way is the site of his last house,

Those sparse and scattered stones where Shakespeare died
At New Place by the glimmer of the Gild . . .

and the surviving grammar school where he was educated: his youth and age within the shortest bowshot. This, with the region round it, is forever Shakespeare's country. His theatre rises massively a few hundred yards from the Great Garden of New Place, and in his work the man of "right happy and copious industry", Ben Jonson's star of poets, is immortal. Genius makes its own rules. Denial of Shakespeare's authorship has become a dull and complicated game with no genius at all behind it, merely a confusion of ciphers or an obstinate insistence—an example of man's delight in seeking a conspiracy where none exists. John Masefield said of Shakespeare: "Imagination, being much neglected in the modern world, is little understood." It is beyond pedantrics and sophistrics. We must regret that the odder forms of imagination have convened a dozen or so aristocratic pretenders (there are more than eighty candidates in all); the general epigraph might be Gilbert's "With all our faults, we love our House of Peers."

Even though he died at 52 and did most of his work in London —ninety-two miles separate the hurly of Bankside and the silence of the Warwickshire Bank Croft—a narrative of Stratford is overwhelmingly a narrative of Shakespeare. Earlier, certain events appear like isolated oaks. There was a Romano-British settlement at Tiddington, a little way above Clopton Bridge. A Roman road from Droitwich and Alcester forded the Avon near the present bridge; a monastery is said to have existed before the Conquest in what today is called Old Town; Domesday speaks of "Stradforde", a manor of the Bishop of Worcester, who had a river mill worth ten shillings yearly, or 1,000 eels. Set between the forest world of Arden and the undulating, spreading champaign and the sheep-walks of the open Feldon to the south-east, Stratford developed into a market town with some celebrated fairs and a good proportion of craftsmen; and with a wooden bridge, later called by Leland "a poore bridge of tymbar", across the broad, willowed stretch of the Avon. By the mid-fourteenth century, thanks to John de Stratforde, a townsman who became Archbishop of Canterbury, it had a college of priests to serve its church—named finely the Collegiate Church of the Holy Trinity.

In the previous century the Gild of the Holy Cross had been formed, and this Augustinian fraternity of brethren and sisters— an association, religious, social, and educational, for mutual benefit—more or less ruled the town until its dispersal by the Chantries Act in 1547. The Gild maintained the grammar school; it had splendid almshouses and its own chapel, the beautiful grey-towered building still in the midst of Stratford, with a fine-drawn look as if age were telling on it. Commissioners who inspected the property in the year the Gild was dissolved, noted that the chapel's central position was

> for the great quietness and comfort of all the parishioners there; for that the parish church standeth out of the same town, distant from the most part of the said parish half a mile and more; and in time of sickness, as the plague and such other diseases doth chance within the said town, then all such infective persons, with many other impotent and poor persons, doth to the said chapel resort for their daily service.

Stratford during 1553 came under the government of a Corporation: a bailiff, fourteen Aldermen and fourteen Burgesses, to whom the property of the Gild was assigned. The borough, as John Leland had considered it approvingly not long before, was "reasonably well buyldyd of tymbar", with a "fayre large" parish church, a "right goodly chappell in a faire street", and its important trade route, the bridge given at the end of the fifteenth century by Hugh Clopton, a Stratford man who had been Lord Mayor of London and who is buried in the City. Before this, when the river was high, many people refused to cross from the east bank by the bridge that was "smaule and ille".

William Shakespeare was born eleven years after the incorporation of Stratford. He was the eldest son (two previous children, daughters, had died in infancy) of John Shakespeare of Henley Street, a glover and curer of skins, and Mary Arden of Wilmcote, three miles to the north-west. Thence everything must fall to insignificance compared with the work and fame of the one townsman. There were such matters as a desolating plague in 1564, the year of William's birth; flood in 1588, Armada year; recurrent disastrous fires; the use of the neighbouring Clopton House as one of the rendezvous of the Gunpowder Plotters; Civil War alarms when Stratford was held once by the Royalists, twice by the Parliament, the town hall was blown up, and Shakespeare's daughter, Susanna (Hall), entertained Queen Henrietta Maria for three nights at New Place. Otherwise Stratford's history seems to have Shakespeare—whom we shall meet again—on every important page.

II

I think at the moment of his portrait. The face haunts Stratford-upon-Avon; we see it on bust, painting and statue; ash-tray, spoon, tobacco jar. We can buy it on the handle of a toasting-fork ("all that was ever writ in brass") or variously upon a score of resolute postcards. We meet it on an eighteenth-century *alto-relievo* in the Great Garden of New Place; here Shakespeare has the kindly but embarrassed look of a man who, during an after-noon's walk, is trapped between two importunate women, one called the Dramatic Muse, the other the Genius of Painting. He is found in the bezel of a signet-ring or else standing, with Comedy and Tragedy, ready to receive Garrick on a distant Parnassus. The actor, as George Carter painted him in 1784, is being propelled through the air in a winding-sheet by a detachment of bored angels. Shakespearean characters, to whom he waves amiably, seem to be as flummoxed as he is.

Shakespeare is recognizable by his domed forehead, curling locks, spreading lawn collar. He looks wise, mild, austere, moving, benevolent, excessively poetic, or just odd. The face is the brand-mark of an industry, and there are industries far less reasonable. Few places have had such a citizen as this: a New Englander once told Gladstone that even in Boston it would be hard to find "ten men the equal of Shakespeare". We can recreate him as we wish, unstarching the Droeshout print, animating the Janssen bust, ask-ing if this can really be the Shakespeare of the last years: the man idyllically in his orchard-close (pruning roses, eating pippins, says Sir Edmund Chambers), less idyllically (say the sceptics) at his desk with "rotten parchment-bonds", or, neutrally, walking up Chapel Street towards the Gild tower which must have been a silver-grey ghost, a mist in the twilight, from the time it was built. Though we have only a blurred idea of his aspect—for none would call Martin Droeshout or Gerard Janssen masters of their craft—we have as many ways of interpreting the clues as of spelling the name, or of seeking a new anagram from the chancel-epitaph that has delighted Baconians. My favourite is: "Francis Bacon wrote here. His cue. Aye aye. Shakespeare." There is also one that says "Chrystepher" Marlowe is buried here.

Most people in Stratford will fix upon three likenesses. The 'Flower' portrait in the theatre picture gallery, which used to be labelled as the Droeshout original, was based presumably on the print: X-ray examination has shown it to be painted over a fifteenth-century Virgin and Child and Saint John. Other Shakespeares, the idealized and the matter-of-fact, are the bust in Holy Trinity and the seated, plinth-raised statue that stares across the main road and the to-and-fro traffic round a ring road and over Clopton Bridge. Neither of these portraits, in limestone or in bronze, has more than a family resemblance to a small white bust on my mantelpiece, I suppose about sixty years old now and from a series once very popular. With its tightly symmetrical curls, broad collar, and expression more pensive than most, it is what a romantic collector would expect a poet to look like: the usual formula behind pretenders brought forward as true portraits.

Certainly I would rather have the face of the Shakespeare on Lord Ronald Gower's monument than that of the Janssen bust in Holy Trinity, even though Janssen's must be nearer to the truth: it was placed in the chancel six years after death, obviously with the agreement of Anne Shakespeare and the colleagues who had known her husband so long. Made of ash-coloured limestone, it occupies an arched recess upon the north wall. It is set between Corinthian columns of black touchstone and surmounted by a mantled shield with Shakespeare's arms; a pair of cherubs aloft represent Labour and Rest, the first with a spade, the other with a torch inverted. Shakespeare's beard, short, pointed, and crudely re-coloured in 1861, is auburn; so is the hair. The eyes are now time-darkened hazel, the doublet is scarlet beneath a sleeveless gown of black, and the hands, a quill in the right, a paper beneath the left, are supported by a cushion which is green above, crimson below, and tasselled and corded in gilt. Here, according to a Latin inscription, is the man who was "in judgment a Nestor, in intellect a Socrates, in art a Virgil: the earth covers him, the people mourn him, Olympus has him".

While agreeing that it looks better from a distance, seen di-agonally, this is to me the presentment of a puffy-faced burgher who gazes across the chancel with pained surprise: for some reason I think of the line, "the thick rotundity o' the world". Opinions on the work of Gerard (or Garrett) Janssen (or Johnson), a mason of Southwark, have clashed wildly. Thomas Gainsborough, the painter, said "A silly, smiling thing". Matthew Arnold said: "Thou smilest, and art still, Out-topping knowledge". W. H. Hutton held that though the full face was almost as heavy as Droeshout's engraving, a side view became "refined, intellectual, humorous". For Alfred Domett from New Zealand, Browning's 'Waring', who visited Stratford in July 1873, the face belonged to a man "with a sort of catching of the breath, going to burst into a roar of laughter". John Masefield, revising in 1963 a book he wrote in 1910, still saw the image of a man "with much vitality of mind . . . an alert and sunny man, energetic and effective". Christian Deelman, modern historian of Garrick's Jubilee, dismissed the bust as a "moon-faced ninny". M. H. Spielmann* rejected the notion of a death-mask. He suggested that "the curious, and at first sight, stupid aspect of the bust" was due to the eyes and nose which were too small for the face. Moreover, the "unskilful and vulgar brush" of the restorer had drawn and coloured the exaggerated pupils; and those "stupidly hard, coarsely-shaped, half-moon eyebrows, more George Robey's than anybody else's", had been accentuated and set too high on the frontal bone. Ivor Brown took it to be a heavy, dull presentment of a heavy, dull person, and "Shakespeare, whatever else he may have been, simply cannot have been heavy and dull." Dr. Dover Wilson thought that "all this might suit well enough with an affluent and retired pork butcher, but does gross wrong to the dead poet." Still, nobody has attempted to dash it to pieces. As the woman says in the Pinero farce: "It is an embarrassing thing to break a bust in the house of comparative strangers."

There, then, it is, the Bust: "repaired and beautified" in 1746 from the proceeds of a town hall performance of *Othello*—very good, on the whole, except for a poor Brabantio—painted white in 1793 at the plea of that dogmatist, the critic Edmond Malone, and tinted again, with too rough a flourish, by Simon Collins in 1861. The bust, in spite of some highly misleading pictures of it, rests as it has done for nearly three and a half centuries; Shakespeare must live for ever in its image and in that of the First

* "Shakespeare's Portraiture" in *Studies in the First Folio* (Oxford, 1924).

Folio's copper engraving of a man some twenty years younger.

Another Stratford portrait is better known than the Bust to casual visitors who do not reach the Church. It is the elaborate memorial by Lord Ronald Sutherland Gower that stands in the gardens near the approach to Clopton Bridge. It turns its back upon the river meadow (the Bancroft), the mass of the Royal Shakespeare Theatre beyond, and further back, round the river curve, the spire of Holy Trinity. Instead, the monument studies the traffic-battered roads—there is, I suppose, the excuse that Shakespeare went across Clopton Bridge to London—a coach and car park, an omnibus station, a snack bar and a screen of poplars. We can help if we wish by extending the range of vision north-westerly to Snitterfield four miles off, the upland village towards which the statue is turned. Shakespeare's father was brought up there, and the church door, for those given to calculations, is level with the top of St Mary's tower at Warwick. But Snitterfield from the Bancroft is for the eye of faith only. The monument was moved across the gardens during the spring of 1933 from a more retiring site and better view behind the round of the old theatre. It seems now to be established everlastingly. Shakespeare, with manuscript and quill, sits in his chair on a high circular plinth upon a pedestal. Round the pedestal are masks, emblems and trophies, with four life-size bronzes to represent philosophy, history, comedy and tragedy: Hamlet—"Prince Hamlet, green as a penny, heaved a bronze sigh," wrote the Cornish poet Charles Causley— Prince Hal with the crown, Falstaff and Lady Macbeth.

This is known to its friends as the Gower, just as the shorthand for the Shakespeare Jubilee of 1769 is the Garrick Jubilee. Few people today can identify Lord Ronald Sutherland Gower. Born in 1845, he was a generous, art-loving dilettante—and a worker as well—with a passion for Shakespeare. Entering the Commons almost direct from Cambridge, he sat for seven years as Liberal Member for Sutherland, then a family perquisite. After 1874 he spent much of his life as sculptor, writer and traveller. His Shakespeare monument took more than a decade to complete. Refusing an offer for it from America, he heard with relief in the autumn of 1887 that Stratford would accept his work as a gift for the new public gardens by the river. Early in the next year he altered his design. Originally, in conventional fashion, figures of Tragedy and Comedy were crowning a bust of the poet. Now all

of these were replaced by a seated figure of heroic size. At the end
of the summer the mass of statuary, sixty-five tons of it—the
bronzes had been modelled and cast in Paris—stood ready for un-
veiling "as a lasting tribute of solemn admiration and reverence".
On 10th October 1888 the Mayoress, Lady Hodgson, unveiled
the memorial on its retired riverside lawn; the Volunteer Band
played "Warwickshire Lads and Lasses"; a luncheon speech by
the journalist, George Augustus Sala—who had arrived that
morning in his "famous astrakhan-lined greatcoat"—rose to a
redoubtable peroration; and Oscar Wilde, who also spoke, called
the Memorial Theatre, with its plum-cake turrets and sham-
Gothic extravagances, "one of the loveliest buildings erected in
Britain for many years". At the ceremony he had read, without
irony, a sonnet by a Stratford poet which slightly over-dramatised
Lord Ronald's gentle Shakespeare:

> Aye so, methinks, by the red embers' glare,
>   Silent he sat, with eagle eyes astrain,
>   And saw the myriad children of his brain
> Take form and semblance on the midnight air.

Through forty-five years the Gower, behind the old sugar-
striped Memorial and staring downstream towards the church,
grew so surely into the riverscape that it was taken for granted.
Visitors liked to be photographed against it. One picture of a
group of straw-hatted actors, Bensonians, catches the tranquil
quality of Stratford at the turn of the century: a town that, without parade, lived quietly on Shakespeare and upon the family sense
of its brief yearly festival. It was already much changed when in
1933, twelve months after the opening of the great new theatre,
the council resolved to improve the main entrance to Stratford,
to move a scatter of sheds and skin-dealers' yards, to turn a dirty
canal basin to an ornamental water and to open up the Bancroft
meadow as a park. By then, as the theatre director, W. Bridges-
Adams, had written,

> Tarmac, chars-à-bancs, cash-registers, motor-boats oiling the face
> of the Avon . . . trippers chy-iking the actors from the opposite
> bank, Birmingham blokes with their girls riding pillion, visiting
> hordes from every quarter of the globe—all these were beginning
> to make that Yeoman-England Stratford . . . a thing of the past in
> 1919. The Petrol Age was taking charge of Stratford.

With the agreeable re-fashioning, as a conference hall, of the first theatre's burnt-out shell, the Gower had to be moved. The theatre governors gave it to the town; and the council committee turned Shakespeare's back upon the theatre. On the old site his back had been turned, but not at so great a distance and in so marked a manner. Drama critics, naturally cynical, at once saw the wrong reason for this. Then within a few months the Gower had settled, unaware of cynicism, into its new landscape; and today it is so obvious, so familiar, that like Chesterton's postman it can go unnoticed. The graceful figure, its eagle eyes not noticeably astrain, is an idealisation, and none the worse for that: John Aubrey might have called Lord Ronald's work "handsome, well-shap't", words to enrage Baconians and Oxonians who will allow no dignity to the "Stratford man". Lord Ronald knew also what he was doing with the young Hal raising the crown, Lady Macbeth wringing her hands and Hamlet with the skull. Only the Falstaff, fourth supporting figure, is too arch, though the sonneteer of 1888 had imagined him "trolling some roystering refrain"—I wish the sculptor had lived long enough to see a performance by Roy Byford, one of the few naturally zestful Falstaffs, who had no need to troll or royster self-consciously. As a whole, it is a gallant group. Shakespeare's face, said to owe something to both the Janssen bust and the swarthily romantic 'Chandos' portrait, is preferable to either. Admittedly there is the fear that at heart we want too mild a Shakespeare. Hugh Kingsmill may have been closer to the truth when, speaking through one of the characters in his novel, *The Return of William Shakespeare*, he wrote: "I saw a man who had suffered and fought, a man who had *wanted* things. . . . It was not, to be quite frank, quite as comfortable as *my* Shakespeare."

We cannot be dogmatic. To everyone his own Hamlet; to everyone his own Shakespeare, whether in mantelpiece bust, in solemn monument, or as something seen in the bowl of a souvenir spoon.

III

Everyone, too, has his personal idea of the region we call Shakespeare's Country. Few writers who describe a face in detail, pore by pore, help us as much as they imagine: it is conscientious but blurring. Granted one feature, one mannerism, we create the face, the person, for ourselves. Shakespeare describes nobody at length, yet all of us have our sovereign ideas of Hamlet, "that unmatch'd form and feature of blown youth"; Cassius, with the "lean and hungry look"; Aguecheek, whose hair "hangs like flax on a distaff"; Richard of Gloucester, "rudely stamp'd", "curtail'd of his fair proportion"; Rosalind, "more than common tall", probably a note on the original boy player.

So it must be with the face of a region. Bred on the tip of a southern Cornish peninsula, I find it hard even now to map in needle-point the coil of lanes and field-paths round the central moor, or the creeks of the estuary, oak-shelved and heron-haunted. It does not matter, for I know the spirit of the place, just how it differs from the rest of the county in its lonely pride. Similarly, I can think of Shakespeare's country without what Jonson called "numbering the streaks of the tulip"; simply indeed as I have thought of it since I first heard a play at Stratford-upon-Avon during the late Twenties—a night when a cinema, its walls alive with gondolas in moonlight, served as a temporary theatre. The play, alarmingly for a pilgrim, was by Sheridan; the remainder of the week, from *Hamlet* onwards, atoned. Stratford was already as crowded in the midsummer afternoons as the piazza of St. Mark; the Avon served as Grand Canal, even if the town's one active gondola, Miss Corelli's *Dream*, was no longer visible. Everything and everyone baked composedly in "fantastic summer's heat"; plum-coloured and cedar-red brick holding and storing the warmth; half-timbered houses, ancient or dubious, and most of them sturdily renovated, leaning cheerfully against each other; the wide Rother Market shimmering in heat-haze round its eccentric American Fountain; visitors elbowing through the Knott Garden of New Place, that set of flower-mosaics among the lavender and box, thyme and sweet marjoram.

In comparison, the country across the river, C. E. Montague's "quintessence of the contained and friendly English midland landscape", seemed to be a world as unassuming, as calm, and yet as welcoming as northernmost Venice after the central tumult. One draws one's own boundaries. Since those days the Shakespeare Country has meant for me the space enclosed by, say, Warwick and its "vast hereditary dwelling" (Henry James), the now tree-covered escarpment of Edgehill on the Oxfordshire border, the haunted shapes of the Rollright circle, the first rising of the Cotswolds, the towns of Evesham in Worcestershire and Alcester in Warwickshire. These are on the perimeter. What lies between appears in the mind to be fenced off as snugly as one of those deer-parks upon an Elizabethan map; "Now are we park'd and bounded in a pale." Within, it remains a summer day. There is no light on any horizon to show that the sea is near, for this is as far inland, midland, as we can get in Britain, indeed what James in 1877 called "the core and centre of the English world; midmost England; unmitigated England"; the omphalos, the central gold. If we like to consider the country in terms of Shakespeare's own portrait, then the Holy Trinity bust might stand for the town of Stratford, and the Gower Shakespeare for those serene pastures of the Avon valley and the Vale of the Red Horse. Though the industrial cities are so close, and out beyond the workshop of Birmingham stretches the Black Country that could have been christened by Professor Tolkien, Shakespeare's land has been for me a place of peace, tranquil, walled, protected; a land of grave content; not a hair dislodged, no topple of crags, or furious tangle of water, or trees stunted and wind-shorn.

We can forget the multiplying traffic on the roads, the sounds in the sky. The Cornish writer, Anne Treneer, who loved Warwickshire, spoke of "low pleached hedges over which the eye swings to so wide a horizon that the sky is a fitted dome". The central plain, gently undulating, can keep that seventeenth-century composure: "The Meadowing Pastures therein [lie] with their green Mantle, one so embroidered with Flowers, that from Edge Hill we may see it as a Garden of God." Somewhere across it glint the rivers, say the Warwickshire Avon and its tributary, the Stour. The note is English plain-song. Though I can quarrel with Mr Peter Hall's film of *A Midsummer Night's Dream*, I have no quarrel whatever with its setting which turns Athens, most properly, to the Shakespearean Athens-by-Arden and puts the entire fantasy within the park, by the lake, and along the woodland rides of Compton Verney: the kind of scene that in its glistening tranquillity is almost classically Middle English.

Ronald Gower used various symbols on his monument: poppies and peonies (sleep and blood) for Lady Macbeth, ivy and cypress for Hamlet, English roses and French lilies for Hal, grapes and hops for Falstaff. For some of us the symbols of Shakespeare's Country are an elm tree in a pasture—though Arden was once dense with oak—a wall of rose-brick, pollarded willows by the river, a hedge sharp with hawthorn. The elm, 'Warwickshire weed', governs the region; but I think yet of an oak, spreading upon a smooth hillock that Bridges-Adams took as background for the *Love's Labour's Lost* of 1934 in what was then the Shakespeare Memorial Theatre. The scene was a park in Navarre. The picture that night was of "unmitigated England", and it was right to see it at the heart of heart, the very core of the gold, in the town of Stratford-upon-Avon.

Stratford is among the only four major towns in Shakespeare's country; the others are Evesham in its vale and those unexpected neighbours, baronial Warwick and decorous Leamington. We can remember Simon de Montfort in Evesham, Richard Beauchamp at Warwick; but Shakespeare's country, plain, river-vales, boundary hills, "eternal stretched velvet" (James again), water-music and formalised tapestry, church and castle and manor and cottage, belongs in spirit to that one man, "Gulielmus filius Johannes Shakspere". Its salient feature is Stratford itself, where, within half a mile, we have the man's presumed birthplace, the house of his last prosperity, his school, the church where he was buried and the great theatre where today his works are preserved in near-permanent festival: Shakespeare's country of the mind. His country can be Snitterfield, which I remember always in lemon sunlight under a pale arch of February sky, or his mother's Wilmcote, or Barton-on-the-Heath. ("Am I not Christopher Sly, old Sly's son of Burton-heath?") It is also the platform at Elsinore, the sea-coast of Bohemia, the Illyrian shore and the enigma of Prospero's island. For all the multitudes in High Street and Henley Street, there are times when, beyond Stratford, the Shakespeare country rests like Alonso's daughter, Claribel of Tunis, "ten leagues beyond man's life".

TWO

UP TO THE BIRTHPLACE

I

The man who rules it must be quickly established: William Shakespeare, who was half an Arden and no uncouth peasant, though the disbelievers wish to equate him with William in *As You Like It*. I used to hear an Oxfordian, who was an expert speaker, raise gales of laughter from an audience (most of which had not the slightest idea what it was all about) by imitating a complacent Touchstone and a rustic William:

> "For all your writers do contend that ipse
> is he; now, you are not ipse, for I am he."
> "Which he, sir?"

and so on.

William Shakespeare was bred in the bustle of a Midland market-town between coppice and pasture, and by the banks of a river that, however silver-slow, could still rise into dangerous flood covering the pale willows and the riparian meadow-land. We have an idea of his aspect, whether we prefer to romanticize it or to take the plain statement of the Bust. We have his work, pavilioned in splendour. His father, presumably born at Snitter-field, to the north-west, by the upland famed for flowers, oaks, and nightingales, was John Shakespeare, a farmer's son who be-came a glover and whittawer (a curer of skins) as well as other things, and who on documents made his mark in the form of a delicate pair of glover's dividers—not necessarily because he could not write. His wife, of a very old line with an evocative name, was Mary Arden, from a family of small landowners at Wilmcote three miles from Stratford, where we can see the comfortably imposing, dormer-windowed, oak-framed farmhouse which used to be described as a cottage, probably because in an urban

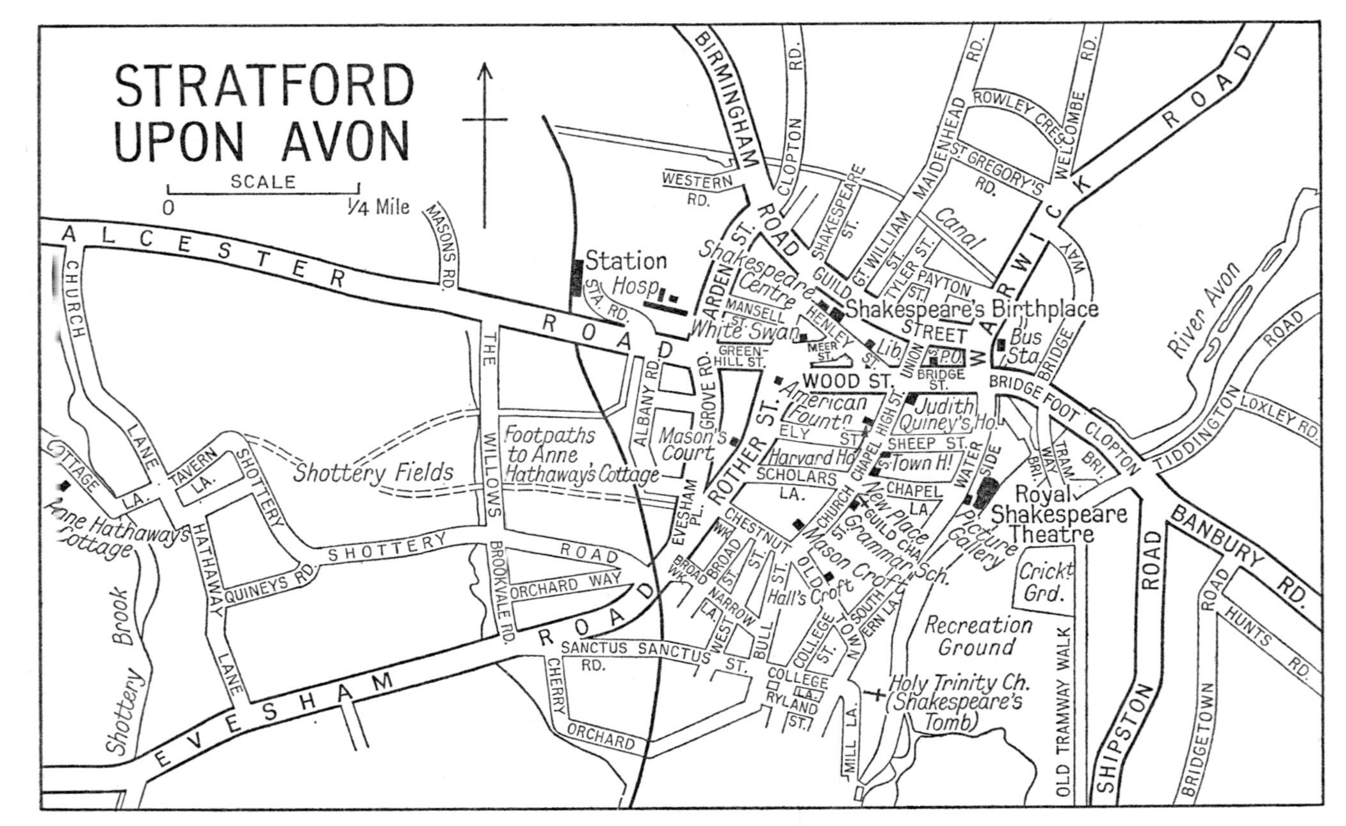

STRATFORD UPON AVON
SCALE
0   ¼ Mile
ALCESTER ROAD
MASONS RD.
CHURCH LANE
EVESHAM ROAD
Shottery Brook
Anne Hathaway's Cottage
COTTAGE LA.
TAVERN LA.
SHOTTERY LA.
HATHAWAY LANE
QUINEYS RD.
SHOTTERY ROAD
Shottery Fields
THE WILLOWS
Footpaths to Anne Hathaway's Cottage
BROOKVALE RD.
ORCHARD WAY
ORCHARD
CHERRY ORCHARD
SANCTUS RD.
SANCTUS RD.
Station Hosp.
STA. RD.
WESTERN RD.
BIRMINGHAM ROAD
CLOPTON RD.
SHAKESPEARE ST.
GT. WILLIAM ST.
TYLER ST.
PAYTON ST.
MAIDENHEAD RD.
ST. GREGORY'S RD.
ROWLEY CRES.
WELCOMBE RD.
WARWICK ROAD
Canal
Shakespeare Centre
ARDEN ST.
GUILD ST.
HENLEY ST.
MANSELL ST.
White Swan
MEER ST.
GREEN HILL ST.
Shakespeare's Birthplace
STREET
Lib.
UNION
P.O.
BRIDGE ST.
Bus Sta.
WOOD ST.
ALBANY RD.
GROVE RD.
EVESHAM PL.
Mason's Court
ROTHER ST.
American Fount'n
ELY ST.
Harvard Ho.
SCHOLARS LA.
CHESTNUT WK.
BROAD WK.
BROAD ST.
NARROW LA.
WEST ST.
BULL ST.
Hall's Croft
HIGH ST.
CHAPEL ST.
Judith Quiney's Ho.
SHEEP ST.
Town H'l
Mason Croft
CHURCH ST.
Grammar Sch.
New Place
Guild Chapel
CHAPEL LA.
OLD ST.
SOUTH ST.
FERN LA.
COLLEGE LA.
COLLEGE ST.
RYLAND ST.
MILL LA.
WATER SIDE
Picture Gallery
Royal Shakespeare Theatre
BRIDGE FOOT
CLOPTON BRI.
TRAM WAY BRI.
Recreation Ground
Holy Trinity Ch. (Shakespeare's Tomb)
Cricket Grd.
OLD TRAMWAY WALK
River Avon
BRIDGE WAY
TIDDINGTON ROAD
LOXLEY RD.
BANBURY RD.
SHIPSTON ROAD
HUNTS RD.
BRIDGETOWN

imagination the country meant a cot beside the hill, a beehive's hum and the short and simple annals of the poor. Mary was the youngest of eight daughters of the landlord of John Shakespeare's father at Snitterfield. In time the yeoman and the "daughter and heir of Arden, a gentleman of worship", had also eight children, William the third of them, the first son and the eldest surviving child. John Shakespeare held various important offices, ultimately High Bailiff, in the borough among the orchards and ubiquitous elms; "Thou art an elm, my husband," says Adriana of Ephesus in *The Comedy of Errors*. Later, though it seems that Stratford generally respected John, he was involved through a long period of adversity in various troubles, principally financial, but also apparently religious. He was a recusant—that is, he did not attend Church services—but his particular shade of allegiance we can only guess. His star rose again, probably because William, growing in repute, was ready to help; and in 1599, two years before his death, John received a grant of arms, drafted three years earlier and described technically as:

> Gold, on a bend sable, a spear of the first, steeled argent. And for his crest or cognizance, a falcon, his wings displayed, argent, standing on a wreath of his colours; supporting a spear gold steeled as aforesaid, set upon a helmet with mantels and tassels.

This blazon, "at all times and places convenient", John Shakespeare and his posterity could bear upon their shields, targets, escutcheons, coat of arms, pennons, guidons, seals, rings, edifices, buildings, utensils, liveries, tombs or monuments. The motto was *"Non sanz droict"*, twice altered on the draft because a comma crept into it (*"Non, sanz droict"*) and was repeated when the phrase was tried with initial capitals. At that stage, as C.W. Scott-Giles has said*, someone seized a pen and printed firmly at the head of the document, *NON SANZ DROICT*.

William, we assume, had been educated in the massive-timbered upper room of the free school at Stratford, known today as King Edward VI Grammar School. The school, by the Gild Chapel, was above the Gildhall, where strolling players would act from time to time and where John Shakespeare, as High Bailiff, entertained them in 1569. The boy would hardly have been there, though he must have gone later, for twenty-three

* *Shakespeare's Heraldry* by C. W. Scott-Giles (Dent, 1950).

visiting troupes came to town between 1573 and 1587; in the last year there were five. There was no reason to doubt the general scope of his education, whatever Ben Jonson, writing from a scholar's height, had to say about his classics; the grammar school was highly reputable. William married in 1582 Anne Hathaway, of Shottery, also from a substantial 'cottage'; she was his elder by eight years, and there is some mystery about their marriage. However, within three years they had three children, Susanna the eldest and then twins called Hamnet and Judith. William is presumed to have left for London during the mid 1580s. With an increasing family, and life in Stratford precarious, London must have seemed the obvious place for a young man in want of fortune. Why live "dully sluggardized" at home? The tradition that he fled after a deer-poaching affray at Sir Thomas Lucy's Charlecote has been much blown upon, but it is a useful passage in the Shakespeare romance which likes every action to be trimmed as handsomely as possible.

A period ensued as mysterious as the 'coal-sack' in the Milky Way and much dredged by the speculative. They have suggested that he was a schoolmaster; maybe it is as reasonable as anything to imagine him transiently an assistant usher at the grammar school. It is held also that he might have gone early as page to a noble family in the neighbourhood; that he had elementary legal experience; that he went to sea (one writer asserts blissfully that he ran away at the age of 13, circumnavigating the world in the *Golden Hind*); and, perhaps inevitably, that he was a soldier. Duff Cooper begins a charming book, *Sergeant Shakespeare*, by suggesting that Shakespeare had served in the Low Countries and had been promoted to non-commissioned rank. Theorist after theorist has been as circumstantial as Sheridan's Crabtree with his tale of a ball that struck against a little bronze Shakespeare, grazed from the window at right angles, and wounded the postman who was coming to the door with a double letter from Northampton-shire; a nice omnibus phrase for the more resolute speculations. All of this derives from the fallacy that an imaginative writer cannot write of anything he has not experienced himself. Shakespeare might have held horses' heads outside a play-house. He might have gone abroad in a touring company. We know, any-way, that he became famous as a man of the theatre, though not particularly as an actor—Solinus, the Duke of Venice, the Ghost of Hamlet's Father and Adam have been tentatively proposed for him—that he lost a son (Hamnet in 1596), made a fortune, bought the big house of New Place at Stratford, owned land near the town, was a major figure of the early Jacobean stage and retired to New Place about 1611. His father had died ten years earlier, his mother in 1608. Browning's Bishop Blougram summarises:

> He leaves his towers and gorgeous palaces
> To build the trimmest house in Stratford town;
> Saves money, spends it, owns the worth of things,
> Giulio Romano's pictures, Dowland's lute;
> Enjoys a show, respects the puppets too.

At New Place he died on 23rd April 1616, supposedly his fifty-second birthday and certainly St. George's Day. A simpler poet than Browning has written simply:

> On an April night in Stratford, when the air was
>   warm with spring,
> There died a weary singer with no more songs to sing,
> And on an April morning they bore him down the nave
> Of the mother church of Stratford to a Stratford
>   townsman's grave.

He was buried, "Will Shakespeare, gent.", not without right, seventeen feet deep within the sanctuary of the great, light-filled chancel of Holy Trinity, a privilege due to him because, as owner of a moiety of the tithes of Stratford (with Old Stratford, Welcombe and Bishopton), he was in fact a lay rector. Upon the tombstone a doggerel rhyme which it would be pleasant not to attribute to him, placed a curse on those who would disturb his bones. Presently the Bust was brought to the north wall. Anne Shakespeare's tombstone lies immediately beneath it in the sanctuary, next to her husband's. She died in 1623, the year of the publication of the First Folio, amaranth of immortality, even though an artisan, after hearing Dr. John Dover Wilson lecture at Stratford during the First World War, said, "We don't think nawt to Shakespeare here. He's a middle-class superstition."

II

True, there are no explicit references to Stratford-upon-Avon in the plays: obviously, say the iconoclasts, a sound reason why Shakespeare was somebody else. If he were really the dramatist, he would have salted the text with local allusions and included a relevant cipher, wrapping his plays carefully round it and appearing, no doubt, as an angry ghost to the not very good printers of the First Folio. As it is, we have to make our cheer with plausible supposition. Nothing could less persuade the unorthodox who will not believe that Warwickshire shines and flows and sings and trembles throughout the Folio, and who are perfectly sure that Bacon or Oxford was responsible for striking clocks in Rome and for the sea-coast of Bohemia. They insist on the name of Stratford, and they do not find it, merely Stony Stratford where the young Prince of Wales lay overnight.

Still, a master of the possible allusion, that learned antiquary, the Rev. Edgar Fripp, deduced that Shakespeare knew the fishing-ground below the mill, beyond Holy Trinity Church, because of the imagery of a passage in *Macbeth* ("if it were done, when 'tis done") that presents a fisherman handling rod and "trammel" on the shallow, sloping edge of a deep pool. The smith in *King John*, who stands with his hammer while his iron cools, listening to a tailor's tidings, is probably Richard Hornby, of Henley Street, listening to William Wedgewood, the tailor who lived beside the Shakespeares. Hornby's forge and smithy came next. The not especially relevant reference to building operations in *Henry the Fourth, Part Two* ("When we mean to build, we first survey the house, then draw the model") derives from Shakespeare's recent purchase and refurbishing of the decaying New Place, where probably he wrote the chronicle. Various bells are severally identified as Stratford bells. The pinfold, or pound, in Tinkers' Lane—or Scholars Lane now, at the intersection of Chapel and Church Streets—may have prompted some of Speed's glum backchat in *The Two Gentlemen of Verona*. Apparently, too, when Celia is explaining to Oliver in *As You Like It* how to reach the cottage in the forest, Shakespeare is giving a direction to Hew-lands Farm (Anne Hathaway's) from Stratford:

> West of this place, down in the neighbour bottom—
> The rank of osiers by the murmuring stream
> Left on your right hand, brings you to the place.

All of this is part of the grand Shakespeare mosaic. Most of us

Stratford-upon-Avon: the Collegiate Church of the Holy Trinity

RONALD GOWER
TO
STRATFORD-UPON-AVON
THIS MONUMENT
WAS REMOVED FROM THE
MEMORIAL THEATRE GARDENS
TO THIS SITE IN THE YEAR
1933
PRINCE HAL.

accept so readily that Constance's profoundly poignant sorrow for Arthur is a reflection of the death of Shakespeare's 11-year-old son Hamnet; or that Holofernes in *Love's Labour's Lost* stands (why not?) for a local schoolmaster, the Lancastrian Alexander Aspinall, that we should be prepared to take a few more suppositions without strain. Certainly it is pleasant to find that both Fluellen and Bardolfe were Stratford names.

III

An overwhelming number of visitors come to Stratford for Shakespeare's sake, not always with much knowledge of "the middle-class superstition", but because the man belongs to the English fabric as much as William the Conqueror, Good Queen Bess, or Sir Winston Churchill, and it is a self-conscious joke, rather like brawling in church, to call him 'Bill' or 'Willie', or to say that, of course, he was ruined for one at school. (What was ruined? Usually *The Merchant of Venice, As You Like It,* or *Julius Caesar,* with that good bit where Caesar enters in his nightgown.) Persuaded Shakespeareans, usually bred on the plays in performance—which is the best way to study them—go to Stratford as the pilgrims of St. Francis to Assisi. There is also another kind of visitor. On a week-end afternoon in summer I suspect that most people upon the Bancroft Meadow have run over from Birmingham or Coventry for a few hours by the river, mild and swan-feathered, and have no interest whatever in the other Swan and in what I heard a schoolgirl call that big red cinema at the end of the town. Stratford is a congenial, if business-like place, easy to wander about in once you have established that it is a small gridiron of streets practically unchanged in form across the centuries. These streets run roughly either north and south or east and west: some parallel to the river, others crossing them at right angles. The road immediately next to the Bancroft, to the gardens beyond the theatre, or to the river, runs between the bottom of Bridge Street and the almost monastic calm of Old Town. In its first part it is named Waterside and takes in several old brick cottages; later, curving between the walls of Southern Lane, it ends near the Church. The second horizontal, beginning at the top of Bridge Street, also ends in Old Town after changing its name three times on the way: first High Street, it enters Chapel

3

Lord Ronald Sutherland Gower's Shakespeare Monument, Stratford-upon-Avon

Street and then Church Street. This is Stratford's processional route. Along it are Harvard House, the town hall, the site of New Place, the beautiful etiolated tower of the Gild Chapel, the Grammar School and the almshouses. The last, most westward, and least important of the three horizontals, runs from, roughly, the American Fountain in Rother Street (or Rother Market) out to the western fringe of the Old Town area. The verticals on the grid are Bridge Street with Wood Street and, at a tangent, Henley Street; Sheep Street, which runs up from Waterside and is continued by Ely (once Swine) Street; and, finally, Chapel Lane beside the garden of New Place and continued westward by Scholars (formerly Tinkers') Lane.

This compact borough, as John Leland put it in the mid-fifteenth century, is set "apin a playne ground on the right-hand or ripe of Avon, as the watar descendithe". Clopton Bridge, sweeping across from the east or left bank, is still "sumptuus"— it was enlarged in 1814—though you can admire the grace of its arches better from a discreet distance than when you are crossing upon its pedestrian footpath, with a bluster of traffic Hugh Clopton never contemplated, clanging by like a race of bulls in an armoury.

Clopton is a Stratford name so revered that there must have been head-shaking when old John Coleman, buckram-bound actor, thundered through his memoirs early this century. He insisted on talking of Clopton House, which he visited during his ludicrous festival *Pericles* in 1900, as Hopperton Hall, making it sound like something from *Jorrocks:* "I was due on Sunday to lunch at Hopperton Hall with the Hodgsons. . . . Sir Frederick ceded us the Hopperton pew in Shakespeare's Church." Clopton House, with its Gunpowder Plot associations—it was leased by Ambrose Rookwood, one of the conspirators—is about a mile and a half to the north of Stratford, off the Birmingham Road. Traces of the family, which died out during the eighteenth century, are visible throughout the town. Hugh Clopton, bachelor, prosperous mercer and Lord Mayor of London in 1491, paid for the bridge's precisely-pitched arches, for the powder-grey miracle of the Gild Chapel, and for New Place, which one day became Shakespeare's at a cost of sixty pounds, not the bargain it may appear in modern value. No man could have done more than that. In Holy Trinity we find the Clopton Chapel, where various members of the family lie cut in alabaster, also the cenotaph of Hugh, the "charitable Gent.", who was buried in St. Margaret's, Lothbury. There is a Clopton claimant to Ophelia's drowning; but it is probable that Shakespeare, if he were thinking of anyone at all except Ophelia, remembered the drowning of "Katharine Hamlett, spinster"—the nominal echo is fortuitous—in the Avon at Tiddington on a December day when she was 16 and he was 15. At the inquest it was decided that Katharine did not take her life wilfully, but that "going with a milk-pail to draw water at the river, standing on the bank [she] slipped and fell in, and was drowned".

It does not do to pause upon the edge of Clopton with too many memories and a fleet of articulated lorries. For a reflective walk the Tramway Bridge is more profitable, a mild red-brick affair a little distance downstream, a footbridge now, but built in 1823 to serve a horse tramway that first ran out to Moreton-in-Marsh, and then on a branch line (1836) to Shipston-on-Stour. Collectors can see by the town approach to the bridge one of the original wagons, a rustic wooden cart with flanged wheels, set on a length of the cast-iron, fish-bellied rail used on the original permanent way of 4 ft 8½ ins. (The rails were taken up in 1916 during the First World War.) Probably—for even the head of the Gower Shakespeare is turned from it—this is Stratford's least-remarked site, something for a conference of industrial archaeologists. There were once wharves quite close, over by the Swan's Nest Hotel (which has been an inn for three centuries and during recent festivals has often housed a brood of drama critics). For about 200 years after 1672 the Avon was navigable from its mouth, and vessels of some thirty tons burthen could use it; in eighteenth-century prints the port of Stratford can look surprisingly active.

Today, standing at the Tramway's northern parapet, you can view in comfort most of the grey thrust of Clopton and its wallflower-starred arches. It is best to go up to the bank by the 'Swan's Nest' to peer more closely at the arch upon the eastern side: home of the eddy, caused by the current turning back on itself, that the Shakespearean scholar, Caroline Spurgeon, observed and drew in 1934. When Captain Jaggard, the bookseller of Sheep Street, described it to her, it reminded her at once of the tale of Collatine's grief in the poem of *The Rape of Lucrece*:

> As through an arch the violent roaring tide
> Outruns the eye that doth behold his haste,
> Yet in the eddy boundeth in his pride
> Back to the strait that forced him on so fast,
> In rage sent out, recall'd in rage, being past:
>> Even so his sighs, his sorrows, make a saw,
>> To push grief on, and back the same grief draw.

It has been said unkindly that the "roaring tide" sounds more like the tumult beneath old London Bridge; but I prefer to leave Miss Spurgeon her eddy. The Avon has had its terrors, as in the boisterous Armada summer of 1588 when the river rose "higher than ever yt was knowne by a yeard and a halfe, and something more": three men were trapped on the submerging bridge, unable to get either forward or back. It may be easier to think, as Nathaniel Hawthorne wrote in his notebooks (1855), "It is very lazy . . . and it loiters past Stratford Church as if it had been considering which way to flow, ever since Shakespeare used to paddle in it." Yet we can take the poet's word: "The current, that with gentle murmur glides, Thou know'st, being stopped, impetuously doth rage." Miss Spurgeon calculated that of fifty-nine river images in Shakespeare, twenty-six are of different aspects of a flooding river; eight are of the river overflowing its banks, eleven are of the impetus, force and overbearing nature of a raging flood.

The downstream parapet of the Tramway Bridge is the place for a sovereign view of what is now the Royal Shakespeare Theatre; the Prince of Wales flew down to open it in 1932 on a gusty Birthday afternoon. In any fine night of summer the building, its windows lit, seems to be floating like a liner upon the Avon; the moon rests, a silver plate, on the river bed. You can hear old Stratfordians speak of it still as the "new theatre", though it is a good forty years after the fuss over the design. Its architect, Elisabeth Scott, planned it for white concrete. The assessors thought brick would tone better with the town. The bricks had first to mellow, and undoubtedly they were a too resolute red when the theatre was opened to a blaze of criticism— "The crudest villa bricks which have not had time to weather;" "Why not white marble?"; "A jam factory" (as though this kind of factory was peculiarly shocking), and so on into the night.

Admirers were equally warm: Sir John Squire, at the opening, praised in *The Architectural Review* "one of the finest brick walls ever built". Lately Professor Pevsner agreed* that at the time the theatre, though highly dated now, was "a radical statement in England, very remarkable in a place of such strong and live traditions". He added: "Modern-minded members of the Design and Industries Association from Birmingham showed it proudly to Gropius one day in 1934 or 1935, and it was embarrassing to see his embarrassment." At this remove we can bear the thought equally. The Royal Shakespeare has merged almost entirely with Stratford—"aged well", says Professor Pevsner. Nobody, I think, would accuse it of bullying its way into the scene; the swans of Avon float by it as contentedly as their forbears passed the other towered and gabled structure, which had a life of only forty-seven years, or the wooden Rotunda on what was then called Banstead Mead. David Garrick recited his "Ode" there on a wet morning in 1769, and masqueraders circulated in the dance on a drenching night when the Avon was up—flooding as remorse-lessly as it had done in the sixteenth century when Clopton was new, or, earlier, the wooden bridge had swayed and tossed in those teeming waters.

IV

Beyond Clopton and its early nineteenth-century toll-house like a small tower, beyond the placid Shakespeare on the left and the menace of omnibus station and traffic-coiling ring road on the right, a slope declines from the original causeway to the foot of Bridge Street and then rises up a wide expanse to one of the most commandingly and theatrically judged bank buildings in the country, formerly a market hall (1821), now Barclay's with its white cupola, dead centre of the stage. It is near the site of the fourteenth-century High Cross and of the Market House that was once mid-Stratford: a structure of timber and plaster, supported by four oaken pillars and crowned by a clock turret—a clock with a single hand. Here, besides the tradesmen's stalls (and John Shakespeare, glover, would have been a principal), were such social amenities as pillory and whipping-post. "I had as lief be

* *Warwickshire* (in The Buildings of England) by Nikolaus Pevsner and Alexandra Wedgwood (Penguin 1966).

whipped at the High Cross every morning," says Gremio in *The Taming of the Shrew*, considering a husband for Katharina. The base of the original cross is in the garden behind the Birth-place in Henley Street.

In Bridge Street every 23rd April the international flags are unfurled—a ritual, patiently organised, which used to be at noon. Now it follows the Birthday luncheon. Though, since 1908, it has been a discredited legend that the flags must mean rain as surely as *Macbeth* must mean disaster, we know that any superstition develops with time, unchecked. True, there is something in the *Macbeth* legend (Stratford gasps yet over Diana Wynyard's crash from the stair during the sleepwalking in 1949.) As for the flags, let me say simply that on the Birthday, wet or fine, white poles in triple rank stand along Bridge Street; others go into annexes in Henley Street or on Waterside. At the hour and signal, the Mayor, at the head of Bridge Street, releases the Union flag, and presently the others (135 on the Birthday of 1969) flare out down the slope in cheerful peacockery, a rush of colour to the head. Ideally, an envoy from each nation is there for the flag. When this is impossible, deputies must be cast on the spot; even stray drama critics have been mobilized in goodwill to all.

Though Bridge Street, without its poles, is not urgently exciting, a medley of Victorian and modern-functional, it is at least wide and airy, and its slope a useful piece of natural scenic design. I like it best at night. You notice a spell-stopped quiet if you slip across the Bancroft lawn during a theatre interval and find your-self looking up that twilit slope, as if it were a broader Coinage Hall Street at Helston, an occasional window glowing and only a few people about: the day's end in a small market town of a farming country. That is eternal Stratford, though Shakespeare hangs round it like a giant's cloak. There is matter for the imagi-native who can summon the then tripartite street as it was in the ebb of the sixteenth century, approached from the "causey" that led to the town from Clopton Bridge across marshy fields, with the Butt Close—where the citizens practised archery—on the left, and a view unimpeded beyond the common pasture of the Bancroft meadow to Holy Trinity tower. At the foot of Bridge Street the lane which is now Waterside ran southward into Bancroft Side. Crossing the Mere at the end of its meander into the Avon from Walkers (Chapel) Lane, the road joined the

Churchway at the entrance to Holy Trinity: "everyone," says Puck, "lets forth his sprite in the churchway paths to glide." Bridge Street itself, guarded by two inns, Thomas Barber's 'Bear' (which in 1595 employed fourteen persons) and 'The Swan', was split into three, a central range, Middle Row, occupied largely by butchers, beer-sellers, glovers and whittawers. On the left was Fore Bridge Street, on the right the narrower Back Bridge Street. Halfway up the first of these was 'The Crown', which during the Commonwealth became tactfully 'The Woolsack'. Modern Bridge Street belongs in season to the visitors; and if Shakespeare does not wildly interest them, they can get at once, without going much further, all they need to remind them of Stratford. I suppose the temporary resident most renowned is the essayist, Washington Irving, fore-spurrer of so many Americans. He stayed during 1815 in the Red Horse Hotel on the right going up—for a time in recent years it was named after him—and his Stratford essay is customarily quoted with reverence.

Published at length in *The Sketch Book*, it became celebrated, among other reasons, because Irving, who could be amiably sentimental, had claimed a small parlour, twenty feet square, as his undisputed empire at the end of the day, the armchair as his throne and the poker as his sceptre. It sounded snug, and at that period snugness was valued. For the rest, Irving was acid about the Birthplace, accepted the young Shakespeare's deer-stealing escapade—a stock tradition about which neutrality seems impossible —and described the Bust as "pleasant and serene, with a finely-arched forehead" and indications of a cheerful social disposition. He had, too, a brief passage for resurrection-men:

> The inscription on the tombstone has not been without its effect. It has prevented the removal of his remains from the bosom of his native place to Westminster Abbey which was at one time contemplated. A few years since, also, as some labourers were digging to make an adjoining vault, the earth caved in, so as to leave a vacant space, almost like an arch, through which one might have reached into the grave. No one, however, presumed to meddle with his remains so awfully guarded by a malediction*; and lest

* The verse on Shakespeare's tombstone reads:
> Good frend, for Iesus sake forbeare
> To digg the dvst enclosed heare:
> Bleste be ye. man yt. spares thes stones,
> And cvrst be he yt. moves my bones.

any of the idle or the curious, or any collector of relics, should be tempted to commit depredations, the old sexton kept watch over the place for two days, until the vault was finished and the aperture closed again. He told me that he had made bold to look in at the hole, but could see neither coffin nor bones; nothing but dust. It was something, I thought, to have seen the dust of Shakespeare.

Indeed, the quintessence of dust. Otherwise, the essay is like several meditations on Stratford, though it does avoid the clammier raptures. A few lines from one of these, on the "bright-eyed boy of glance divine", can speak for all. It was published during 1888 in *The Theatre*, a journal given to this kind of thing:

There was his young mind rocked in a cradle of sweet thoughts and tender fancies; and this sweet store of thoughts in riper years came back to him, and so was given to us, and to those that shall come after us, moulded into things immortal.

V

Of the two ways directly before us at the head of Bridge Street, that bearing left is the busily unremarkable Wood Street—cast for general utility—which glances up, with a few old houses (Nos. 44-45 are sixteenth-century) towards the broad space of Rother Street—naturally a site for a market; it is still used for the purpose. Someone has said rightly that it is like a paved village green, or, if you will, a Venetian *campo*, funnelling off southward to a street of ordinary width. Here, as much as anywhere, we get an idea of the openness and the generally low roof-line of Tudor Stratford. Here also, by no means Tudor, is the American Fountain (and clock) which George W. Childs, proprietor of *The Philadelphia Ledger*, gave to Stratford at Queen Victoria's Jubilee, 1887, in token of Anglo-American amity. The first plan was for a memorial window in the Parish Church; then a fountain was proposed, accepted, designed in Birmingham and unveiled during October by Henry Irving. It proved to be a plump and fussy dwarf spire that always reminds me of a kind of Gothic Rockall, the tip of some huge building, *cathédrale engloutie*, lost below. Collectors are glad, I dare say, that the finials of these crocketed gables represent Puck, Mustardseed, Peaseblossom and Cobweb. Oliver Wendell Holmes wrote for the first ceremony a daunting poem that Irving read undaunted: it hinted that nightingales would sip there and eagles stoop to drink. Irving himself, eagle of the moment, drank the first cupful in a toast to the Immortal Memory. "We were preceded by an execrable brass band," wrote Lord Ronald Sutherland Gower, who had come down to stay with the Hodgsons at Clopton and who walked in the procession up to Rother Street. "The ceremony was a rather long one, and there was a jam of newspaper reporters all around us, and two Roman Catholic priests insisted on standing all the time on my feet." I hope he recalled Mr. Winkle at the Rochester review when Mr. Pickwick asked, "Can anything be finer or more delightful?" "Nothing," replied Winkle, who "had had a short man standing on each of his feet for the quarter of an hour immediately preceding".

One inscription upon the fountain is from *Timon of Athens*, "Honest water which ne'er left man in the mire", sound temperance doctrine and a judicious choice of play because in it occurs the line, "It is the pasture lards the rother's sides"—a reference to the red oxen which give their name to the market. Strangely, the word was altered to 'wether' when *Timon* in 1967 had the most recent of its few Royal Shakespeare revivals, with Paul Scofield in idiosyncratic splendour. There is also a quotation from *Henry the Eighth*, a chronicle by Shakespeare, or Fletcher, or both, according to choice. If Heminge and Condell included it in the Folio, knowing it to be a collaboration, why, I wonder, did they omit *The Two Noble Kinsmen?*

Immediately across from the Fountain, on the north side of the Rother, is the White Swan Hotel, occupied as a tavern in about 1450; a man named Perrott owned it in Shakespeare's day when its sixteenth-century murals from the apocryphal book of Tobit were new—figures in Tudor costume painted boldly in colour. We can say of them as Washington Irving says of Shakespeare—it is in his essay and also upon the fountain—that they "gild the dull reality of life with innocent illusions". Shakespeare and his wife would choose for their eldest daughter a name from the Apocrypha, Susanna, not much used then.

VI

To reach the birthplace of the man Irving and so many others have insisted on calling the Bard, an unhappy word that has gathered comic-ironic overtones, it is convenient to cut from the Rother behind Wood Street and down Meer Street where the brook used to run. Beyond is Henley Street and one of the half-dozen best-known houses in Britain. Henley Street, which today, apart from the Birthplace and the glistening Shakespeare Centre, is a gentle muddle of shops, pleasantly small-town, is also approached directly by bearing half-right from the top of Bridge Street. The house described as the Birthplace, isolated up on the northern side with a low iron railing before it, is a substantial, half-timbered, three-gabled, latticed and dormered dwelling, so over-exposed—for it has been photographed, painted in oils, etched, charred in poker-work, beaten in brass, embroidered on tablecloths, knitted in coloured wools—that you may feel you are making a routine call on an ancient relative. The nature of the greeting must depend on your response to birthplaces in general. Not noticeably romantic (you supply your own clouds of glory), the building is as stable as some of the Shakespearean anecdotes are flimsy. Stratford is not a town for those insistent upon decay as an evocative agent; and the Birthplace, fiercely preserved, is caulked and bitumed like the chest of Thaisa. Built upon a low limestone ground-sill—stone from Wilmcote—its walls have vertical oak timbers from Arden, close-studded and narrowly spaced, with a rectangular panelling of beams higher up. The west end holds more of the original external timbers. On the roof great chimney-stacks pin the fabric.

When William was born the building was in two separate but contiguous houses. John Shakespeare, in his versatile capacities, kept the eastern house for business; some have described it as the Woolshop. The family lived, no doubt, on the west. Upon his father's death the property went to William; it passed to various members of the family, finally in 1670 to Shakespeare's grand-nephew, Thomas Hart, and with the Harts it stayed until 1806, when Thomas Court purchased it for £210 and about 1,000 visitors a year were coming to see it. The lower part of the west house was then a butcher's shop; the eastern house an inn. Long under the sign of 'The Maidenhead', it was 'The Swan and Maidenhead' in 1847 when nearly 2,500 people came to the Birthplace. That year the houses and the garden behind them, bought for £3,000 by public subscription, were vested in the Stratford

Birthplace Committee*, saviour of what an auction poster proclaimed to be "the truly heart-stirring relic of a most glorious period, and of England's immortal bard". Before rebuilding, begun at once, the house had been pulled about unconscionably; in 1847 it must have been at its shabbiest. Today, in the isolation which helps to protect it against fire, it is staunchly, as the late Christian Deelman put it, "an excellent restoration of an Elizabethan house known to have existed in something like its present form when Shakespeare was born". Traditionally, it is the blessed plot. We must believe that Shakespeare was born within the walls, giving (said Benjamin Haydon, predictably ecstatic), "the first puling cry which announced he was living and healthy".

It had been a showpiece during a century before its purchase. At present well over 300,000 people a year, or more than twenty times the population of Stratford, come to Henley Street from perhaps 150 countries. Two centuries ago the notoriety of Garrick's 'Jubilee' first encouraged more than a trickle of visitors, and the Harts made thoughtful provision. Thus the Honourable John Byng, of the Torrington Diaries, who came in 1785, saw Shakespeare's Chair, shown to him by the Mrs Hart of the moment:

> "How do you do, Mrs. Hart? Let me see the wonders of your house."
> "Why there, Sir, is Shakespeare's chair and I have been often bid a good sum of money for it. It has been carefully handed down on record by our family; but people never thought so much of it till after the Jubilee. And now see what pieces they have cut from it, as well as from the old flooring in the bedroom."

Promptly Byng bought a slice "equal to the size of a Tobacco Stopper". Later, he bought the lower cross-bar. Washington Irving, refusing to romanticize the Birthplace, saw it as a "small, mean-looking edifice of wood and plaster", with various squalid rooms. It was shown to the public by "a garrulous old lady, in a frosty red face, lighted up by a cold blue anxious eye, and garnished with artificial locks of flaxen hair, curling from under an exceedingly dirty cap". This was a Mrs. Mary Hornby, wife of Thomas Hornby, cousin of a Hart from whom he rented the Birthplace. She lived there from 1793 until 1820 (as a tenant during

* The Trustees and Guardians of Shakespeare's Birthplace were incorporated in 1891.

the last fourteen years), acted as a guide, was herself a playwright, of slightly less fame than Shakespeare—her plays, I gather, included *The Battle of Waterloo* and *The Broken Vow*—and was ready at all seasons to gloat over the shattered stock of the weapon with which Shakespeare shot the deer; his tobacco-box; the sword with which he played Hamlet, and which apparently the Prince Regent coveted; the lantern with which Friar Laurence discovered Romeo and Juliet at the tomb; and, in Irving's phrase:

> An ample supply also of Shakespeare's mulberry tree, which seems to have as extraordinary powers of self-multiplication as the wood of the true Cross; of which there is enough extant to build a ship of the line.

A neighbour, a Mrs. Hawkins, prepared in 1819 a list of Mrs. Hornby's relics—or, if you wish, her circumstantial double letters from Warwickshire. It covered:

His chair in the chimney-corner;
The matchlock with which he shot the deer;
His Toledo [blade] and walking-stick, which seemed of vine, and
    was elegant in its form;
A small bugle-horn;
His reading glass;
The bench and table near his bedside where he wrote;
The glass out of which he drank without rising in his bed in his last
    illness;
A cup and basin;
His christening bowl;
His child's chair;
A superb table-cover, embroidered in gold, given him by Queen
    Elizabeth;
His easy-chair;
His bed complete;
The images that seem to have been posts, and four panels of a tri-
    angular form which appear to have been made a half-tester,
    though no longer part of the bedstead;
His lantern;
His coffer, with some money;
His pencil-case;
His wife's shoe;
A bolt taken from the door of the room;
A portrait of him put together from fragments by Dr. Stort, Bishop
    of Killala.

In the previous year, 1818, Sir Richard Phillips, editor of *The Monthly Magazine* and a sheriff of London, visited Stratford and went up to Henley Street. Later he wrote in his magazine:

> Mrs. Hornby shows a very small deep cupboard, in a dark corner of the room in which Shakespeare was born; and relates that a letter was found in it some years since, which had been addressed by Shakespeare from the playhouse in London to his wife. She asserts that this letter was in her possession, and that she used to show it to visitors; that one morning, a few years since, she exhibited it to a company, who went from her house to the church; but presently sent a message to beg that she would send the letter for further inspection at the tomb,—a request with which she complied. She saw nothing further, however, of her letter; but the parties, on leaving Stratford, sent her a shilling and their thanks! Persons in Stratford doubt the truth of this relation; but the woman persists.

Unquestionably she was persistent.

In about 1820 Mrs. Court, who lived at the inn, decided to take over the butcher's shop and dispossessed Mrs. Hornby. In dudgeon, crying a plague o' both your houses, the guardian of matchlock, lantern, bugle-horn, bolt, pencil-case and coffer (with some money), moved, frosty-faced and blue-eyed, to an address across the street, in acute if transient rivalry. Though she flitted to other houses in Stratford, her day soon waned: Shakespeare could not go on tour. Meanwhile Mrs. Court, in sole command, invited members of the nobility and gentry who happened to be in Henley Street, to satisfy their laudable curiosity and to see the home of the immortal poet of nature. Many of them came, responding to the Birthplace as to the Bust and to local shrines in general. Thus Benjamin Haydon, in 1828, was "lost, quite lost" in Stratford. He fell into a trance; when he emerged it was hard to talk to waiters and chambermaids about tea and bread and butter. "To feel that they were requisite, to think of eating and drinking at all, was a bore and a disgust." A Shakespearean editor, the Rev. William Harness, Mary Russell Mitford's friend, visited the Birthplace in 1844 and heard from the aging Mrs. Court that the Stratford Corporation "don't care about Shakespeare. Strangers—Americans, people from the Indies—care much more about him than people here do." Visitors from America and the Indies have never failed to arrive.

Today, under the care of the Birthplace Trust and its learned director, Dr. Levi Fox, the matchlock-and-mulberry era, the world of Hornby and Court, has slipped into primeval myth. In the western, or domestic, part of the Birthplace, furnishings are in key with the period and spirit of the house. On the eastern side a museum, presenting the poet's career and later life, has such documents as the purchase deed of New Place—Shakespeare from William Underhill—and the Quiney letter. Richard Quiney*, a Stratford mercer, wrote this at 'The Bell' in Carter Lane, London, on 25th October 1598. Asking Shakespeare, "my loving good friend and countryman", for a loan of thirty pounds, he said, "You shall friend me much in helping me out of all the debts I owe in London." There is evidence that Shakespeare agreed immediately. He may possibly have remembered his Bassanio's phrase two years earlier, "to get rid of all the debts I owe". By then he was obviously a prosperous man, for £30 in 1598 would be something like £1,000 now. The survival of this letter is quite extraordinary. Edmond Malone discovered it in the summer of 1793 while at Stratford, "rummaging" in the Corporation's stores. During ten days—so he wrote to his friend, Thomas Percy, Bishop of Dromore, on 21st September 1793—he

unfolded and slightly examined not less than three thousand papers and parchments; several of which were as old as the time of Henry the Fourth and probably had not been opened for two centuries. From the whole mass I selected whatever I thought likely to throw any light upon the life of Shakespeare, on which I am now employed; and these the Mayor very obligingly permitted me to pack up in a box and to bring with me to London, that I might peruse them at my leisure. . . . I was not fortunate enough to meet with a single scrap of his handwriting, though I have got the signatures of almost all his family and friends; but I have found a letter *to* him when in London, a very pretty little *relick*, about *three inches long by two broad.* His answer to this letter, the object of which was to borrow some money from him, would have been a great curiosity: and what is provoking is, it ought to have been in the bundle where this was found (a parcel of letters to and from a Mr Quiney whose son afterwards married the poet's daughter) and this *should* have been among the papers of Shakespeare's granddaughter, wherever they are.

* Or Quyney.

The simplest theory is that Shakespeare and Quiney met before the letter was sent. Possibly Shakespeare could have come to 'The Bell' to see his "countryman"; if so, Quiney would have explained verbally what he wanted. He died less than four years afterwards, during his second term (1602) as Bailiff of Stratford, and his papers, including the undelivered letter, would have gone into the archives that Malone, after two centuries, was "rummaging".

From the Birthplace museum we get to the bedroom, at the front of the first floor of the western house, where our imaginations must take charge. "As people are generally born in bedrooms," said Haydon sagely, "why this upstairs room probably gave birth to the poet." Tradition guards it. Garrick plumped for it; and during the Jubilee pomps of 1769 a huge transparency, symbolizing the struggle of the sun through clouds ("Thus dying clouds contend with growing light"), was hung in crimson and blue and scarlet over the bedroom window. On the window-panes are the scratched signatures of many people (from Walter Scott to Ellen Terry) eager to agree that this is the place. "I was seized with a sort of enthusiasm and wrote mine," Tennyson said after his Stratford visit with Edward Fitzgerald in 1840; "I was a little ashamed of it afterwards; yet the feeling was genuine at the time, and I did homage with the rest." What the friendly, islanded building most lacks is a sense of continuity, any real feeling that life has coursed through it for centuries. You find Shakespeare more surely in the garden at the back, planted with the trees, flowers, and herbs from the plays; everything from mulberry and medlar to marjoram, camomile and (a Cornishman is glad to report) saffron: "I must have saffron to colour the warden pies."

Next door, overpeering the garden, is the splendid Shakespeare Centre, designed by Laurence Williams, built by the Birthplace Trust with aid from many nations, opened in the Quatercentenary spring (1964) and controlled by Dr. Fox, whose natural fastidiousness has kept the major properties of the Trust—the others are Nash's House, Hall's Croft, Mary Arden's House and Anne Hathaway's—from stiffening into the cold museum-pieces they might have been. The crowds, inevitably, must be a trouble: for some people any sight-seeing in convoy is a penance. There is no comparable worry at the Centre, quick forge and working-house of the profession that has grown up about John Shakespeare's son.

The books and the documents are here, with room to study them and such bonuses as John Hutton's glass panels; his Titania, spirit of another sort, reminds me of a performance by Dame Peggy Ashcroft, the play of her hands, the wavering shimmer and ripple at "Pale in her anger, washes all the air".

VII

The Centre was not dreamed of when, new to Stratford, I used to walk in the summer evenings from the late Georgian blandness of Payton Street, named for an inn-keeper who was an important figure in Garrick's time and later thrice mayor. A reasonably active crow could have flapped onto the Birthplace in under ten seconds. I took longer to cross the Birmingham Road, clanging with traffic; to penetrate a slit that led to Henley Street beside the Free Library, and then to move up past what in those days were the flaking walls of Meer Street towards the 'Temporary Memorial Theatre'. Here in Greenhill Street—once Moor Towns End—on the way to the station, Bridges-Adams, as civilized a director as Stratford had ever known, was staging the Shakespeare Festival in a cinema. John Shakespeare once owned a house in Greenhill Street, long vanished, that some writers have proposed as the Birthplace; I doubt whether this particular heresy occurred to many playgoers at the cinema. It was during the late twenties, the interregnum after the fire, when the new Memorial was nothing but a hole and some foundations beyond a stout board fence across the Bancroft. For a while the Stratford stage had to be a makeshift; it could not have been happier. Those July evenings were very still: hushed on purpose to grace harmony. The day's crowds had melted. Audiences on the rake of the temporary theatre, between its moonlit and semi-Venetian panels, listened as I had seldom known audiences to listen. For me, even today, the ghosts of Stratford are not Elizabethan and Jacobean townsfolk, Quineys and Badgers, Sadlers and Walkers, Shaws and Sturleys, who would not matter much to us if they had not been Shakespeare's fellow-citizens. (A word for Alderman George Whateley, who owned nineteen stalls of bees with their hives and "wax-honey and other things in the apple-chamber".) Rather, the streets are haunted by men and women who worked for Bridges-Adams in 1929 and 1930: George Hayes, wearing in Westminster

The Birthplace, Stratford-upon-Avon
Clopton Bridge across the Avon at Stratford

THE
FALCON
HOTEL

Hall the robe and gold cross of Richard the Second; Wilfrid Walter and Roy Byford; Dorothy Massingham, Cleopatra as Veronese painted her; Kenneth Wicksteed, among the few who have animated Touchstone. Wicksteed, with the splintery voice, played in more Shakespeare than any actor of his period. Stratford people loved him not only because he was a comedian (which went far), but also because he loved the town he had adopted. During those brief festivals Stratford always felt grieved that Bridges-Adams, after the stress of preparing the repertory, would go away and not return until the season's end. They warmed to somebody like Wicksteed who would stop in High Street to chat about old Double or a yoke of bullocks. He could carry off the Fools and Clowns,* and that is no easy business when a single-minded Shakespearean, as persistent as Mrs. Court, is apt to be plagued by such a nightmare as this:

Enter a pair of Fools, with a Second Citizen.
Touchstone (after excessive mirth): Shall I nominate in order now the degrees of the lie?
Second Citizen (a wag): All, sir, for truly all that I live by is by the awl.
Lavache (glumly): As fit as a pancake is for Shrove Tuesday.
Touchstone: Thou say'st well. It is a figure in rhetoric that drink, being poured out of a cup into a glass, by filling the one, doth empty the other. It is meat and drink to me to see a clown.
Immoderate laughter. Enter Launcelot Gobbo, with Grumio.
Launcelot (richly): I do beseech you, turn up on your right hand at the next turning, but at the next turning of all, on your left.
Second Citizen: Of awl! Good, i'faith.
Grumio: Fie, fie, on all tired jades, on all mad masters, and all foul ways.
Touchstone (at the top of his form): Amen. A man may, if he were of a feeble heart, stagger in this attempt. Concerning the cut of a certain courtier's beard. . . .
Oddly, Juliet's Nurse crosses the stage.
Nurse: 'Wilt thou, not, Jule!' quoth he; and, pretty fool, it stinted and said 'Ay.' (*Long and rusty laughter.*)
Several Voices: Ay, let's be red with mirth!
Touchstone (rising to it): Nay to your 'Ay's' if naught but neighing contents your ears. There was a certain knight that swore by his honour they were good pancakes . . .

* Much else besides. He was a splendid Leonato, caught in Miss Norah Taylor's miniature of him as "an Elizabethan Gentleman".

4

New Place Garden, Stratford-upon-Avon
The Guild (Gild) Chapel, Stratford-upon-Avon

*General delirium; and screams of "O, here's a wit of cheveril that stretches
from an inch narrow to an ell broad."*

Oxfordians prize the last words—supporters, that is, of the
theory that Edward de Vere, Earl of Oxford (d. 1604) was
Shakespeare. If we take away the first two letters of 'inch', making
it therefore "an inch narrow", and arrange for the 'il' (or 'ell') to
be turned into "an ell broad", the word 'cheveril' can mean
'Inch E. Ver ell'. This is to say, Edward de Vere's wit, equal
to all occasions, will stretch effortlessly, like soft leather, from an
inch to an ell. It seems more probable to me that the phrase was
written by a dramatist who knew something about a glover's shop.

Beyond Greenhill Street (where this pun was never explained
to us) Stratford peters out, though we can get across swiftly to
Shottery on the left. I used to delight in the station which for
years the Great Western Railway labelled "*on*-Avon". Dwindling
now to an exhibit of industrial archaeology, it has memories from
the railway meridian. Here Lord Ronald Gower and Sir Arthur
Hodgson went to meet George Augustus Sala and his astrakhan
coat a few hours before the Gower Memorial was unveiled. Here,
at festival time, the players would alight to see the station decorated and half the town waiting for them outside. Here Stratford
met Frank and Constance Benson after the actor had been
knighted in London at the Shakespeare Tercentenary matinée.
The station that day was beleaguered; Lady Benson, lost among
the lilies, and Sir Frank, with a chaplet of bays, were borne to an
open landau in which players and townsfolk drew them through
the streets to the Shakespeare Hotel, and on to the theatre. From
Stratford station also, during April 1911, Marie Corelli, the local
lady-in-residence, inaugurated "in clear, silvery tones" a device
called the Railophone: a system of wireless telephony for sending
messages to and from trains in motion. It was being tested then
upon a stretch of line between Stratford and the village of Kineton
beneath Edgehill: a curious route when the 'railway years' are
fading, but in 1911 matter-of-course. The Stratford-upon-Avon
and Midland Junction Railway maintained a steady service: nine
minutes from Stratford to Ettington, seventeen to Kineton, thirty-
six to Fenny Compton, and beyond this again the edge of the
world.

The station stands within the old fringe of the Forest of Arden.

Lodge's *Rosalynde* is set in the Ardennes; but we can hardly believe that when Shakespeare dramatized the novel, he turned his back on a local Arden. In the words of Jaques, "the why is plain as way to parish church". We might well return now to mid-Stratford from its outer bound and take that way ourselves from the Birthplace door to Holy Trinity.

THREE

OUT TO THE CHURCH

I

Flower-carriers from the Birthplace, on the afternoon of 23rd April, move through Stratford towards Old Town with all convenient speed. Earlier, at a luncheon in the Conference Hall, that re-fashioned shell of the burnt-out theatre, speeches are sententious if not always very sharp: certainly pleasant without scurrility, learned without opinion, and (sometimes) strange without heresy. To burnish the central toast of 'The Immortal Memory' must challenge any orator who feels that Shakespeare said it in two words: "Let be." After the flags have been unfurled, the procession is homage as eloquent as speech. A band plays; the Mayor and leading visitors follow it, the Beadle and mace-bearers before them, and behind them anyone who wishes to join. At the head go ceremonial chaplets and wreaths; at the tail are rosemary and violets, knots of primroses, bunches of garden and hedgerow flowers that presently will be heaped and mingled over Shakespeare's tombstone in the chancel. The doggerel warning—like a snatch from *Pyramus and Thisby*—is covered in a drift of blossom —a scene, without any special pomp or ritual, that does linger as if it were Perdita's flower speech. As Charles Edward Montague, the great Manchester drama critic who loved Stratford, wrote more than sixty years ago:

> One trembles at the thought of an unsymbolistic race essaying this joint act of emotional symbolism, unhelped by the Gallic passion for such effects. Yet all goes well, and is simple and not hugger-mugger. The time I saw it a couple of thousand persons were there, mostly women; most of them carried bunches of daffodils, wallflowers, primroses, anything. . . . Everyone filed past the poet's grave, all looking, in a surprising degree, as if it mattered to them that he had lived.

Montague's last sentence is valid on the afternoon of any Birthday. Yet this anticipates. We are in Henley Street, moving eastward to the corner by the white mass of the bank; then round it, and forward on a progress along three linked streets that curve suavely to the south across the history of Stratford-upon-Avon. The first is High Street. Once I liked it particularly because it had a "chymist"—it still has—and because over a bookshop door the legend, "Come and take choice of all my library, and so beguile your sorrow," should have urged theatre-men to consider *Titus Andronicus* long before the tough old play responded in 1955 to the genius of Peter Brook and Laurence Olivier. High Street goes on reminding me of Charles Lamb when he was superannuated: "I walk about, not to and fro." There are few pleasanter streets to walk about in without fixed aim. Some streets reproach us; they are for business, nothing else, and a loiterer slips into the shadow. Not so High Street, which welcomes loitering, though its pavements are fuller than they were, and some hours are better than others for a study of the Garrick Inn lozenges and the bell-shaped upper bracings of Tudor House, or a discussion of 'lattenayles' (which were wooden pegs for fastening tiles to roofing laths), 'spykyngnayles' (which were large wooden pegs used for driving through the timbers when mortised together), or 'sparrys' (which were just spars or rafters). I cannot loiter in central Stratford without remembering *The Merry Wives of Windsor*, written at speed to match a late Tudor sense of fun, and speaking in mood for Shakespeare's own town as surely as it does for Windsor topography. Not because of the false trail of Justice Shallow and the "luces" at the outset, but simply because the play has Stratford in its eyes. George Page, whose fallow greyhound was outrun on Cotsall, and Frank Ford, possibly reminiscent of a notoriously splenetic Stratfordian (try Nicholas Barnhurst); the Wives themselves, High Street neighbours; the town gossip, Quickly, who asks "Does he not have a great round beard, *like a glover's paring-knife?*"; Hugh Evans, parson and schoolmaster, who could have derived from Thomas Jenkins, of the Stratford Grammar School: all may have their stage home in Windsor, but can we doubt that Shakespeare, in a hurry, transplanted them from more familiar streets? Falstaff is not the mighty Sir John, yet he fits into the scene, and the decorations count. For years it was one of Stratford's favourite plays, "smelling April and May" in spite of its winter setting. Presumably because it was not 'relevant', it slid from fashion during the late fifties and most of the sixties; but in 1968–9 it returned in a rather muted production that moved from farce to social comedy, the new Windsor bourgeoisie teaching a lesson to a visitor who condescended from the fringes of the Court. It was ruled by the frenzy of Ian Richardson. His Ford, running a feverish temperature, delivered speech upon speech as if he were suddenly bounced off a trampoline.

II

The flower procession, entering High Street, passes the Bridge Street corner with the house, much-restored, where Shakespeare's second daughter, Judith, Hamnet's twin, lived from 1616 after her marriage to Thomas Quiney. He was a tavern-keeper and vintner, son of Richard of the "loving friend" letter of 1598. The house was once the town gaol: a fact somehow fitted to Thomas, a debatable character, if by no means untalented.* Hard upon his marriage and just before the death of his father-in-law (who seemed to distrust him), he confessed to "incontinence" with a Stratford woman who had died later with her child. In years ahead he was fined for swearing and for "suffering townsmen to tippell in his house". He left Judith, according to some accounts, in 1652, and we do not know where he died. She died ten years later, leaving neither children (for her sons had predeceased her) nor grandchildren.

We have plenty of people to remember in High Street—if we mean to be on terms with everybody Shakespeare knew, which is not invariably profitable. Antiquaries have worked it out so exactly that they could deliver posthumous greetings to any address in Elizabethan and Jacobean Stratford. It can be enough in High Street to name Daniel Baker, the Puritan Bailiff of 1603 (grimly, "Master Baker's year"), who stopped travelling players from acting in the Gild Hall; Hamnet Sadler, a baker, and his wife Judith, after whom Shakespeare's twins were probably christened; an apothecary, Philip Rogers, who sold such things as Venice turpentine, Burgundy pitch, corrosive sublimate, and, surprisingly, ale and "tobecka"; Richard Quiney, the mercer,

* Consider the pleasant letter he wrote to his father in Latin, at the age of 11.

Thomas's father; another mercer, Henry Walker, to whose son Shakespeare, as godfather, left a gold piece of 20s; and an agreeable couple, as frenzied as Ford, if not for the same reason, whom we can summon near the modernized corner of High and Sheep Streets. These were George Badger, Catholic woollen-draper, and Nicholas Barnhurst, another draper and a Puritan, who were unwilling neighbours. After a rumpus at a meeting in 1597, the council expelled Barnhurst for his "lewd and bad speeches", for calling George Badger *knave* and *rascal,* and for "using other abuses to the rest of the company". Though he apologized and was forgiven, he offended again, and this time received no quarter. The council would not endure provocative thumb-biting; soon Badger also lost his aldermancy.

A few years earlier the enemies had suffered in one of the fires which caused repeated local havoc. Those of 1594 and 1595 consumed 200 houses, did £12,000 worth of damage, and obliged the corporation to seek relief from the Queen. Other outbreaks were in 1614 and 1640. Stratford's thatch and timber could be perilous: hence the abnormal height of the chimney-stacks, so built to carry any sparks safely above the roofs. The first fire, in September 1594, driven by a pelting south wind and with nothing but the most primitive methods to fight it, involved four streets and endangered the Birthplace. Luckily it did not cross the "mere" (stream) above Hornby's smithy, that served here as a "moat defensive to a house". The second blaze, in April 1595, was especially destructive round Sheep Street and Barnhurst and Badger's properties.

For amateurs of timbering the western side of High Street is the better. Together, in a *corps d'élite,* are Harvard House, the Garrick Inn, and what is known as the Tudor House. Other towns are timbered; Stratford shivers them because no rival can stand up to a Shakespearean association. It is like the bargaining in *The Taming of the Shrew:*

> "What, have I choked you with an argosy?"
> "Gremio, 'tis known my father hath no less
> Than three great argosies; besides two galliasses,
> And twelve tight galleys; these I will assure her,
> And twice as much, whate'er thou offer'st next."

Harvard House, mostly from 1596 and later, is one of the great argosies. Belonging now to the American university at Cambridge, Massachusetts, it was the home of Alderman Thomas Rogers, a wealthy butcher, maternal grandfather of John Harvard, an English Puritan minister and the university's founder. Its front riots in late Elizabethan carved ornament; its interior is heavy with oak panelling. The back, and older, part survived the fire of 1595. Next door is the house (the present Garrick Inn) rebuilt after the fire for William and Roger Smith; in the earlier building on this site a weaver's young apprentice was the first victim of the Stratford plague of 1564, followed shortly by his master's wife. Southward again, on the Ely Street corner, is the three-storeyed 'old Tudor' house (John Wilmore's) with overhanging front; also from the year of the fire, it has immensely ornate timbers and some grotesque brackets. We meet here that determined Lady Bountiful, Marie Corelli. The town owed to her the restoration of Harvard House and the 'Tudor 'House. After buying the first to preserve it, without deciding what to do next, she met, on a cruise with Sir Thomas Lipton, a wealthy American, Edward Morris of Chicago and his wife. Morris bought the house, and when in 1909 it was restored—"almost oppressively antique" somebody said—he presented the title-deeds to Harvard.

Across the road, after a modern inlet where the Corn Exchange used to stand, High Street ends at the Sheep Street junction. On the corner of Sheep and Chapel Streets the Town Hall is a modest affair of Cotswold limestone, inseparable from the Garrick celebration of 1769. Originally there was a market hall of Charles I's reign, shattered in 1643 by a gunpowder explosion while Parliamentary forces held the town. Repaired, the building hung on shakily for a century and more; a single column exists in New Place gardens. In the old hall, on 9th September 1746, the John Ward company, good solid provincial pomping folk, had given a performance of *Othello* in aid of the Bust; "through length of years and other accidents" this had become as "much impair'd and decay'd" as the hall itself. Tickets for *Othello* were half-a-crown and a shilling. We can believe that the players, led by Ward, grandfather of John Philip and Sarah Kemble (Siddons), performed as at a Solemn Musick. They must have been extremely competent; according to the Rev. Joseph Greene*, headmaster of

* See Dr. Levi Fox's admirable edition of *The Correspondence of the Reverend Joseph Greene* (H.M. Stationery Office, 1965).

the grammar school and a mighty man of Stratford, they were "much the best set I have seen out of London", in spite of an elderly Brabantio (never a rewarding part) who did "some things well, others wretchedly". Greene supplied a prologue, spoken by Ward with "the most exact propriety", which ended:

> Hail, happy STRATFORD!—envi'd be thy name,
> What City boasts, than thee, a greater fame?
> Here, his first infant-lays great SHAKESPEARE sung!
> Here, his last accents falter'd on his tongue!
> His Honours yet, with future Times shall grow,
> Like Avon's streams, enlarging as they flow! . . .

Garrick in 1769 presented to the new town hall a statue of 'great Shakespeare', John Cheere's copy in lead of Peter Scheemaker's revision for Lord Pembroke of the Westminster Abbey statue. Leaning on a pile of books, the poet looks thoroughly benign, though he is not the "silly, smiling thing" Gainsborough found in the Bust. He commands Sheep Street from an ornamental niche on the town hall's north front, remembering possibly a morning when Garrick at full pitch in the Rotunda by the river, apostrophized him during the "Jubilee Ode":

> Look down, blest spirit! from above,
> With all thy wonted gentleness and love;
> And as the wonders of thy pen,
> By heav'n inspir'd,
> To virtue fir'd
> The charm'd, astonish'd sons of men!

We might say of Garrick and Greene, as of Mr. Woodward's Brabantio, that they did "some things well, others wretchedly".

III

At the corner by the town hall, Sheep Street, contented and expansive, begins its slope down towards Waterside; its buildings are the expected Stratford medley, but it does have a sense of age, a patina, that Bridge Street wants. Traffic is not so exacting. Moreover, from the southern pavement the passage-and-yard called Emms Court—in the West Country it would be an 'Ope'—has a First Folio look about it, and on the north is the

Shrieve's House, tall and grave, clearly a length of agreeably sententious blank verse. Once it was owned by William Rogers, who rebuilt it—inevitably—after the fire of 1595. He was a Serjeant-at-the-Mace in a jerkin of canary-coloured leather; Stratford saw in him what Kent saw in the face of Lear—authority. Part of the house he kept as a tavern where he sold ale and aqua vitae; his wife, who took it over after his death, was a sister of Henry Walker, Shakespeare's friend; and if Shakespeare were in Stratford during October 1613, he might reasonably (Edgar Fripp says) have attended at the Shrieve's House the wedding feast of young Elizabeth Rogers and Master Matthew Morris. Across the road lived Richard Tyler, very likely a schoolfellow of Shakespeare; he had, when he was 22, a runaway marriage with a girl of 16 from Shottery Manor, whose wealthy grand-father promptly cut her off. Tyler went on to a long and com-fortable life in Stratford as a wealthy gentleman, and he received in 1616 Shakespeare's bequest of 26s. 8d. for a mourning ring. Sheep Street, in general, makes one remember an essay of C. E. Montague from 1924*: "What urban countenance is so amusingly demure as that of Stratford-upon-Avon, with its air of contained geniality, animated leisure, ordered complacency, everything with a note of reference in it to the auriferous Bard."

Back in Chapel Street now, on the processional road to the church, we pass the majestically nine-gabled Shakespeare Hotel (the façade insists upon "hostelrie"), set back a little from the town hall, which pushes itself forward out of the line of the street. This renowned hotel, with its bedrooms appropriately in key—you can sleep, if you like, in 'A Midsummer Night's Dream'—dates on its north from the sixteenth century, and on its south from the later seventeenth. Another decorative hotel, 'The Falcon', much of which would have been more than a century old when Shakespeare lived in New Place, is farther up the street on the west. New Place itself, even if next to nothing remains, still heads the cast around here. At the intersection with the present Chapel Lane, Hugh Clopton (according to Leland) "builded close by the north side of the Chappell a praty howse of bricke and tymbre". We can see the foundations of what was probably the "praty howse", though some antiquaries contest the attribution. We have to go first through the building that

* In *The Right Place: A Book of Pleasures* (Chatto and Windus, 1924).

adjoins the site. Once owned by Thomas Nash, who married Shakespeare's granddaughter, Elizabeth Hall, it contains New Place Museum, administered by the Birthplace Trust. Elizabethan England is the theme in aspect and exhibits; also Stratford's own history from the Romano-British daybreak. Good; but many may find it freer outside, where the foundations lie in a fragmentary mosaic that needs to be explained technically, and which I have always imagined in spring among a tracing of primroses. The spangled coils of the Elizabethan Knott Garden are a few yards away. Beyond again, across the latticed fence, is the Great Garden and its topiary.

Shakespeare in 1597, a man of only 33, returned triumphantly to his town, buying the indifferently preserved New Place, "a messuage, two barns, and two gardens", from William Underhill for £60. It sounds easy enough, but owing to a rich burst of melodrama the transaction was not completed until 1603, when he got two orchards as well. Two months after the first purchase, Underhill, a Catholic recusant and an unlikeable man, died suddenly of poison near Coventry; his elder son, Fulke, a demented boy of 18, was found guilty of the murder and executed at Warwick; and the family estates were re-granted, after forfeiture, to the prodigiously-named younger son, Hercules, who did not come of age until May 1602. At once Shakespeare assured himself of the title of New Place by getting a revised deed. There, fourteen years later, he died. The house, with its frontage of sixty feet, stayed in the family until 1670. During the Civil War Queen Henrietta Maria lodged there for three nights as Susanna Hall's guest, the corporation supplying her and her retinue with £15 worth of provisions (and fodder for the horses). In the last quarter of the century the property returned, by a roundabout way, to the Cloptons, one of whom, Sir John, "thoroughly repaired and beautified" it in 1702—so thoroughly that the Tudor New Place vanished beneath Queen Anne brick behind iron railings, a house that Shakespeare would not have recognized in any feature. It was sold in 1753 to the Reverend Francis Gastrell, a wealthy and splenetic clergyman from Frodsham in Cheshire; he was also a Canon Residentiary of the cathedral at Lichfield. Gastrell wanted New Place simply as a summer home; he had not the remotest feeling for its Shakespearean associations, and he could not, or would not, understand what it meant to be custodian of the mulberry tree and its relevant legends.

IV

The tree rose in the Great Garden. We do not know whether Shakespeare delighted in mulberries, for he has not much to say of them. The birds fed Adonis with mulberries and "ripe-red cherries"; Titania ordered the fairies to offer purple figs, green grapes and mulberries to Bottom the weaver; Thisbe died while "tarrying in mulberry shade"; and Volumnia, in the third act of *Coriolanus*, speaks of "thy stout heart Now humble as the ripest mulberry That will not hold the handling". We do know that a Frenchman brought many trees to the Midlands about 1609, a period when King James had issued *Instructions* to increase the number of mulberries for the sake of silkworm-breeding. Presumably Shakespeare planted a tree himself. The tradition hardened; certainly the growth flourished. Edmond Malone recorded in 1790 that the Stratford parish clerk's 85-year-old father, Hugh Taylor, who once lived next to New Place, asserted that until Shakespeare's planting there was no mulberry in the neighbourhood—a tradition preserved in the Clopton family as well as the Taylors'.

I am not much haunted at New Place by thoughts of the tree, or, for that matter, of Shakespeare's various business dealings and controversies in his last years at Stratford. But I can never walk round there without thinking of the last plays, of the Bohemian sheep-shearing that comes straight from Cotswold or the Vale of the Red Horse, and of Granville-Barker's note on Autolycus's rogue who "compassed a motion of the Prodigal Son, and married a tinker's wife within a mile where my land and living lies". Granville-Barker liked to suggest that Shakespeare happened upon that puppet-play at a Stratford fair, with Autolycus behind it.

More strongly still at New Place—warm and enclosed retreat at the quiet centre of England—I think of Shakespeare's love of the distant sea and its imagery. Through life he had an inland man's curiosity about the "main of waters", the "salt flood". He lived in that rapidly expanding world of the great navigators, at a time when the noise of far-off seas stirred in London streets. Though we need not suppose that he went to sea himself, he must have read much and known many sailors, not the kind of adventurers to appear suddenly in a riverside orchard. The sea moves often through his last plays. In *Pericles* "the brine and cloudy billow kiss the moon." The Queen in *Cymbeline* speaks of England as "Neptune's park ribbed and paled in with rocks unscalable and roaring waters". In *The Winter's Tale* the Clown, on the dubious coast of Bohemia, describes "the ship boring the moon with her mainmast, and anon swallow'd with yest and froth, as you'ld thrust a cork into a hogshead." If we wish, we can imagine Shakespeare in the utter calm of New Place conjuring Prospero's storm, the terror of the wreck, and the thunderous seas that environ the isle. New Place, however tranquil, however retired among the flowers of a midland summer, must ring with the waters of *The Tempest* "mounting to the welkin's cheek", and the Boatswain's cry, "What care these roarers for the name of king?" New Place is for me Stratford's seaway, not an orchard-close, the home of the mulberry, or that summer-house where Kipling, in one of his last and least familiar stories, *Proofs of Holy Writ*, established Shakespeare and Jonson at an afternoon's task: it is Shakespeare's duty to render five verses of the sixteenth chapter of Isaiah for the translators of the Authorized Bible. In this pleasant speculation Kipling reveals his own craftsman's mind.

V

We have to return, as at one period everybody did, to the mulberry shade. More than 130 years after Shakespeare's death Francis Gastrell discovered that in the town his mulberry, the tree he had bought with the house, was regarded as a public possession. So many people came to see it and to ask for leaves or twigs as souvenirs, that Gastrell, testiest of misanthropes who was never really at home in Stratford on his holiday visits, lost what rags of patience and good temper he had: he could never have had much. What peace could a man expect, he asked, when strangers were continually hammering at his door to do obeisance to a tree; a tree, moreover, that shadowed his windows and "rendered the house . . . subject to damps and moisture"? For three years he suffered "the frequent importunities of travellers"; then he hired a man called John Ange to cut the tree down. Helpless and furious, Stratford people could do nothing but protest, "review with tears the fallen tree" (as a writer said some time afterwards), or, as a quite useless gesture, smash to flinders the New Place glass. Only Thomas Sharp, a young clock-and-watchmaker, remained resourceful. He bought the wood, and, as he affirmed in a solemn statement on his deathbed in 1799, "out of a sincere veneration for the memory of its celebrated planter, employed one John Luckman to convey it to my own premises". There he

> worked it into many curious toys and usefull articles. . . . And I do hereby declare, and take my solemn oath, upon the four Evangelists, in the presence of Almighty God, that I have never had, worked, sold, or substituted any other wood than that what came from, and was part of, the said tree, as or for mulberry-wood.

Those "many curious toys and usefull articles" included cups, snuff-boxes, tobacco-stoppers, standishes, toothpick-cases, and a box in which David Garrick received the Freedom of Stratford in 1769. The accumulation explains why Washington Irving found the mulberry to have had "as extraordinary powers of self-multiplication as the wood of the true Cross".

Francis Gastrell did more than fell the mulberry, cut down a legend and start a traffic; he destroyed the fabric of New Place itself. Though he could visit Stratford for only a part of the year—during the rest of the time he lived in Lichfield—his servants occupied New Place, and the corporation demanded from him the usual poor-rate, payable then on any house in the town valued at more than forty shillings a year. At length, "in the heat of his anger, he declared that his house should never be assessed again" (R. B. Wheler), and on a day in 1751 he gave orders for complete demolition and the sale of the materials. When the house was a chaos of brick, stone, and timber, the townspeople could do nothing, merely to vow, impotently, "never to suffer a man of the same name to reside in Stratford". I have wondered now and again whether this still holds; whether there is any sort of Civic Vigilance Committee that can rap on a Gastrell's door in the dead vast of the night and conduct him to the limits of the borough. Though Francis Gastrell was both angry and impetuous, we cannot say that he destroyed Shakespeare's New Place, for the decorous house that he pulled down, pedimented and sash-windowed, was barely as old as the century. Yet, on the evidence, I am quite sure that if the old building had stood, he would have had no fret of conscience but disposed of it as bluntly as the other: about Shakespeare he was even less inquiring than the Reverend John Ward who, soon after he had become vicar of Stratford early in the Restoration, confided to his journal, "Remember to peruse Shakespears plays, and bee versed in them, yt I may not bee ignorant in yt matter."

Today all that remain of New Place are the foundations of some of the walls, a part of the cellars and two wells; in aspect it is like an eccentric Knott Garden. If one is ignorant in the matter, it is a few yards to the Knott itself, flower patterns, violet, blue, scarlet, tessellated among lavender and thyme and box. In the adjoining Great Garden the turf is bowling-green malachite. Here are yews and box clipped by a topiarist, though no longer into peacocks and other curious fowl; and an arbour where Benedick could have concealed himself on the evening when Don Pedro, Claudio and Leonato "fitted the hid-fox with a pennyworth"*—took revenge on him, that is, for eavesdropping. The lawn has a central mulberry† of possibly historic provenance: it may be a descendent of the original. We can quote, if we like, from Garrick's "Address to the Ladies", spoken (mulberry wand in grasp) during the 1769 Jubilee:

> Spite of all Malice—here I glorying stand—
> That Shakespeare's Tree produced this little Wand:
> From this to me, such Heart-felt Transport springs,
> As Staffs to Gen'rals, Sceptres give to Kings!
> The Parent Tree from whence its life it drew,
> Beneath his Care, its earliest Culture knew,
> And with his Fame, the spreading Branches grew.
> How once it flourish'd feeling Crowds can tell;
> Unfeeling Foes will mention how it fell.

Boswell thought this was lively; and maybe he would have applauded the redoubtable *alto-relievo* of Shakespeare and the Muses which used to stand in London outside Boydell's late eighteenth-century Shakespeare Gallery in Pall Mall. It is on the eastern side of the garden. Beyond, the tower of the Royal Shakespeare Theatre, seeming as a rule to be stippled with white-

* *Much Ado About Nothing*, II, iii, 41.

† Bernard Shaw, not to be outdone, planted a mulberry tree in Priory Park, Malvern (1936), to celebrate his eightieth birthday.

wash, rises from the Bancroft. Away to the south is Holy Trinity spire; across Chapel Lane, in the south-western corner, the worn presence of the Gild Chapel; and to the north-west a rumple of weathered roofs. The narrow Chapel Lane, quiet in leaf and rose-brick, which slips down to Waterside past the garden of New Place, has been called in its day Dead Lane and Walkers' Street, 'walker' meaning a fuller: the fullers used in their craft the stream that flowed through the lane.

The area must always move me more than Henley Street does. Shakespeare would have looked every day at the buildings of which the "right goodly" Gild Chapel is the lovely phantasmal centre: tower, porch, and nave rebuilt by Hugh Clopton in 1496–7, and a much earlier chancel. Within, a naïvely vigorous Day of Judgment, or Doom, overlooks the chancel arch. Beyond and behind the chapel is the half-timbered grammar school of ancient lineage. After 1553 the school functioned in the massively oak-framed upper room of the early fifteenth-century Gild Hall, where a governing ghost is Alexander Aspinall, a consequential Oxford man from Lancashire, who lived in Stratford from 1582 as schoolmaster and in various borough offices. Shakespeare might have studied under three predecessors, of whom the second, Thomas Jenkins, a Hugh Evans figure, would have given a Welsh enthusiasm to his *hig, hag, hog* and his "focative" case; but Aspinall was the most complete pedagogue. Probably Holofernes of *Love's Labour's Lost*, the man lives as I remember Mark Dignam playing him at Stratford in 1956, tetchy and pedantic, with a burnt-toast rasp in the voice; talking at large as a wind-blown thorn-bush, with a roving eye, might talk if it had a love of Latin and a gulping laugh (a kind of *ricanement*) to punctuate its tags. Quivering with irascibility, his hair "full of oaties", as they say in the old Scots farce, the actor—a mint of phrases in his brain— was gloriously in command. Below Aspinall's schoolroom is the long, low hall where the Gild of the Holy Cross used to hold its feast as prescribed in the original ordinances, brothers and sisters each giving twopence a year at an annual gathering held in

Easter Week, in such manner that brotherly love shall be cherished among them, and evil speaking be driven out; that peace shall always dwell among them, and true love be upheld. And every sister of the Gild shall bring with her to this feast a great tankard;

Stratford-upon-Avon: Bridge Street, crowded in mid-season

RESTAURANT
EVENING
TELEGRAPH

and all the tankards shall be filled with ale; and afterwards the ale shall be given to the poor. So likewise shall the brethren do; and their tankards shall, in like manner, be filled with ale and this also shall be given to the poor. But before that ale shall be given to the poor, and before any brother or sister shall touch the feast in the hall where it is accustomed to be held, all the brethren and sisters there gathered together shall put up their prayers, that God and the Virgin and the venerated Cross, in whose honour they have come together, will keep them from all ills and sins. And if any sister does not bring her tankard, as is above said, she shall pay a halfpenny. Also, if any brother or sister shall, after the bell has sounded, quarrel, or stir up a quarrel, he shall pay a halfpenny.

Here, too, in rather less amity, the corporation would meet after 1553, and strolling players—when a bailiff was as tolerant as most of them were before Master Baker—would act at the upper end of the hall: the Queen's Men, or Leicester's, or Worcester's, or Derby's. Next to the grammar school on the south is the soberly timbered range of fifteenth-century almshouses; these, with their overhanging upper storey, continue to lodge twenty-four deserving old people of Stratford. We are in Church Street now; and we drop abruptly from Shakespeare to Marie Corelli. Probably few people in the flower procession have a thought for her when they pass on the Birthday the house called Mason Croft. It is on the western side of Church Street: scraped and austere in its early eighteenth-century brick, but in Marie Corelli's time held together by a mass of rustling creepers rather like her prose.

VI

Marie Corelli (who in childhood could have been Minnie Mackay) genuinely wanted to help Stratford; to do what she could for Shakespeare's town and the town of her adoption: a pleasing coincidence. Unluckily, she approached everything with the self-conscious air of the lady of the manor alighting at a humble cottage; and she was hurt and surprised when the ungrateful peasants refused to touch a forelock or to make an aproned bob. Stratford people had shuddered away from condescension. Some of them, though not all, disliked Marie at once. In spite of her generous instincts, she was vain and humourless:

5

George Carter's picture "The Immortality of Garrick"
Auditorium of the Royal Shakespeare Theatre, Stratford-upon-Avon

she saw herself, in a sense, as Shakespeare's executrix, charged to watch over literature, art and aesthetics generally, in the shrine of Stratford-upon-Avon. Moreover, she hated to be crossed. What she said was the law from Sinai, and who dared to contradict? In stature she was very short, and aware of it. Like many small people, she sought to assert herself, and her authoritative ways, which would have been shrugged off in London, gave offence to a town that had long understood and controlled its own affairs.

We have to assume that she was the illegitimate daughter of Dr. Charles Mackay, the writer, journalist and popular poet of "Cheer, Boys, Cheer!" Her stepbrother, Eric Mackay, to whom she was deeply attached, wrote verse. He apostrophized Beethoven:

> An angel by direct descent, a German by alliance,
> Thou didst intone the wonder-chords which made despair
>   a science

and again

> O Sire of Song! Sonata-King! Sublime and loving Master,
> The sweetest soul that ever struck an octave in disaster!

Marie herself began and abandoned a career as a pianist. She also wrote some lush sonnets that appeared during the eighties in *The Theatre*, then edited by Clement Scott. The first (1883) was on Rosalind and directed at Orlando. It ended:

> What! Canst not spy beneath the shepherd's vest
> The bounteous wave of Rosalind's fair breast?
> As boy she kissed thee. By that touch divine
> Wert still in doubt with *her* sweet lips on thine?

Music and poetry were not enough: in 1886, when she was 31, she turned novelist and *A Romance of Two Worlds* appeared. Thenceforward she continued for the rest of her life to turn out these cascading romances, bounteous waves, that would be praised from time to time, and, inexplicably, by such personages as Tennyson, Gladstone and Meredith. Maurice Rostand translated her into French. She came to live in Stratford during the early summer of 1899, first renting the Dower House and Hall's Croft, and settling at length in 1901 at Mason Croft in Church Street. Here, with her friend Bertha Vyver, she lived through the rest of her life, twenty-three years. Her novels, fierce in scrambled syntax and urgent absurdity, took her name into countries she would never see, but would be quite prepared to describe in rapturous detail. At the end she was still being read for other reasons: a lexicographer told me that he had studied her books to examine the art of complicated bad writing. Even he allowed that Marie Corelli's sincerity, her belief in herself, could carry her through the most clotted pages. She was never an Amanda Ros (who called her "the greatest and most famous novelist who ever lived"), though I must admit that Amanda is more amusing to read. She never deviates into sense; occasionally Marie Corelli does.

My father, a merchant skipper, used to take to sea on any new voyage a fresh crate of books—Carlyle to Corelli, Conrad to Caine—and leave the previous collection at home. Gradually he accumulated a full shelf of Corelli. Between 8 and 10 I was reading *Wormwood*, an awful warning against absinthe that did not shock me as grievously as it should have done; *Vendetta*, in which somebody had been buried alive; *The Sorrows of Satan*, which I was to meet later on a repertory stage, red fire crackling and fizzing uncertainly round the devilish form of Prince Lucio; *Thelma*, in which Marie pulled the Norwegian scenes from her imagination; *A Romance of Two Worlds*, with its theory of "the electric origin of the universe" (" 'Remind me why these wonders exist,' he said, turning to my guide, and speaking in those dulcet sounds which were like music and yet like speech"); and *The Treasure of Heaven, A Romance of Riches*, prefaced by a portrait "in order to prevent any further misleading of the public by fraudulent inventions". That was published in 1906; she went on to use the same portrait until nearly the end of her life. *The Treasure of Heaven*, which Meredith, of all readers, is said to have admired, has a few passages of special feeling. Thus: "I daresay all the little towns and villages in this neighbourhood are full of petty discords, jealousies, envyings, and spites." A word, too, about reviewing:

Criticism from fellows who just turn over the pages of a book to find fault casually wherever they can—(I've seen them at it in newspaper offices!) or to quote unfairly mere scraps of sentences without context—or to fly off into a whirlwind of personal and scurrilous calumnies against an author whom they don't know, and perhaps never will know—that sort of thing is quite useless to me. . . . It is a mere flabby exhibition of incompetency—much as if a jellyfish should try to fight a seagull!

She expressed her undisciplined jellyfish-and-seagull imagination in a frenzy of dashes and italics. Curiously, she never essayed what Henry Labouchere exhorted her to do: to "write a novel bringing in Shakespeare and Anne Hathaway, and with local colouring". The great company of the faithful, away from Stratford, would have received it reverently, and it would have had a spirited plot. She enjoyed plotting. Her books were like mats of mesembryanthemum on the Cornish cliffs, blobby, bright and luxuriant. Readers squelched across them in the least expected places. My father remembered a voyage to Iquique when his ship, fore and aft, was lightning-split by a debate over *The Sorrows of Satan*, the novel with a paragon whose initials are M.C., Mavis Clare. In a South American port he found a Brazilian customs official spelling earnestly through *Wormwood*. One of the sternest of preachers took *God's Good Man* into a Cornish village pulpit.

In Stratford-upon-Avon, where she used to relax on the river in a gondola, *The Dream*—her first gondolier, a Venetian professional, was sacked for inebriety—Marie's books were discussed less freely than her character. She was warm-hearted. She loved Stratford's past and sought where she could, to save any threatened building. Yet, fatally, she remembered that she was a genius, Stratford's pride, and exempt from rules. Her last years were calmer; passion spent, she was too tired for major fights or minor frictions. In April 1924 she died, and during the Birthday procession soon afterwards, the band, in salute, stopped playing as it came up to Mason Croft.

The house, in its early eighteenth-century brick, was down-at-heel when she and Miss Vyver entered it. Rapidly it was renovated: its front covered abundantly with creepers, its window-boxes filled in season with tulips, pansies, and hyacinths. In the garden Marie had a pavilion for work, and she acquired beside the house a building that she made into a music room. Once established, she began her often tactless philanthropy, her intrusiveness into local affairs, ecclesiastical, municipal and—this was to be expected—theatrical. She stopped Sir Theodore Martin from erecting a mural bas-relief in Holy Trinity chancel as a memorial to his wife, the actress Helen Faucit: this dispute ended in the Court of Arches. She fought for old houses. With some cause she attacked the Memorial Theatre's bowdlerized 'Flower' texts of Shakespeare. Involved in a libel action with a local resident, she received a farthing damages. It was a prickly life, yet those nearest to her respected her intentions. Conceited, petulant, basically kind, her personality lingers, though most of her books have fallen to dust. She is not Marie Corelli the novelist, but the Miss Corelli, who would arrive, fatuously, as 'Pansy' at an Edwardian fancy-dress ball, or drive round the town in a pony-chaise drawn by two Shetlands, or refuse to change the clocks of Mason Croft from "God's time" to "Summer time".

After Marie died and was buried in Stratford Cemetery under an angel of Carrara marble, Miss Vyver lived on in Mason Croft until her own death in 1941. The terms of Marie's will had then to be considered, and they were alarming. She had designated Mason Croft as the future meeting-place "for the annual or provincial meeting of scientists connected with the Royal Institution of Great Britain", and as a home for "distinguished persons visiting Stratford-upon-Avon from far countries, who should be selected and recommended to the trustees by the Council of the Society of Authors, and who would otherwise seek their quarters in a hotel". She "absolutely excluded actors, actresses, and all persons connected with the stage"—Marie never forgot her differences with the Memorial Theatre and with Mrs. (Lady) Benson—and she also banned strictly the employment of "any person or persons connected with Stratford-upon-Avon officially or otherwise". It was all more than a little wild; and Marie Corelli had not foreseen that, with failing royalties, there would be no money to maintain the house.

Inevitably the provision was declared void. The house and its contents had to be sold, and some of Marie's possessions went for absurd sums. A picture for which she had paid £525 fetched two guineas, with the easel (which the purchaser most coveted) thrown in; and a complete set of the novels, bound in blue leather and signed, went for £29. The gondola did better (sixty-seven guineas), but a pantomime impresario paid only thirty-two guineas for the pony-chaise. In time Mason Croft became the Stratford home of the British Council; today—and this is work Marie Corelli might have acknowledged—it is the Shakespeare

Institute of the University of Birmingham. I think of a spacious, cheerful building with doors innumerable; of a bedroom in which a certain Jane Collins, sometime during the late eighteenth century, scratched her name upon the window-glass; and of the music room, where so many speakers have lectured from the point of view of scholar, director or critic. It is well over two decades since the façade was decorously restored. An authority speaks with cold reserve of a "seven-bay brick front of two storeys, with raised quoins". That would not have been Marie Corelli's way of putting it. Some may regret the old, lavishly floral aspect like the unrestrained tangle of a Corelli novel: "Seest thou yonder planet circled with a ring. It is known to the dwellers on Earth, of whom when in clay thou art one, as Saturn. Descend with me."

VII

Dwellers on Earth, in the procession from the Birthplace, discover that Church Street gives eventually upon Old Town, core of the settlement in the dim, pre-Conquest age when a monastery (invariably monks knew the right places to build) stood roughly where Holy Trinity Church stands now. It is less than a hundred years (1879) since much of Old Town, including Hall's Croft and the Church, was brought within the borough boundaries. Now it is a gentle way through history, guarded by such buildings as Hall's Croft and the former Dower House of the Clopton family, where the centuries kiss and commingle, and where the staircase could very well be Shakespeare's own, removed by Sir John Clopton after the rebuilding of New Place about 1700. Shakespeare's son-in-law, Dr John Hall, a Puritan, a physician much-regarded in Warwickshire "as also in the counties adjacent", and a man of marked independence, lived at Hall's Croft with Susanna Shakespeare after their marriage in Holy Trinity in June 1607; she was eight years his junior, and he was only eleven years younger than his father-in-law. We can be fairly certain that Shakespeare respected him. It may not be fortuitous that the most affectionately presented doctor in the canon, Cerimon in *Pericles* ("In reverend Cerimon there well appears The worth that learned charity aye wears") arrived when John Hall and Susanna had not long been married. I am unsure whether the General Medical

Council would have allowed Cerimon, "a lord of Ephesus", to practice; but he spent his time studying physic and employing "the blest infusions that dwell in vegetives, in metals, stones", and Ephesians thought it was the natural thing to consult him. His restoration of Thaisa, thrown ashore in the caulked and bitumed chest, her body shrouded in cloth of state, "balm'd and entreasured with full bags of spices", is a scene that must linger from the Levantine journey. To the music of viols, and in the warmth of Cerimon's chamber, Thaisa stirs:

> Gentlemen, this queen will live; nature awakes;
> A warmth breathes out of her; she hath not been
> Entranc'd above five hours; see how she 'gins
> To blow into life's flower again!

Upon awakening, she faints; but Cerimon and the bystanders bear her into the next room: "Come, come; and Aesculapius guide us." Let us hope that John Hall was pleased.

We do not see the earlier crown of Shakespearean doctors, Gerard de Narbon, for he was dead when *All's Well That Ends Well* opens. His skill was "almost as great as his honesty; had it stretch'd so far, would have made nature immortal, and death should have play for lack of work." A man indeed; but he had gone, and the King of France had abandoned other physicians, "under whose practices he hath persecuted time with hope; and finds no other advantage in the process but only the losing of hope by time". Luckily, Gerard left to Helena, his daughter, "some prescriptions of rare and prov'd effects", among them "a remedy, approv'd . . . to cure the desperate languishings whereof the King is rendered lost". Soon Helena is with the King, telling him of the receipt that was the "dearest issue" of her father's practice. Fresh from the gloom of the "most learned doctors" and "the congregated College", he is not sanguine. Helena stakes her life upon a cure to be performed at speed, saying so in couplets that, however reprehensible they may be, have clung to capricious memory since I read Shakespeare first and shouted the rhymes (see-saw, Margery Daw) across the cove and valley of Caerthillian:

> The great'st grace lending grace,
> Ere twice the horses of the sun shall bring
> Their fiery torcher his diurnal ring;
> Ere twice in murk and occidental damp

> Moist Hesperus hath quench'd his sleepy lamp;
> Or four and twenty times the pilot's glass
> Hath told the thievish minutes how they pass;
> What is infirm from your sound parts shall fly,
> Health shall live free and sickness freely die.

We know that Helena succeeded—in one Stratford production the restored King leapt over a bench—and that she also won the reluctant Bertram, the main object of her toil. Though I have never liked the child, and have wondered what the "congregated college" said of her, we must remember that Shakespeare took his plot from the third day of the Decameron: the narrators were then discussing those who, by effort and determination, either obtained what they greatly admired, or regained what they had lost.

Earlier yet, Caius is the comic French doctor of *The Merry Wives of Windsor*. We cannot blame actors for what is called extravagance; Shakespeare has set down clearly enough how the man must be played. Mistress Quickly gives the word in her first speech: "If he find anybody in the house, here will be an old abusing of God's patience and the King's English." Caius's first words on entering are: "Vat is it you sing? I do not like dese toys. Pray you, go and vetch me in my closet *un boitier vert*—a box, a green-a box: do intend vat I speak? a green-a box." We go on from there. Every actor in memory has played the man like a jumping-jack. He belongs to the section, 'Farce', and to its sub-section, 'All Foreigners Are Funny'.

Friar and Apothecary in *Romeo and Juliet* do not come within our reckoning. *Macbeth* has an English doctor who appears solely as a cue for Malcolm's speech on the King's Evil and Shakespeare's flattery of James. Later, a Scot, unhappiest of all, in castle practice at Dunsinane, is obliged to watch the Queen's sleepwalking (where the true disease is beyond his practice) and to receive frenzied instructions from the King. A last couplet, "Were I from Dunsinane away and clear, Profit again should hardly draw me here," surprises nobody. A Doctor's part in *King Lear* is, simply, to attend at Lear's awakening in the French camp before Cordelia and Kent; the King must wake to music as Thaisa does in the house of Cerimon. No griefs there for John Hall; and I daresay he would have approved of Cornelius, physician in *Cymbeline*, who knows something of poisons, those "movers of a languishing death ... though slow, deadly", and who refuses to trust the

Queen with drugs "of such damn'd nature". Instead, he arranges for her to be "fool'd with a most false effect"; everything will be well when Imogen—each of them unaware—receives the drug from a faithful servant. Cornelius appears among the cumulated denouements of the fifth act to announce that the Queen is dead. "Who worse than a physician would this report become?" exclaims Cymbeline with some pungency, John Hall concurring.

Doctor Butts, physician to the King in *Henry the Eighth*, looks in simply to tell Henry that Cranmer waits humiliatingly at the Council door " 'mongst pursuivants, pages, and footboys". Whereupon the King observes, "By holy Mary, Butts, there's knavery;" and there is. These will serve, though we note that in *The Tempest* old Gonzalo, no medical man, says "You rub the sore when you should bring the plaster." In any predicament, my first call would be for Cerimon, with fire, cloths and music— and Aesculapius guide him. John Hall was guided, even if his book, *Select Observations on English Bodies**, written in Latin, and, after his death, "put into English for common benefit" by another practitioner "in physick and chirurgery", shows him to have been a man of frightening ideas. One of his poultices was of "swallows' nests, dirt, dung and all, boiled in oil of chamumel and lilies, beaten and passed through a sieve", to which was added "white dog's turd, one ounce, the meal of linseed and foenagreek, each one ounce, ointment of Diathea and hen's grease, each half an ounce—and so make a poultice—it is applied hot". Undeniably Hall, applying most things hot, adorned his profession; but one might have felt happier with his wife, whose epitaph in Holy Trinity begins with the couplet, "Witty above her sex, but that's not all; wise to salvation was good Mistress Hall." Both she and her husband, he in 1635, she in 1649, died at New Place, where they went from Old Town in 1616 after Shakespeare's death, traditionally of a "feavour"† that even John Hall could not abate. The Croft, oak-firm, many-gabled, with overhanging upper floor and a walled garden, "circummured with brick", is now one of the Birthplace Trust properties and the picture, internally,

---

* The full title was *Select Observations on English Bodies; or, Cures both Empericall and Historicall, performed upon very eminent Persons in desperate Diseases.*

† John Ward, vicar of Stratford 1662–1681, wrote in his journal (1661–1663): "Shakespear, Drayton, and Ben Jhonson, had a merry meeting, and itt seems drank too hard, for Shakespear died of a feavour there contracted."

of a middle-class Tudor home; room also for Dr. Hall's dispensary, with herbs, pills, pestles and mortars and apothecaries' jars. On the purchase of Hall's Croft in 1949, Shakespeare's Birthplace, the site of his last Stratford home and the houses linked with the names of his mother, his wife, and his daughter, came under one control.

On the opposite side of Old Town is the inconspicuous College Street, roughly the site of the college built in 1353 for housing the priests of Holy Trinity. In the mid-sixteenth century it was a large private house—separated from the Church by Mill Lane— that was demolished eventually in 1799. Garrick would have had glum recollections of it during those drenching days in 1769 when it served as Jubilee headquarters. College Street means rather more to me than the ancient foundation, simply because through one long summer, while working in Fleet Street, I would hurry down whenever possible for a few hours in Stratford—walking out after dark from the station (then normally equipped with trains), and going by way of Chapel Lane and Southern Lane. The last was then high-walled on both sides, its bricks warm to the touch in a resplendent June. At the end of Southern Lane, where Holy Trinity spire—it seemed, with its bells, to be in our garden—rose dimly on the left, a yellow cat would purr down from its chosen tree. On the walk I might have overtaken the actor, George Hayes, who lodged next door in College Street, and who would be nursing a headache if it were one of the nights when he was playing Macbeth in Theodore Komisarjevsky's fevered idea of the part: less of a fallen angel, Lucifer, star of the morning (Masefield's conception) than a dangerous neurotic given to nightmares in one of which he spoke the entire cauldron scene.

Just beyond College Street, at the curve of Old Town, is Stratford's Collegiate Church among its limes, plumed elms and riparian tombs. Dixon Scott, of the *Manchester Guardian*, wrote some sixty years ago: "As the spire emerges and passes up against the sky, you get a sense that you are watching the uprising of some great figure commanding silence. You will probably feel inclined to obey." The visitor is expected to pay for his homage, and the toll equates the church with a museum—a pity, even if we know that a fabric must be maintained. Holy Trinity is approached along Puck's "churchway path", between a grove of limes that put out their ruby buds at the Birthday season.

Shakespeare would not have known the present octagonal stone spire, a landmark from the roads into Stratford. When he went to the church, on the edge of town and river, there was a wooden spire covered with lead and only half the height; it was replaced in 1763. The charnel house on the north side of the church has gone as well. Otherwise Shakespeare would recognize much within and without the great cruciform building with its odd 'skew', or inclination of the chancel to the north. He would know the sanctuary knocker on the door of the north porch, Hugh Clopton's cenotaph of Caen stone, the carved misericords in the chancel (St George, angels, a dromedary, an eagle, a mermaid and so forth) and the rhymed epitaph written in four languages— Hebrew, Greek, Latin, and English—upon a townsman of his youth: Richard Hall, a grazier and thrice bailiff of the borough, who died in 1593. The inscription says winningly:

> Here borne, here lived, here died, and buried here,
> Lieth Richard Hill, thrice bailif of this borow:
> Two matrones of good fame, he married in Godes feare,
> And now releast in joi he reasts from worldlie sorrow.
> Here lieth entombed the corps of Richarde Hill,
> A woollen draper beeing in his time:
> Whose virtues live, whose fame dooth florish still,
> Though he desolved be to dust and slime.
> A mirror he, and paterne mai be made,
> For such as shall suckcead him in that trade:
> He did not use to sweare to glose eather faigne
> His brother to defraude in barganinge:
> He would not strive to get excessive gaine
> In ani cloath or other kinde of thinge;
> His servant S.I. this trueth can testifie
> A witness that beheld it with my eie.

We might call it a select observation on an English body.

Full of air and light, Holy Trinity has a springing grace. Its architecture covers several centuries and several idioms. The central tower (Early English) is from about 1210; the transepts are also Early English; the aisles and columns of the high, broad nave are in the Decorated style (about 1330); and the clerestory, porch, and the shining, flowering chancel built by a Dean Balsall (he "reedified the quier") are Perpendicular. The Clopton Chapel, all painted alabaster and lying-in-state—observe, too, a sculptured flourish of gunpowder-barrel, cannon and flags—speaks strongly for Stratford's great household. Elsewhere I think of a memorial tablet to actors who fell in the First World War, with a Kipling quatrain*, and the dark green marble pulpit that in 1900 was Sir Theodore Martin's tribute to his wife, Helen Faucit, a Victorian actress who played several Shakespeare heroines and wrote about them, and who had a youthful attachment to her leading actor, William Charles Macready. She was Beatrice in *Much Ado* on the opening night of the Shakespeare Memorial Theatre in 1879. One of the alabaster statuettes round the pulpit is of the Empress Helena, but the face is Lady Martin's. When I hear Helen Faucit's name, it summons not a slightly oracular retired actress—properly remembered by a pulpit—but a flirtatious, clinging girl who, in the late 1830s and early 40s, had such an infatuation for her fatherly but easily susceptible manager that he had to debate its ebb-and-flow in his nightly journal. He even wrote for her album a poem that began:

> Tis not the dove-like softness of thine eyes
>   My pensive gaze that draws, however fair;
> A holier charm within their beauty lies,
>   The unspotted soul, that's mirrored always there.

("My muse," he murmured, "is cold—she never had much vitality".) I suppose that only one visitor in 10,000 may remember Helen Faucit. All 10,000 will go straight to the chancel of Holy Trinity where the Bust overlooks five plain gravestones within the sanctuary rails: those of Anne Shakespeare; her husband; Thomas Nash (son-in-law of Susanna and John Hall); and the Halls themselves. Touching as the chancel tombs must be to anybody unashamed of emotion, it can be more touching outside the church in the fall of a late summer afternoon. There, from the river parapet of the churchyard, we look across the Avon to a droop of willows and the mildly-rising Midland pastures. Not far off is the everlasting water-music of the weir. It is a place of unstained simplicity. We realize the aptness with which that Stratford scholar, the late Frederick Wellstood,

---

* We counterfeited once for your disport
  Men's joy and sorrow; but our day has passed.
  We pray your pardon all where we fell short—
  Seeing we were your servants to the last.

varied Byron's lines on Petrarch at Arqua:

> They keep his dust in Stratford, where he died:
> The midland village where his latter days
> Went down the vale of years; and 'tis their pride—
> An honest pride—and let it be their praise,
> To offer to the passing stranger's gaze
> His birthplace and his sepulchre; both plain
> And venerably simple, such as raise
> A feeling more accordant with his strain
> Than if a pyramid form'd his monumental fane.

VIII

Sometimes, even in Stratford churchyard I find guiltily that while my words fly up, my thoughts remain below. They cannot extricate themselves altogether from a page in an obscure auto-biography by the Victorian actor-dramatist, Edward Stirling, with the misleading title, *Old Drury Lane*. He wrote it in 1881, but the tale is undated.

STRATFORD-UPON-AVON, SHAKESPEARE'S CHURCHYARD:

Watching a sexton, removing an old gravestone bearing the date 1661 [wrote Stirling], my abstraction was disturbed by a hand on my shoulder.

"Excuse me, sir, I see by your face you like my fellow-townsman, Shakespeare. I'll show you a relic of him." Here was a real surprise. "Walk with me." I did, to his lodgings. Carefully wrapped up, he brought forth—what?—a rusty old weather-cock, inscribed "1573".

"This vane," said he, "blew down last year. I luckily picked it up. If it could speak, wouldn't it tell us how often and often sweet Willy looked up at it to see which way the wind blew!"* (a very natural deduction). "I daresay you wonder who I am?" *(bowing)*.

I did.

"A French horn."

"What?"

"Yes, I travel with a menagerie up and down the country, blowing my inside out for twenty-two shillings a week. I'll turn it up, and go on the stage. Shakespeare did, and he went to the same school that I did."

After so much confidence on the part of my new acquaintance,

---

* I am surprised that no scholar has yet connected this with Borachio and Conrade in *Much Ado About Nothing*, III, iii: "Didst thou not hear somebody?" —"No, 'twas the vane on the house."

I ventured to state that I was connected with Drury Lane, and thanking him for his interesting communications, bade him good-day. To my no small astonishment, a few weeks after, came this proposal from the French horn:

Stratford-upon-Avon

Dear Sir,

According to promise i rite and if you can do anything for me i am not afraid but that i can give you satisfaction. i can imitate the Cornet Saxhorn Clarinet Harp Violoncello &c. can sound four octaves sing old Jowler with imitations of the huntsmans horn hounds in full cry death sound at the distance i was with Offemans in the name of Herr Herlong two months left not likeing the party i took the lead in the first March song bass in the glees played second in the rest of the tunes i was born in the same street as the immortall Bard had hold of a deer in the same park that he stolen is from the day after last Christmas have never been in London yet but thought i should have liked to have come with the deer if you can do anything for me you will oblige your humble servant

JOHN KEMP
No 15 Scholars Lane
Stratford-upon-Avon

Sing comic or sentimental

I immediately replied to "Herr Herlong", advising him to replace the deer in Lucy's park, forget "Will", and stick to the French horn and Old Jowler.

IX

Scholars Lane, where the French Horn lived, runs up from the intersection of Chapel and Church Streets, almost opposite Chapel Lane. This was the old Tinkers' Lane that contained the pinfold, or pound, for straying cattle. We have yet to penetrate Stratford's minor streets and to beat its outer bounds, those areas like the petticoat-fringe of Rosalind's tactless analogy. Though casual visitors are seen there as rarely as a scurrying tourist in the parts of Venice round Sant' Alvise or behind San Francesco della Vigna, most people in love with the town do find themselves very soon on the path round to the mill, averting their gaze from the silo, examining the record of high-water marks (when the Avon has "drowned its shores"), crossing the footbridge over a river that can be frothed uncomfortably with detergent, exploring the decent red-brick cottage streets behind Old Town, hearing

that long ago a portable melodrama fit-up used to glorify the
evenings in Sanctus Street, and looking for a lost and secondary
railway station that in a primitive world could have despatched
them to Marylebone.

If we go from Old Town westward along Chestnut Walk, and
turn into Rother Street, towards the fountain, we move of a
sudden into the early fifteenth century. The house called Mason's
Court, on the left-hand side, is a crumpled building that, with its
crooked timbers, over-peering eyebrows of wavy roof and thin-
bricked chimney-stack, is keeping itself upright by force of will.
When it was built it had a central hall open from ground to roof.
Compared with Mason's Court, Payton Street, only a century
and a half old, has yet to grow up. To the north of the town, the
canal behind it, it is the first left-hand turning off the Warwick
Road. I stayed there during my early visits to Stratford, close to
a Baptist chapel with a columned and pedimented front. The
house was late Georgian, stuccoed, its porch pillared, its staircase
curved graciously, its garden stretching at the back between plum-
bloom walls towards the then weedy canal. When the street, with
others, was developed in the Regency from an area known un-
compromisingly as the Gild Pits, it was named after an important
Stratford man of a generation just gone. Landlord of the White
Lion in Henley Street, John Payton had been on the council when
the new town hall was built, and he helped to plan the Garrick
Jubilee. For this he looked after the general catering ("300 dozen
of pewter plates . . . 50 dozen of stewpans and kettles, and 300
waiters"); also he nearly doubled the size of his own inn, a
speculation less profitable than he had hoped. Later he served
thrice as mayor: he might be pleased to know that there are two
streets, not far from his own, that are called Shakespeare and
Mulberry—neither, alas, inspires. There is nothing at all for
Thomas Sharp.

When I knew Payton Street one of its houses belonged to a
veteran actor who looked more actorish than anybody had a right
to be. A pavement was a stage; if he entered a room the curtain
rose. He gave to his Shakespearean parts the amplest top-dressing
of Edwardian style. Even now, an April midnight in this street,
where laburnum and lilac trail across the brick copings, must
always be his, just as Scholars Lane must always be the personal
property of Edward Stirling's friend, the French Horn.

FOUR

BACK TO THE JUBILEE

I

Stratford-upon-Avon is the capital of the Shakespeare Country of the plays: an empire, obliterating time, that unites the plains of Troy and the wolds of Gloucestershire; Sicily and Elsinore and Navarre, the Levant and Illyria, Agincourt and Philippi; tumult at the Boar's Head, news on the Rialto, the Cypriot alarum-bell and the Bohemian bear. No empire has been more closely fought over; its historians thrust at each other as A. E. Housman at the former editors of Manilius, or Mr. Pott at Mr. Slurk. Example: "It is nothing short of wicked that the biography of the greatest writer in our language should be made such nonsense of. This is the importance of getting it right." Every Shakespearean tries to get it right, to a chopped comma. In about 1854 Browning was apostrophizing

> You, Gigadibs, who, thirty years of age . . .
> Believe you see two points in Hamlet's soul
> Unseized by the Germans yet—which view you'll print.

It is a rich flurry when the exegetists are at odds. Only Shakespeare himself knows what has not been printed, though how he would regard the piled cairn of books we cannot guess. That starry-pointing pyramid is erected above plays that if we listen to them often enough in the theatre, their true place, can declare themselves at once.

Shakespeare might have expected them to be heard at Stratford while he was alive. In 1601 he wrote in *Hamlet:*

> Good my lord, will you see the players well bestowed? Do you hear, let them be well used, for they are the abstract and brief chronicles of the time; after your death, you were better have a bad epitaph than their ill report while you live.

80

Shakespeare's Bust in the chancel of Holy Trinity Church
Frank Benson (1858–1939): portrait (1910) by Hugh Rivière

Two years later the bailiff, aldermen and burgesses of Stratford-upon-Avon banned the players from the town. It was 'Master Baker's Year', and Daniel Baker, puritanical enemy of the stage, was unlikely to fear the "ill report" of a strolling actor. So the trumpets ceased to blaze in High Street. Young people grew in Stratford—a town literate and thriving—without knowledge of "young Hamlet, old Hieronimo, kind Lear, the grievéd Moor, and more beside". This was the position in 1612 when Shakespeare —we would say still in his prime, but lives were shorter then— had retired to his great house with barnyard and two barns, two gardens, two orchards, and everything handsome about it. Almost concurrently—and in 1613 Daniel Baker had his second term as bailiff—the council renewed its ban and increased the penalties. Plays were unlawful, and "the sufferance of them againste the orders heartofore made, and againste the example of other well-gooverned citties and burrowes"; any convicted actor would have to pay £10 instead of 10s. Shakespeare continued to write, but a late Member of the King's Men, a "housekeeper" of the Globe, and "the applause! delight! the wonder of our stage!" went down the slant of life in a town where his plays were forbidden and his friends, the players, were unwelcome guests.

Six years after he died, and in the year before John Heminge and Henry Condell edited the First Folio, the King's Men, Shakespeare's old colleagues, were on tour in the Midlands: Leicester, 8th June; Coventry, 9th June. They came over to Stratford, probably to see the tomb-maker of Southwark's coloured bust in Holy Trinity. The council hastily forbade them to perform, but remembered at the same time that these were the King's Players, with special licence "freely to use and exercise the arte and facultie of playing Comedies, Tragedies, Histories, Enterludes, Moralls, Pastorelles, stage-plaies . . . and such other like". Some compensation was advisable. Hence a serio-comic note in the accounts of the borough chamberlain of Stratford. It reads with obstinate simplicity: "To the King's Players for not playing in the Hall, 6s." No more; and nothing importantly theatrical occurred in Stratford for over 120 years, a period during which Sir William Dugdale (in the *Antiquities of Warwickshire*) wrote that the town "gave birth and sepulture to our late famous Poet Will. Shakespeare."; and in London, after the Puritan hiatus, Shakespeare was being mangled, rewritten, edited, popularized,

6

Stratford-upon-Avon: the Royal Shakespeare Theatre from the air

and in one form or another persistently acted. In 1741 he gained recognition in Westminster Abbey, a soulful monument by the sculptor, Peter Scheemaker.

Stratford hardly shared in the growing cult. It continued to prosper as a market town for corn and malt and cattle. For a time, with the opening of the Avon navigation, it expanded into a small inland port. Shakespeare it barely considered, even if the vicar of Holy Trinity, in the early Restoration, reminded himself to read the plays—the man, after all, was a former parishioner and somebody might ask about him. Early in the eighteenth century Thomas Betterton, the leading British actor, came to discover what he could and picked up a variety of legends. In 1742 a new young leader, David Garrick, a short man with extraordinary eyes, visited Stratford with Charles Macklin to see the mulberry tree at New Place and the shabby house in Henley Street. Everything, pre-Gastrell, was placid during a stay in which Garrick would have gone round to look at the Bust, decaying like the fabric of the Birthplace; visitors already had a trick of breaking off bits of the soft stone as souvenirs. Hence, in 1746, the town hall performance of *Othello*, that 'benefit' for the Bust to which John Ward, the actor-manager, had "very genteely agreed". It raised £17, enough to pay John Hall, a Bristol limner, to revive the old colouring, renew the gilding, and repair ("with ye original materials, sav'd for that purpose, whatsoever was by accident broken off"*). Having looked to the Bust, Stratford again neglected the plays, though more people began to arrive for Shakespeare's sake. Horace Walpole, writing to George Montagu of a visit in 1757, described it as "the wretchedest old town": he had hoped to find it "smug, and pretty, and *antique, not old*". As for the repainted Bust, "Lady Caroline Petersham is not more vermilion."

II

Then David Garrick reappeared, by now unquestionably at the head of the stage, and amiably aware of it. There might not have been a celebration, and Shakespeare in Stratford might not have been magnified for many decades, if the corporation had not wanted a new town hall. The old one, with the stage of *Othello*,

* *Correspondence of the Rev. Joseph Greene*, edited by Levi Fox, p. 171.

was crumbling as the Birthplace was and the Bust had been. There must be a new building, Cotswold stone in a Tuscan style, and Francis Wheler, an attorney, Steward of the Court of Records for the borough, suggested that if Garrick could give something, "some very handsome bust, statue, or picture", it would offer the publicity and spur they needed. Why not make him a Freeman of Stratford and enclose the scroll in a box made of Shakespeare's mulberry tree? Through Wheler the corporation told Garrick that it was "ever desirous of expressing gratitude to all who do honour and justice to the memory of Shakespeare", and that it was "highly sensible that no person in any age hath excelled you". If he would present some statue, bust, or picture of Shakespeare, it would be equally pleasing to have a picture of Garrick himself and to perpetuate them together. The council then procured a piece of the fertile Thomas Sharp's mulberry wood and arranged for Thomas Davies, a craftsman of Birmingham, to make from it "a small, neat chest", costing £55. Upon the front Fame held a bust of Shakespeare, the Three Graces crowning it with laurel leaves, and the mulberry tree behind. On the ends were figures of Tragedy and Comedy; Garrick, as Lear in the Storm scene, from Benjamin Wilson's painting, was carved on the back. The box stood on four small plinths, each supported by a gold-eyed, ruby-tongued dragon emblematic of Envy. Within lay the scroll of the Freedom, a document in which the Council, leaving nothing to chance, was

fully sensible of the extraordinary accomplishments and merits of [Shakespeare's] most judicious admirer and representative, David Garrick, Esq., a Gentleman who has not only raised the dignity, and increased the lustre of the Drama in general, but happily traced out the source of, and thereby added (if possible) to that pleasing command over the passions, which Shakespeare in a most eminent degree, and in numberless instances possessed.

Garrick decided, rightly, that this was a compliment. But though in October 1768 he was elected, with pomp, an honorary burgess of Stratford-upon-Avon, the box itself took a long time to make; on the north side of the town hall, the niche that waited for a new statue remained empty. The box did arrive in May 1769. Mr. George Keate, a minor poet, duly attended (with Wheler) upon Garrick in London, receiving as his reward from the council a "neat writing-standish" carved from the usual golden tree. Delighted, Garrick wrote from Southampton Street, saying that the Freedom "sent me in such an elegant and inestimable box, and delivered to me in so flattering a manner, merits my warmest gratitude". Why not, then, a festival, a Jubilee, an elaborate tribute to Shakespeare by the Avon itself, something to be repeated perhaps every seventh year?

Already he had fixed on a Jubilee symbol: the mulberry. Meanwhile he could, and did, send to Stratford John Cheere's leaden copy of a revised version of the Scheemaker statue in the Abbey,

> Untouch'd and sacred be thy shrine,
> Avonian Willy, bard divine,
> In studious posture leaning!

With it was a rather gloomy domestic portrait of Shakespeare by Benjamin Wilson, instead of a new one, as he had hoped, from Gainsborough. That artist had had a luckless notion, never completed, of "showing where the inimitable poet had his ideas from, by an immediate ray darting down from his eye, turned up for the purpose". However, Gainsborough was ready for sixty guineas to paint Garrick at full length, standing in a grove and leaning nonchalantly, cross-legged, against a Shakespeare bust*. The corporation, ready to pay for this, found other expenses rising: not that these mattered with the Jubilee ahead, the worship of the blest mulberry and, it followed, of Garrick himself. It filled the actor's mind and overflowed into his verse. A Drury Lane audience heard about it that May, in an exclamatory epilogue at the close of the spring season:

> My eyes till then† no sights like this will see
> Unless we meet at *Shakespeare's Jubilee!*
> On Avon's Banks where flowers eternal blow!
> Like its full stream, our gratitude shall flow!
> There let us revel, show our fond regard;
> On that loved spot first breathed our matchless Bard;
> To him all honour, gratitude is due,
> To him we owe our all—to him and you.

The dates chosen were very early in the autumn, 6th, 7th and

* This fine picture was destroyed during the fire in Stratford Town Hall, December 1946.

† i.e. until the following season.

8th September—no Shakespearean anniversary but Stratford Race Week. Massive preparation filled the summer. Because the heart of the Jubilee must be "on Avon's banks", nothing, Garrick thought, would be more serviceable or look better than a wooden copy of the Rotunda at Ranelagh, London's octagonal and modish pleasure dome. Obviously, though some wanted a site behind John Payton's 'White Lion' up in Henley Street, the place was the Bank Croft meadow on the west or town bank of the Avon, where Stratford people in Shakespeare's time could pasture their cattle for an hour daily: "all horses, geldings, mares, swine, geese, ducks, and other cattle" found there against the regulations were impounded by the beadle in the Tinkers' Lane pinfold. In 1769 the meadow, a pastoral water-colour, had many willows upon it—half of these by permission of the Duke of Dorset, who owned the land, and his lessee, Dionysus Bradley, were promptly cut down; thus, as Garrick would say later, the ravish'd eye of Stratford swains could have

A rich command
Of widen'd river, lengthen'd plain,
And op'ning skies.

The fallen willows were bought by a Church Street carpenter and auctioneer who sold them to a Sheep Street maltster—in partnership, remarkably, with Mr Thomas Sharp.

The octagonal Rotunda, even if it would be derided as "a gingerbread amphitheatre", looked solid enough. It covered 560 square yards. Able to hold 1,000 people and an orchestra of more than a hundred—this was important in Garrick's scheme—it had a central circular arcade of Corinthian columns seventy feet in diameter, a painted dome and a number of elegant chandeliers. Gilding, painting, embellishments, shone in a diffused glow of wax candles; it seemed a pity that Shakespeare's Hall, as Garrick named it—though it was also the Rotunda or the Great Booth— could have a life of only a few days. Its building was troublesome. Tactlessly, workmen had been imported from London: painters and carpenters from Drury Lane Theatre were busy under the seldom ravish'd eye of Stratford swains. Not long before the date the builders ran out of timber, and local carpenters, pleased to be as unco-operative as possible, refused to help or to lend their tools. Further, certain lamps sent down from Drury Lane for external "transparencies" devised by the lighting master, Signor Dominico Angelo, reached Stratford in fragments. By the end of August Garrick must have wondered what his trouble was worth. Only two actors of name had offered to help him; and all he heard elsewhere were prophecies of failure.

Resiliently, he toiled on. A warehouse opened in Stratford to sell masquerade costumes. Rainbow-hued Jubilee ribbons and favours, made at Coventry of a soft, thick silk, were ready for the week: "Shaksperian ribbands of various dyes" (Boswell) for which the sponsoring haberdasher had used Johnson's line, "Each change of *many-colour'd life* he drew": it was Johnson's only link with the Jubilee. Medals, designed by Davies of Birmingham, the man of the Freedom 'box', were struck in copper, silver and gold with Shakespeare's likeness. The organizers hired sedan chairs from Bath and London. Signor Angelo, fresh lamps procured, completed his transparency for the façade of the Rotunda: great figures of Tragedy and Comedy, with Shakespeare, led to Immortality by Time, between them. There were to be more transparencies for the town hall windows: Lear and Caliban (drinking from Stephano's keg) on one side, Falstaff and Pistol on the other. Garrick had proposed for the window of the designated Birthroom in Henley Street, a scene that would show "the sun struggling through clouds to enlighten the world". Beyond a great scarlet and crimson and deep blue transparency (with many lamps behind it) that almost obscured the house, sat a Londoner, Mr. Thomas Beckett, "grand bookseller to the Jubilee". Boswell mused that Time would show "whether inspiration poetical hath impregnated him".

Garrick in June had said hopefully, "I have no doubt but that we shall be able to amuse the attenders upon ye Jubilee, to their, and our own, Satisfaction." But in September even he was anxious. Advertisements had drawn crowds to rural Warwickshire. Many people drove down early to make sure of rooms, wretched and expensive. Carriages converged upon the town which lay under ominous cloud. There had been severe rain; and the Avon, turbid and swelling, looked anything but the current that with gentle murmur glides. It was crowded, too, with small craft, because in those days Stratford—with the river navigable from Bristol for boats of up to thirty tons—was technically a port, its centre near the 'Swan's Nest' inn at the eastern end of Clopton

Bridge. On the brink of the Bank Croft, where the Royal Shakespeare Theatre stands today, thirty cannon were ready to be fired; Angelo had provided a battery of fireworks in the meadow across the river. Superficially, everything seemed hopeful, and yet there was an odd foreboding. Garrick could not think of anything he had omitted. It had never occurred to him that a dramatist is honoured in performance, and that a Shakespeare festival might be odd without a Shakespeare play.

III

As he and his wife Eva-Maria—guests of the town clerk—woke at daybreak on Wednesday, 6th September, Garrick heard the Bank Croft cannon booming into the cold September air, and presently bells pealed across Stratford. It was five o'clock. Already serenaders from Drury Lane, fantastic in period costume ("in disguise", Boswell said) had begun the Jubilee with song. To the notes of guitars, hautboys, flutes, and clarionets, they sang Dibdin's aubade, "Let beauty with the sun arise, To Shakespeare tribute pay", followed by the Steward's best ballad, all seven verses. It began:

> Ye Warwickshire lads, and ye lasses,
>   See what at our jubilee passes;
> Come away, rejoice, and be glad,
> For the lad of all lads, was a Warwickshire lad,
>   Warwickshire lad,
>   All be glad,
> For the lad of all lads, was a Warwickshire lad.

It went on to:

> Old Ben, Thomas Otway, John Dryden,
> And half a score more we take pride in,
> Of famous Will Congreve, we boast too the skill,
> But the Will of all Wills, was a Warwickshire Will,
>   Warwickshire Will,
>   Matchless still,
> For the Will of all Wills, was a Warwickshire Will.

> Our Shakespeare compar'd is to no man,
> Nor Frenchman, nor Grecian, nor Roman,
> Their swans are all geese, to the Avon's sweet swan,
> And the man of all men, was a Warwickshire man,

> Warwickshire man,
> Avon's swan,
> And the man of all men, was a Warwickshire man . . .

And it ended:

> There was never seen such a creature,
> Of all he was worth, he robb'd Nature;
> He took all her smiles, and he took all her grief,
> For the thief of all thieves, was a Warwickshire thief,
> Warwickshire thief,
> He's the chief,
> For the thief of all thieves, was a Warwickshire thief.

Many other visitors, who had spent a night less agreeable than Garrick's, responded to the last line. Stratford was not shaped to receive guests. There was only one really major inn, the 'White Lion' (Garrick had an official suite there), so townspeople had to make room among themselves; several, knowing the chance would not recur, charged extortionately for the shabbiest accommodation. Among the visitors was the lame Samuel Foote, Cornish-born dramatist and comedian, a wasp with a sharp pleasure in stinging Garrick. He travelled to Stratford with the theatrical freelance, Arthur Murphy, and it could not have helped Garrick to meet this mocking pair at an hour of tension. Other patronage comforted him: the presence of the Duke of Dorset, High Steward of the borough, who had allowed the Bank Croft willows to be felled; and such people as the Duke of Manchester, the Earls and Countesses of Plymouth, Hertford and Northampton, the Earls of Carlisle, Shrewsbury and Denbigh, Lords Beauchamp and Grosvenor, Lady Pembroke and Mrs Clive, not to speak of James ('Corsican') Boswell, then 28 and in tearing spirits. All of these except Boswell, who got typically into disaster on the journey down, had shelter for the night; others who had not troubled to bespeak rooms, had to 'bivouac' in carriages and chaises that would soon slop axle-deep in mud. Foote was delighted.

It had not begun to rain when Garrick rose on the morning of the 6th, assumed a suit of mole and amber velvet, gold-trimmed, with a lining of ivory taffeta, and hurried to the town hall. Here the mayor and corporation formally and superfluously appointed him Steward of the Jubilee. On his breast "the short punch man, very quick and entertaining", wore a mulberry medal of Shakespeare, set in gold; in his white-gauntleted hands he carried a long, thin mulberry wand of office. Cannon thudded from Avonside; bells clashed from the church; and the Jubilee began in such a way that Garrick felt the affair he would later call his "foolish hobby-horse" might have real success. Wednesday, in fact, was a choral prelude. After a public breakfast, when tea, coffee and chocolate were served in the town hall, the company moved to Old Town, to the lime avenue, and to Shakespeare's church where flowers lay upon the grave, laurel wreathed the Bust, and the musician, Dr. Thomas Arne, conducted his oratorio of *Judith*, to words by Isaac Bickerstaffe. It was "a very numerous and polite audience", says Wheler, the Stratford historian, but nobody could stir much excitement. Inquirers asked why the work had been chosen; attendant wits replied, that because there was no oratorio called *William*, this, with a title that might do for Judith Shakespeare, must be the next best thing. At the end, Garrick, plumply expectant, led the singers round the town, past the Birthplace where "Nature nurs'd her darling boy", and down to the meadow and the Rotunda. The nobility and gentry came behind in coach and chaise; lesser folk plodded on foot. Music accompanied them relentlessly:

> This is a day, a holiday! a holiday!
> Drive spleen and rancour far away;
> This is a day, a holiday! a holiday!
> Drive care and sorrow far away.

At three, after more songs in the Rotunda or Shakespeare's Hall, 700 guests sat down there to dinner, not served until nearly four o'clock and proving then to be a "grand and sumptuous public ordinary", with turtle and madeira and "all the rarities the season could afford". They stayed in the amphitheatre, beguiled by wine and song, catch and roundelay, until it was time to disperse to various expensive lodgings and dress for the night's assembly. The songs were simple, many of them Garrick's own, such as an address to the inevitable mulberry tree:

> Behold this fair goblet, 'twas carved from the tree,
> Which, O my sweet Shakespeare, was planted by thee;
> As a relick I kiss it, and bow at thy shrine,
> What comes from thy hand must be ever divine....

and "Sweet Willy, O", in which Shakespeare became a familiar friend of the family:

> He charmed 'em when living, the Sweet Willy, O,
> And when Willy dy'd,
> 'Twas Nature that sigh'd,
> To part with her all in her Sweet Willy, O.

It was a placid afternoon. When the company met again at owl-light, coming down to the assembly in a soft cobwebbed evening (no rain yet), and through an illuminated town where drums beat in the background, one might have called the Jubilee a success. Undeniably so while minuets formed and re-formed between the blue Corinthian pillars. From midnight until three in the morning there was a flurry of country-dancing, and even Sam Foote must have wondered moodily if Garrick were carrying it off.

IV

Next day, the 7th, he had his answer. Rain drenched Warwickshire and concentrated on Stratford. It turned Bridge Street to a cascade, endangered the Rotunda by the verge, soaked flags and transparencies, clogged the meadows and poured down any runnel. Garrick's barber, who had celebrated on the night before, cut him "from the corner of his mouth to his chin", a gash awkward to staunch. The Steward, a trifle ruffled, came downstairs to trouble. There was to have been a long progress of Shakespearean characters, with a triumphal car for Melpomene, Thalia and the Graces, drawn by six persons habited like satyrs. But in a flood none would willingly risk either the Drury Lane ostrich plumes—the theatre property might be "damnified £5,000"—or the health of the satyrs and Melpomene, so the pageant was put off until next day. "God's judgment on vanity and idolatry", observed the appalling Foote. Garrick did not reply; he would go forward to the Rotunda and to the "Ode upon Dedicating a Building and Erecting a Statue to Shakespeare at Stratford-upon-Avon". Outside it rained as though a new Ark might take to the water. The Avon lurched beneath Clopton arches in a mud-stained flood; the Bank Croft was a bog; the Rotunda roof leaked. Within, standing below the statue of Shakespeare he had given to Stratford, and heedless of drumming upon the roof, Garrick, still in his mole and amber suit and gilded waistcoat, and suffering from a cold, embarked upon the winding river of his "Ode". The choir, under Arne, sang interspersed airs and choruses; Garrick the actor did all that a technician could. James Boswell, after leaving Stratford, wrote about it in a *London Magazine* letter:

> The performance of the dedication ode was noble and affecting: it was like an exhibition in Athens or Rome. The whole audience was fixed in the most earnest attention, and I do believe that if anyone had attempted to disturb the performance, he would have been in danger of his life. Garrick, in the front of the orchestra, filled with the first musicians of the nation, with Dr Arne at their head, and inspired with an awful elevation of soul, while he looked from time to time at the venerable figure of Shakespeare, appeared more than himself. While he repeated the ode, and saw the various passions and feelings which it contains fully transfused into all around him, he seemed in ecstasy, and gave us the idea of a mortal transformed into a demi-god, as we read in the Pagan mythology.

For once, apparently, Boswell was right; Garrick's voice stilled the 2,000 people crammed there, wet and uncomfortable; and the performance so moved Lord Grosvenor that his veins and nerves "quivered with agitation". The demi-god's poetry, resolute and florid, could have caused this; but Garrick had written for himself, and he knew how to utter his lines, however strange they look in print:

> Now swell at once the choral song,
> Roll the full tide of harmony along;
> Let Rapture sweep the trembling strings,
> And Fame expanding all her wings,
> With all her trumpet-tongues proclaim,
> The lov'd, rever'd, immortal name!
> Shakespeare! Shakespeare! Shakespeare!

Consider, too, a final recitative:

> Look down, blest spirit! from above,
> With all thy wonted gentleness and love;
> And as the wonders of thy pen,
> By heav'n inspir'd,
> To virtue fir'd
> The charm'd, astonish'd sons of men! . . .
>
> Can British gratitude delay
> To him, the glory of this isle,
> To give the festive day,

The song, the statue and devoted pile?
To *him*, the first of poets, best of men?
"We ne'er shall look upon his like again!"

The "Ode" had gone triumphantly; it did not seem to matter a great deal when, in the tumult and the shouting, several benches and part of a wall collapsed. A door fell upon Lord Carlisle, but no one else was injured badly. Order re-established, the audience was depressed, not so much by Garrick's descent to prose, "a most genteel address" (Boswell), as by the Drury Lane comedian Tom King's laboured mock-serious attack upon Shakespeare in the figure of a carping critic. Boswell thought the joke out of touch with an occasion so solemn. Some Stratfordians believed King to be genuine in his lunge against Shakespeare, the Steward and the Jubilee. Visitors from London listened in boredom to a skirmish of inferior comedy and consoled themselves by admiring King's suit, fashionable blue ornamented with silver frogs. Garrick then delivered "a poetic epilogue" to the ladies, and the audience adjourned into the rain, returning at four o'clock to the Jubilee dinner, where the turtle weighed 327 pounds, and to still more glees and catches, one the slightly hysterical "Sacred be thy Shrine, Avonian Willy, bard divine!". Avonian Willy's shrine was moist. It was raining harder; the Jubilee was only half-way through, and there would be little point in another day and a half's eating and singing. Though Angelo had arranged an immense set-piece on the other bank of Avon, in such weather as this anything would have fizzled. Rockets stayed firmly on earth, catherine-wheels were immobile. After half-an-hour's shivering inaction, the watchers vanished to their bare rooms to put on masquerade costume and to pretend that they enjoyed it.

That night's ball should have been the crown. On cue, the ungrateful Avon, which Garrick had addressed as "soft-flowing", broke its banks. The meadow sogged to a swamp and disappeared in a flood. Indomitably, guests reported at the Rotunda, some expensively disguised; some in costumes "of the meanest sort" that had cost four guineas each to hire—Jubilee prices prevailed here as well—others merely masked, a few with faces blackened, and some others advancing without even the concealment of a domino. It was a mad picture after dark, lanterns dancing and weaving like agonized fireflies, in a steamy mist, duckboards slapping out across the mud-bath of the meadow, carriages in splash and lurch through the puddles, glutinous mud tossed from their wheels, and—everywhere and ceaseless—this Jubilee rain. Inside the Rotunda the atmosphere was at least fairly dry and the night glittering. Wax candles illuminated a "company of nobility and gentry, the rich, the brave, the witty, and the fair" (Boswell), all trying to ignore an unprecedented flood. Garrick, his good temper holding, was at the centre like an urbane Capulet. At midnight, with rain even heavier, the masquerade began. Nearly 1,000 guests had dared the weather for the Jubilee and Garrick's sake. Lady Pembroke, Mrs. Payne and Mrs. Crewe, as the three Witches, moved in a sinister group among a dazzle of silk, satin and brocade; Lord Grosvenor, whose veins had ceased to swell, wore a magnificent Eastern habit; a "gentleman from Oxford" impersonated Lord Ogleby, the charming old beau of Garrick and Colman's *The Clandestine Marriage;* there were Merry Wives, shepherdesses, Shakespeare's Ghost and a not very popular Devil whom somebody called "inexpressibly displeasing". Boswell, without a mask because a mask did not suit a bold Corsican, made an entry that, as he reported, "drew universal attention". Wearing a black and scarlet dress, he carried the words "Paoli" and *"Viva la Libertà"* blazoned in gold across his cockaded, blue-feathered cap; stiletto and pistol were in his belt, a musket hung at his back, and in his hand he carried a vine stalk. He had written for the occasion a poem that began, a little irrelevantly: "From the rude banks of Golo's rapid flood, Alas! too deeply tinged with patriot blood . . ."; and those round him, fearing a long haul, stopped him whenever a gust of verse was dangerously near. However. like Puff, Boswell meant to print it, every word: about two in the morning his printer, braving the rude banks of Avon's rapid flood, brought a proof across the sodden planks. Though work could not be finished in time for Boswell to distribute the broadsheets himself, he enjoyed the night which went on until past six o'clock in the morning.

The company had then to disperse in the piercing rain of a frigid daybreak; Avon was like Tiber chafing with her shores, Coaches had their wheels two feet deep in water; and the fantastically garbed guests, told to leave rapidly because the river now threatened to carry off the whole building, found they must wade through mires that trapped horses and carriages and were full of hidden ditches. At length, in growing light, everybody had escaped from the Rotunda. It swung now, a perilous island in a swampy lake; and Garrick, as he went to bed for an hour or two, must have known that, in effect, his Jubilee was over, rained out.

V

He had a third day to get through. Again, on the Friday morning, the pageant, triumphal cars, "all kinds of machinery", had to be abandoned. No bust could be crowned outside the Birthplace; it was nearly impossible to reach the Rotunda through the morass; and, doubtless to the relief of Lord Grosvenor's quivering veins, Garrick could not keep a gracious promise to repeat his "Ode". Carriages and expensive chaises, thick with gouts and dabs of mud, began to push out of Stratford on the road home. Remaining guests sought the racecourse at Shottery Meadow—another sound Shakespearean name for any programme. Garrick had offered a fifty-guinea cup for a Jubilee race in (according to advertisement) "a scene too delicious for description". It was certainly wet, and much of the course was under water.

Still the rain eased, and the race in which five colts competed was won by a groom called Pratt, on his own mount; he did not know much about plays or Master Shakespeare, but he knew a horse and could ride it, or swim with it. Gloriously now, though the skies were charged, it had stopped raining. Nobility and gentry drove back to Stratford, dressed for the last time in lodgings gloomily familiar to them, blinked at Angelo's fireworks—some of them functioning at last, a sky powdered with sudden stars— and kept going with minuets and country dances in the upper room of the town hall until daybreak paled. Mrs. Garrick, Eva Violette, "danced a minuet beyond description gracefully". After four in the morning the Steward of the Jubilee removed his mulberry medal, laid it by his wand, and wondered if it had been worth the trouble:

> ... See, in crowds, the gay, the fair,
>   To the splendid scene repair,
> A scene as fine, as fine can be,
>   To celebrate our Jubilee.

He was by no means sure; the words did not ring.

Samuel Foote, of course, led the Noes.

A Jubilee [he wrote as soon as he could] . . . is a public invitation circulated and arranged by puffing; to go posting without horses to an obscure borough without representatives, governed by a Mayor and Aldermen who are no magistrates; to celebrate a great poet whose works have made him immortal, by *an ode* without poetry, music without melody, dinners without victuals, and lodgings without bed; a masquerade where half the people appeared bare-faced, a horse-race up to the knees in water, fireworks extinguished as soon as they were lighted, and a cardboard amphitheatre which tumbled to pieces as soon as it was finished.

It was inexplicable that Foote, ready for anything to annoy Garrick, had not realized the lack of Shakespeare: the only phrases heard were those Garrick had adapted to slip into his "Ode".

James Boswell spoke for the Ayes. He wrote in the *London Magazine*:

Much noise has been made about the high price of everything at Stratford. I own I cannot agree that such censures are just. It was reasonable that Shakespeare's townsmen should partake of the Jubilee as well as we strangers did; they as a jubilee of profit, we of pleasure. As it lasted for but a few nights, a guinea a night for a bed was not imposition. Nobody was understood to come there who had not plenty of money. Towards the end of the Jubilee many of us were not in very good humour, as many inconveniences occurred, particularly there not being carriages enough to take us away but in detachments, so that those who had to wait long tired exceedingly. I laughed away spleen by a droll simile: Taking the whole of this Jubilee, said I, is like eating an artichoke entire: we have some fine mouthfuls, but also swallow the leaves and the hair, which are confoundedly difficult of digestion. After all, however, I am truly satisfied with my artichoke.

Though Boswell had hoped that there would be a return every seven years, the 1769 artichoke proved to be the only one of its kind. When Stratford in 1771 asked Garrick to undertake an annual event, he refused—to nobody's surprise but Stratford's. In the autumn of 1769 he had contrived to wring success from calamity. Boswell wrote with foreknowledge when he said: "Nature seemed to frown on a jubilee in honour of the *thief* who had 'robbed her of all she was worth.' But as no cost has been spared on the pageant, I hope Mr. Garrick will entertain us with it in the comfortable regions of Drury Lane." That is what Garrick did, seeking to recover some of his heavy losses by staging the pageant at the 'Lane' as an afterpiece entitled *The Jubilee: in Honour of Shakespeare*. Here, on 14th October 1769, were a comfortable theatre, no rain and "a comic fable in which the inferior people of Stratford, and the visitors, were represented with great pleasantry"*. Garrick set one scene in the swirl and flurry of a Stratford inn courtyard, probably the 'White Lion', and turned the overcrowding to what comic purpose he could. Moody played an Irish visitor forced to sleep in his chaise. There were various street scenes; and the pageant, without danger to the ostrich-feathers or "the valuable health of the fair performers", included a procession of Shakespearean characters, Garrick as Benedick, satyrs, Muses, triumphal car and all, Shakespeare's ghost included—perhaps as propitiation. No trouble anywhere, even with the ineffable lyric of "Sweet Willy, O". Whatever Foote might say, this was the autumn's song.

Triumph at the 'Lane' ended a business that, in spite of Stratford's determined delight—various courtesies were exchanged—Garrick would never contemplate with happiness. With memories of processional exhilaration, glees and dances and ritual solemnity in the Great Booth of Shakespeare's Hall, went the puddling of mud, the noise of the turbulent Avon, a swishing of rain and the mockery of Foote's laugh. Asked to go back in 1771, he declined charmingly and—maybe with less charm—implored the council to see that its town was kept well paved, clean and lighted: "Allure everybody to visit the *Holy-land* and let it not be said . . . that this Town, which gave birth to the first genius since the Creation, is the most dirty, ill-pav'd, wretched-looking town in all Britain." There still remained the "small, neat box" of blest mulberry. Garrick was at least an honorary burgess and warmly regarded (the statue stood now in the Town Hall niche)—no man could have paid so exorbitantly for the honour. He may not have reflected—and why should he?—that the Jubilee, as a scholar, Marthe Winburn England, insisted in 1956, was "a clear prefiguration of characteristic romantic attitudes towards Shakespeare, and the varied reactions to it in England, France, and Germany were premonitory of the varied courses romanticism would follow".

* Arthur Murphy's *Life of Garrick*.

Stratford-upon-Avon 1948: Paul Scofield and Claire Bloom in Hamlet
Stratford-upon-Avon 1968: Helen Mirren and David Waller in Troilus and Cressida

In the popular mind the Jubilee lived on in such vague memories as those of Luke Hansard, printer to the House of Commons. While editing his papers, I noticed that, as late as 1827, he recalled in meandering fashion how

> many of the characters which had been made in wood, and painted, and much of the scenery, found their way into our pleasure gardens, and places of fashionable resort, as the bazaars, and such places of the present day—to the additional gratification, and I thought, instruction too, of the middle ranks of people.

For years, at Dobney's Bowling Green and racquet court, at Islington in the fields, the players were watched by Falstaff and Richard the Third, Henry the Fifth and Lear, lay figures brought up from Stratford—last remnants of

> this celebrated jubilee of genius . . . not a piece of farce and rodomontade, as many of the envious sons of our Roscius attempted to make us believe, but an elegant and truly classical celebration of the memory of Shakespeare. (Boswell.)

Probably; but the honorary burgess of Stratford-upon-Avon never returned, even if—though Cowper chose it as an example of man's extravagant praise of man—he might have valued a few words from *The Task*:

> For Garrick was a worshipper himself;
> He drew the liturgy, and form'd the rites
> And solemn ceremonial of the day,
> And call'd the world to worship on the banks
> Of Avon, fam'd in song. Ah! pleasant proof
> That piety has still in human hearts
> Some place, a spark or two not yet extinct.

Stratford holds some of the proofs of Garrick's piety. Thus a case in the Royal Shakespeare Picture Gallery, part of the old redbrick buildings which survived the fire of 1926—another of many fires in Stratford record—contains such things as mulberry ornaments; a pair of gloves that John Ward, the actor, gave to Garrick in 1769, and which fallible tradition assumed to be Shakespeare's; a plate, part of Garrick's fifty-four-piece "garnish of pewter" that had become Marie Corelli's; and, most pathetic, a decorative ticket, signed by George Garrick, David's brother,

7

Stratford-upon-Avon 1955: Laurence Olivier and Vivien Leigh in Titus Andronicus
Stratford-upon-Avon 1950: Barbara Jefford and John Gielgud in Measure for Measure

admitting its bearer to the oratorio, dedication ode and ball in the Great Booth. In the matter of gloves, Garrick received three pairs that were "Shakespeare's own". Ward wrote:

> I have sent you a pair of Gloves which have oft covered His hands, they were made me a present, by a descendant of the Family, when my self and company went over There from Warwick in the year (46) to perform the play of Othello, as a Benefit, for repairing his monument in the Great Church. . . . I am led to Think **I** cannot deposit Them for the purpose, into the hand of any Person so proper, as our Modern *Roscius*.

There hangs in the picture gallery that absurd tribute to Roscius, George Carter's Academy exhibit of the Apotheosis of Garrick from 1784. I have mentioned it already, but it needs to have its full official description:

> A Sarcophagus, supported by Lyric Poetry and the Belles Lettres. In the centre is a Basso Relievo of Nature deploring the loss of her Son; she is weeping over a medallion of Garrick. Attending are two Loves, one with his bow unstrung, the other extinguishing the Hymenial Torch; beneath are Emblems of his Art, and this Motto —'He never shall return'; with a Group of seventeen of his Friends who had figured it upon the great Theatre of Life with him, and are come in their favourite Habits of Shakespeare, to pay their Funeral Obsequies to his Shrine; while aërials triumph over Death, by soaring with the Body to Parnassus, Thalia, Melpomene, and Shakespeare advance with Wreaths, to receive him, to conduct him to the Summit of the Mount, and to the Presence of Apollo and the Muses.

We shall return to other picture gallery players, who are in a particular sense Shakespeare's countrymen in their "favourite habits". Meanwhile, just beyond the building is the Bancroft meadow, tamed and unrecognizable since Garrick's year, but agreeable at most times, especially towards midnight on a summer evening when nobody is about and lights still glitter in the tall chestnut trees along the promenade. It is a pity that the Gower Shakespeare has his back to it all, including the site of the Rotunda, the Great Booth; but for that we must blame a Stratford town council of nearly forty years ago.

FIVE

ON TO THE PAVILION

I

The world, a small world as yet, was quite prepared to continue worshipping on the banks of Avon, fam'd in song. Now that Garrick had discovered Stratford, others must post to Warwickshire—a follow-my-leader progress that delighted the Harts, Mrs. Court and Mrs. Hornby, and a tedious and fraudulent poetaster named John Jordan. Besides being a Stratford wheelwright, and presumably attending to his trade at spare moments, he wrote much babble-verse, hustled victims round the town, probably took a commission from Thomas Sharp's mulberry shop, and would turn up with new Shakespearean fragments as required. These included a jingle about eight villages near Stratford, "Piping Pebworth, dancing Marston", and so on—we shall meet it again—that once it is spoken becomes as inescapable as Mark Twain's "Punch in the presence of the passen-*jare*". Dramatic entertainment was scarce, though some pomping folk at the "New Theatre at the Unicorn"—which must have been rooms by a tavern—did try *The Merchant of Venice*, "this celebrated comedy taken from a real fact which occurred in Venice"; and *Hamlet*, followed—it was a long evening—by a comedy with music, *The Padlock*.

Such a formidable Shakespearean as Edmond Malone came down in 1793 and insisted to the vicar of Holy Trinity that the Bust, from which the hues were flaking, should be painted a uniform and penitential stone colour—just, indeed, as plaster and stucco had blinded so many of Stratford's timber fronts. Malone had his share of the egregious Jordan, who supplied him with a hitherto unknown Shakespeare couplet, richly stuffed-owl:

> Misery, trodden on by many,
> Being bold, is not relieved by any.

During the same summer (the Bust had not been painted then) the Irelands visited Stratford. Old Samuel, the artist—a very bad one—hunted for picturesque views to distort. With him was his still innocent son, William, whose later forgeries Malone was to expose, and who complicated Shakespearean fever with a passion for the Gothick, the Romantick and the Chattertonian image of genius untimely blighted. Jordan, finding them the simplest prey, took them to buy costly mulberry "bagatelles" from Sharp, and sent them goose-chasing to Clopton House. There he knew he could rely on the farmer-tenant, who enjoyed a practical joke, and who told his agonized visitors that he had only lately destroyed several bundles of papers with Shakespeare's name on them. Maybe the shock encouraged William to provide several bundles by himself.

During the Napoleonic Wars Stratford let Shakespeare rest. (Jordan died in 1809.) What the widows might do at the Birthplace was the relentless women's own private venture. At this period the town, which had been growing very slowly, had a population of about 2,300, only 200 more than in Garrick's year and seven times smaller than now. Visitors, in perfect goodwill, had a habit of condescending to it. Thus the traveller Carl Phillip Moritz had reported in the seventeen-eighties that a row of one-storey cottages, "neat though humble", along the bank of Avon—that is, upon Waterside—"impressed me strongly with the idea of patriarchal simplicity and content". Still, Stratford prospered, if it did not expand. Many vessels frequented the navigable Avon. In 1816 the canal, an important commercial link, twenty years in making, was opened between the Worcester and Birmingham Canal at King's Norton and the river at Stratford; a tunnel opening, a mile out of King's Norton, bears a plaque with a carved head of Shakespeare. During the late Regency twenty-four main-road coaches rattled into and through the town every day. The busy little place had not forgotten its asset in Shakespeare— a valuable, if imponderable, property—and in 1816 some of its leaders insisted on marking the bicentenary of the birth. Upon the "natal day", according to R. B. Wheler, writing to the *Gentleman's Magazine*, "the merry bells struck up", and at Welcombe, behind the Warwick Road, George Lloyd, Esq., repeatedly let off six cannon. At ten o'clock 116 ladies and gentlemen attended a town hall breakfast, and doubtless seventy-five gentlemen were in even better spirits at a four o'clock dinner when appropriate healths were drunk, Garrick's included. Memories of poor Angelo in the rain were restored at a firework skirmish on the Bancroft, attended by "a band of musick", and the old pattern went as far as the ball which did not end until five in the morning; it had been kept safely up in the centre of the town, far from any possible ravages of Avon. Also according to Garrick ritual were a ribbon from Coventry and a medal from Birmingham. Wheler added sadly and circuitously:

> Some entertainment in a literary and dramatic shape was originally intended, and would have been highly desirable; but, in consequence of the difficulty and expense of procuring assistance to render it generally attractive at a season when most of the gentlemen whose attendance would necessarily be required were unavoidably engaged in London (though Mr. Elliston liberally offered his own and that of his company from Birmingham) the want of such performances was sufficiently excused.

The only theatre in those days was a small gaff, a fit-up, in Greenhill Street or Moor Town's End; the corporation did not favour stage performances so soon after the war with France. Shakespeare in Stratford had to suffer a great deal from his bailiffs and mayors.

Just before Christmas 1820 the eccentric comedian Charles Mathews the elder, nervous, tetchy and capricious, but generally a man of ideas, spent a night at Stratford, presenting in the town hall the entertainment he had entitled "Country Cousins and the Sights of London". At the tail of his poster he added a note saying that, after the entertainment,

> Mr. Mathews will have the honour of submitting to the audience the nature of some proposals that have been suggested for the purpose of erecting in the form of a Theatre in Stratford, a National Monument and Mausoleum to the immortal memory of Shakespeare.

Good words, and well pronounced; his audience applauded the submission, but nothing more happened, and Mathews was not the kind of man to concentrate for long on the same scheme.

Then in 1824 the famous and still thriving Shakespeare Club began work with a dinner at the Falcon Hotel for a dozen people; it was the club that arranged presently, during 1827, what it hoped to be the first of a sequence of triennial festivals—in the Garrick mode as usual, with that everlasting procession of

Shakespearean characters, the crowning by Melpomene and Thalia of a bust outside the Birthplace, and (this was agreeably fresh) the foundation stone-laying of a new theatre on part of the site of Shakespeare's Great Garden. It was followed, superstition disregarded, by a rendering of Locke's frivolous music for *Macbeth*. The second day provided a public breakfast, a masquerade at an amphitheatre in the Rother, again a comfortable distance from the Avon, and the usual crackle of fireworks. A third day declined to a mixed amateur-professional concert in the 'White Lion'. The Chapel Lane theatre itself, of which not a stone survives, was run up for £1,200—a modest affair that was called unsightly, and probably was. It opened as a matter of routine, with *As You Like It*. Later, to keep Garrick's name going, the company did his perversion of *The Taming of the Shrew*; and later still an inventive manager found a way to publicize *King Lear* with a poster that said, "Royal Edgar Challenges Usurper to Mortal Combat". A few potentially notable players appeared in Stratford, among them the laborious Charles Kean, Edmund's "Charley"; as the figure of St. George during the pageant of 1830, he rode on a grey horse, and at night, as Richard the Third, he offered his kingdom for one. Effort was long and fruitless. Townsfolk stayed away eagerly; and in 1842, puzzled by the neglect of a theatre begun on Shakespeare's day in Shakespeare's garden, the shareholders rearranged the auditorium, removed the stage which ought to have been made of mulberry wood, and re-christened the building the Royal Shakespeare Rooms; Charles Kemble gave a reading. The change was just as unprofitable. Doomed by the *Macbeth* music, the building lingered on as one of a small town's nondescript, maid-of-all-work public halls, ready at anybody's service for any sort of function. Hopefully, during 1869 in what must have been a foolhardy spasm, it reverted to its original form, once more becoming a theatre. Three years drained the owners' patience. After Mr. and Mrs. Rousby had acted Hamlet and Ophelia on 30th April 1872, the doors were slammed for good and the posters peeled off; the fabric was sold and demolished, and the site gradually returned to the open garden of New Place.

Much had happened in Stratford before then: other festivals, balls and masquerades, expansive breakfasts, polychromatic pageants, salutes of cannon. The Shakespeare Club held regular

Birthday banquets, addressed by such people as the actor, George Jones, and the protean Sheridan Knowles. William Wordsworth, then Poet Laureate, could not come in 1847 and appeared unaware that anything had occurred in Stratford before—today this would be called a non-event. That year the Birthplace was bought for the nation, not a minute too soon. The *Illustrated London News* said just afterwards:

> Of what it was in 1564 no notion can be gathered from what it is in 1847. There is something, indeed, most painful in the contrast of its present wretchedness, and our idea of its condition as the comfortable home of Shakespeare's parents. The low, crazy frontage—the crippled hatch—the filthy remnant of a butcher's shamble, with its ghastly hook—on the outside, and the squalid forlornness of the rooms within, convey together such a sense of utter desolation as merges all those feelings of respect and awe which such a relic should inspire. Let us hope the result of Thursday's sale has saved this interesting property from further desecration.

In the ensuing summer Charles Dickens, always a relishing amateur actor able to put into a part something of the flourish of his prose, was touring with friends—George Cruikshank, the artist (still in his pre-Temperance days), Douglas Jerrold, John Leech and several more—to raise money for a Stratford project of their own. The Birthplace was saved. Then why not endow as its first curator the actor-dramatist, Sheridan Knowles? True, he had been a convivial Bohemian, fond of such societies as the Owls—"Come to our Nest next Tuesday; jolly whooping and woo-wooing." He had also been among the most prolific and acceptable dramatists of a thin time; unexpectedly now, he was a Baptist preacher, and he was in debt. A benefit production of *The Merry Wives of Windsor* went cheerfully in London and in several northern cities, Dickens contenting himself with an excellent Shallow. A good deal of money was raised; Knowles shared a large sum with a second beneficiary and paid off his debts. That was all. He never reached Henley Street in a Stratford that may have felt uncomfortable about his jolly woo-wooing.

II

A good mixed trio, Benjamin Webster, Charles Kemble, and James Vandenhoff, spoke oracularly at the Shakespeare Club's "theatrical commemoration" in 1853 without saying much to the purpose. Six years later there were whispers of the approaching Tercentenary of 1864. It would be a convenient date, for in 1861 the railway at last discovered Stratford, and the town was more accessible than it had ever been. That year, in Holy Trinity Church, a London picture restorer, Simon Collins, scraped away the stone colour or whitewash, and put back the original hues of the Bust. (Doubtless somebody asked if Shakespeare could have been thinking of himself when he made Mercutio say of Benvolio, "Thou wilt quarrel with a man for cracking nuts, having no other reason but thou hast hazel eyes.") Next summer public subscription purchased the whole of the New Place property, including Nash's House next door. Suddenly, the Tercentenary loomed: 300 years since the birth—and let there be no argument—in Henley Street.

There is nothing to show where Garrick's ephemeral Rotunda rose upon the Bancroft; but behind the houses of Old Town, and behind the western brick wall, the dark, plant-pot russet, of Southern Lane, we can see a ring of tall poplars; from the air they are especially prominent. The trees mark the place of the Grand Pavilion of 1864; a duodecagonal timber building, 152 feet in diameter, set upon foundations of masonry, with galleries, a wide orchestra and a stage that was seventy-five feet in width and fifty-six deep. Stratford, which had done little enough to honour Shakespeare in the theatre—entertainment in a dramatic shape—was resolved not to botch its tercentenary festival. In "these railway times", said the mayor, Edward Fordham Flower, head of the local brewing family, the town saw a chance of summoning the nation to Warwickshire for the first time since Garrick, and of proving that Shakespeare's kinsfolk knew their own man. The trouble was that a London group wanted the festival for itself. Shakespeare had left Stratford to do his main life-work in London; thus, their argument ran, he was of Bankside, not Bank Croft. Stratford in competition, said the haughtier Londoners, was a country mouse's nibble. The local committee, smiling at grief, planned and replanned: Shakespeare was theirs, birthroom, school and grave; he would remain so.

From his Warwick Road house, 'The Hill', Edward Fordham Flower wrote to *The Times* on 8th December 1863, a plain man's letter. Stratford had a tercentenary scheme too ambitious for local labour and money alone, and he demanded sympathy for a position "from which we cannot escape", not that they wished it:

> We are plain men of business, engaged in a simple duty which we have not sought. As such, however, we have claims which are entitled to respect. It was only the other day that *Punch* accused various persons who propose to build monuments to Shakespeare of only wishing to raise pedestals to their own glory. I do not know whether this sarcasm is merited, but at all events it cannot apply to us. We have no selfish object to serve; we have no literary reputation to buoy up by pushing ourselves needlessly forward.

Stratford would go on to fulfil its simple duty; but in those Arcadian nights next May, when the Grand Pavilion waited to be pulled apart, when no one was hiring opera-glasses or flapping a playbill, and when the festival had dwindled to a memory, many newspaper columns, and a cupboard or two of correspondence, no plain men could have been happier that the business was well ended. They had had to deal with the acting profession; something of which Shakespeare's town, not bred to the stage, had only the haziest idea, though one day it would know more about it. Had Shakespeare been alive, and not merely a book of plays and a Bust, he could have told them much.

At this period Stratford had been described shortly as peaceful, clean (Garrick would have been pleased to hear it) and ancient. With most of its timbering hidden, various raw brick terraces ribboned on its outskirts, and the Shakespeare Rooms neglected in New Place garden, it seemed anxious to deny the final epithet. Yet a stranger would understand at once who ruled the town. The engine of his train would be inscribed 'Will Shakespeare'. On the station he would see a notice that the grandson of an alderman at the Garrick Jubilee now kept the Shakespeare Hotel. Half a minute from the station was a Shakespearean Foundry; and only a few steps farther lay Garrick Court. In the Rother Market the principal building was a Shakespearean Needle Works. Once in the middle of the town, with a Shakespearean bookshop and printing establishment and a Shakespearean book and print warehouse, the name was blazoned on all sides. During April 1864 Stratford must blazon it to the nation; and, whether London approved or not, the town was resolved (said the *Daily News*) to try "an onerous and costly scheme in deference to the public voice of demand". The original onerous and costly scheme involved a festival of four days, beginning with "a banquet for ladies and gentlemen", and continuing with guided journeys to places near Stratford-upon-Avon "illustrative of incidents in Shakespeare's life" (a pity John Jordan was no longer present for piping Pebworth, dancing Marston); critical analyses of the plays, a grand oratorio, a Shakespearean fancy ball, a miscellaneous concert and, inevitably, the comedy of *As You Like It* by "a combination of metropolitan and provincial talent". As a gesture, the committee, which never lost sight of what Ulysses called "degree, priority, and place", allotted one day exclusively to "popular amusements".

In London a National Shakespeare Club did nothing but gaze at these rustics from a great height and reel off a list of vice-presidents for some celebration of its own yet sitting in the stars. On 20th January *The Times* thundered in Stratford's favour, though it was dubious about a monumental memorial, one of two "substantial objects"—the other would be university scholarships from Shakespeare's school—that the festival might possibly finance. (At that stage Stratford expected a large sum.) But *The Times* was flattering; clearly the main celebration must be in Warwickshire. Already the committee had progressed. It had secured for the oratorio, which Garrick had shown to be indispensable, the services of Tietjens, Sainton-Dolby, Sims Reeves and Alfred Mellon. Grateful to a fashionable preacher and elocutionist, the Rev. J. C. M. Bellew, who had coaxed the artists to accept, Stratford appointed him a member of the committee, a vice-president, a member of the entertainments committee, and corresponding secretary in London, which ought to have been enough for any man. Soon, over-weighted by his titles, he would fail to walk the hair-line of tact.

It was early morning. Serenely, and with variable luck, the Committee began to trawl for eminent Shakespeareans. Fanny Kemble, who was going to the continent, could not read *A Midsummer Night's Dream*. That was unfortunate, but plays must come before readings. An invitation went to Helen Faucit, Mrs Theodore Martin, who had been Macready's leading lady during the great years*. Yes; she would help, but what part did the committee suggest? And—she touched on this lightly—would there be any other performance on the same evening? Benjamin

---

* From retirement at Cheltenham, the tragedian, always with a hint of the schoolmaster, sent ten guineas to the scholarship fund.

Webster and Samuel Phelps, good solid figures, placed themselves formally at Stratford's disposal. It was hopeful until someone blundered irretrievably. Charles Albert Fechter, the modish actor from France (born actually in London, among the foreign colony of Hanway Yard, behind Oxford Street) was then playing at the Lyceum. A man of 40 who could have passed for 25 in the dark with the light behind him, he was a romantic, a practised stage lover, a master of fence. His accent fluttered into odd emphases; but his emotional certainty and his aspect—"lymphatic, delicate, handsome, with long flaxen curls, fine eyes, and sympathetic voice," said George Henry Lewes—made of him the transient toast of London. As Hamlet he was unorthodox: according to Dickens, "a pale, woebegone Norseman . . . making a piratical swoop upon the whole fleet of little theatrical prescriptions without meaning, or, like Dr. Johnson's celebrated friend, with only one idea in them, and that a wrong one". Stratford coveted him as an actor everyone would be talking about; and in the middle of December—after Mr. Bellew had joined the Committee—Fechter was invited to play the Tercentenary Hamlet.

It was a fatal decision, for the rugged Samuel Phelps then led the English stage,

> Unrivalled Phelps, who art by genius blest,
> Of all our Shakespeare's students, truest, best.

Eighteen seasons that transformed the minor theatre of Sadler's Wells had established him as a major actor (if without the ultimate inspiration). It was no excuse for Stratford to say, ingenuously, that Hamlet was not his favourite character, and that nobody would mind if a foreigner were engaged. Moreover, splendidly unaware of theatrical politics, the Stratford Committee had no idea that Phelps and Fechter were at war. Phelps was not a businessman. On leaving Sadler's Wells he had been persuaded to act (when needed) under Fechter's management at the Lyceum, for three nights a week at a curiously low salary. He would not credit friends who told him it was merely a way of keeping him off the stage. This was true: for months he was never approached. The end came when Fechter, telling Phelps that *Hamlet* would be put up next, asked what part he would prefer. "Hamlet, of course," Phelps replied. "Oh," said Fechter, "but I play that myself. I thought, perhaps, you would play the Ghost." "The Ghost to your Hamlet—*yours*," growled Phelps. "Damn your impudence!" A more cautious report explains that he "gave a sharp reply through his acting manager". Certainly Phelps would never consent to third or fourth fiddle. Fechter refused to pay his salary; whereupon, after a sparking of legal squibs, the matter was referred to an arbitrator, Charles Dickens, who advised Fechter, as a concession, to play Iago to the elder man's Othello. Fechter refused to be conciliatory; the agreement was cancelled, and Phelps left for Drury Lane. It was a sad period; his wife was painfully ill. Away from Islington he felt worried, tired and insecure.

His profession backed him. When Stratford, leading from ignorance, invited Fechter to the Tercentenary, it alienated more people than it knew. Correspondence with Phelps lasted for three months, at the end of which, to vindicate his professional position in the country, he had it all printed. It opened with a storming sentence of more than 200 words, one that, like Richard the Second's "Draw near, and list what with our council we have done," (Phelps never acted Richard) needed uncommon breath control. In effect, it said that his pride had been hurt.

Everything was muddled. Originally, Robert Hunter, first secretary of the Stratford Committee, had sent with an invitation to Phelps to appear "in the dramatic performances in April", a private note saying he would like to see him as Hamlet, Othello, or Macbeth. It was left that the dazzling Mr. Bellew would call upon Phelps to discuss the business. There would be no dramatic performance on the Birthday, but *Hamlet* (no actor's name given) was planned for 26th April. Bellew did not arrive; and Phelps, in mid-January, asked with some hauteur what the position might be. That evening Bellew rose from his trance. Stratford had now decided upon *Cymbeline* for 26th April, and he wrote proposing that Phelps, "as the foremost of English tragedians", might play Iachimo. The foremost English tragedian smouldered. Stratford must not ask an actor to play Hamlet (or so he understood) and then fob him off with the "slight thing of Italy". He waited for an official letter from Stratford; when it came, after four days, it said merely that "a gentleman would call" which was where the business had started. Phelps promptly wrote to Bellew, declining to appear. At the moment that the thunderbolt dropped from

Canonbury Square, Bellew, though dazed, picked up his pen, "Bedford Chapel, New Oxford Street, January 20, 1864– 5 p.m.", and begged Phelps to think. Everyone wanted him to act with Helen Faucit. It was unlucky about *Hamlet*, but "the Committee specially requested another gentleman" to appear in the part. (Phelps boiled over.) Yet, if he desired *Macbeth*, or *Othello*, or any other play, it should be got up for him, as far as possible in accord with his wishes. Bellew sounded most accommodating.

Phelp's reply, less accommodating, clanged back next day. It began in italics:

I claim the right, upon the following grounds, to be considered the foremost man in my profession in a demonstration meant to honour Shakespeare. I have produced worthily thirty-four of his plays, which no individual manager ever did before. They were acted in my theatre four thousand times, during a period extending over eighteen years. I acted to the satisfaction of a large *English* public all his heroes—tragic and comic—and to that public I shall appeal and publish this correspondence. The Stratford Committee have insulted me by asking any man in this country to play Hamlet on such an occasion without having first offered a choice of characters to

> Yours faithfully,
> S. PHELPS.

Faintly, Bellew hurried the letter to Stratford. At once that most honest of plain men, Edward Fordham Flower, wrote off to soothe Phelps and to protest. Stratford had sent to him before anyone else; there had been no attempt at an insult; he had been given the whole range of Shakespeare's plays. Yet even Flower could not deny that another man had been offered *Hamlet*. The reply, Phelps growled, aggravated the affront. Flower and his committee, thoroughly out of temper, talked of "professional jealousy", consoling themselves with the knowledge that Fechter had promised the resources of the Lyceum; J. B. Buckstone, of the Haymarket would stage *Twelfth Night*, and Webster had been with them all along. Thanks to Miss Faucit and others, there would be a third play, every character worthily cast. What was the newspaper nonsense about a "discreditable intrigue"?

III

Again lightning struck the committee. Just two months before the festival, Benjamin Webster abandoned it; if Fechter were to play, then he would decline. The profession had set itself stubbornly beside Phelps. A delegate sent to London to solicit help was "so encumbered and embarrassed" that he wrote to Stratford, reporting that no good would come of the business while Fechter remained. The committee crumpled the letter and announced a provisional programme headed by an intimidating drum-roll of vice-presidents, patronesses and stewards. First, the national memorial. At noon on the Birthday, if the "arrangements of the Monumental Committee were sufficiently advanced", there would be a procession to the stonelaying. Later in the week, visitors—pouring in by all roads—would be sustained by an oratorio, a grand concert, Buckstone's Haymarket company in *Twelfth Night*, followed by "Mr. Sothern (Lord Dundreary) . . . in a short one-act Entertainment of a peculiar construction"; Fechter and the Royal Lyceum company in *Hamlet;* Ellen (*sic*) Faucit in *As You Like It*—no mention of *Cymbeline*—and a grand fancy-dress ball without "masks, dominos, or pantomime characters". As a sop, "a series of popular entertainments" in the pavilion would last four days: a patronizing throw-away, lesser actors at lower prices, that angered local people, pageant-starved. They wanted (*Stratford-upon-Avon Herald*) "an embodiment of the characters through whom [Shakespeare] imparted to this benighted world such a blaze of intellectual light".

The committee ignored a mutiny from below stairs. The Grand Pavilion, containing four tons of nails, and slightly re-planned to include alterations to stage and proscenium that Fechter himself had wished, rose in the Southern Lane paddock. Scarlet cloth was fitted to the principal seats; William Telbin designed a drop-curtain of Shakespeare's statue in a vestibule, surrounded by pillars and curtains, Holy Trinity Church in the distance. Nearly 7,000 copies of the programme were printed, and no sooner were these out than the hapless committee began to announce change upon change. Tietjens, for some reason, would be unable to sing; "delicate health" prevented Mrs. Keeley from acting Celia in *As You Like It;* and, most terrible, Edward Flower opened a letter postmarked on 24th March from Ventnor in the

Isle of Wight. It arrived at Stratford on 26th March. Dated three days earlier, it was signed "H. Barnett", and it contained the news that Charles Albert Fechter would not play Hamlet.

IV

Barnett was acting manager of the Lyceum. Fechter, so he wrote bluntly, "declined the honour of appearing" because of a "false and injurious statement spread about by one of your members, and published by unfriendly papers, viz: that Mr. Fechter, by undercurrent and trickery ways, forced on the choice of his Hamlet". Tossing his torch into the gunpowder, Mr. Barnett remained the committee's obedient servant. Edward Flower replied with dignity—though it would not have been strange if the plain man had never entered a theatre again—that the letter was incomprehensible. At length it seemed through the smoke that Fechter was complaining because Bellew had been dismissed from the Committee. Edward Flower had written a letter that blamed Bellew for offending Phelps, an act that "far more than outbalances any advantages that could accrue to us from the most zealous advocacy of yourself or any other person". Therefore Stratford had tacitly recognized Phelps. Therefore he had been justly insulted by the assignment of Hamlet to Fechter. Therefore Fechter was insulted. Therefore it went on, on and on. With a few weeks to go, Stratford was left without the Prince of Denmark—merely because in a happy December when everything gleamed (and soloists for the *Messiah* were already booked) it had seemed easy enough to count on Fechter and to push aside Phelps. Now, when they would have been happy with either, both the dear charmers had gone, and left nothing but a hint of sulphur, a pamphlet, some cuttings from the *Morning Star*, and a bill for altering the Grand Pavilion according to Fechter's wishes.

The committee feared that for a night it might have to close the pavilion, an enforced act of contrition. But George Vining, manager of the London Princess's, had a proposal. On the former *Hamlet* night, Stratford could have the fashionable French girl, Stella Colas, in *Romeo and Juliet*, and those broad comedians the brothers Webb, as the Dromios in *The Comedy of Errors*. Promptly, the committee accepted—and just as promptly Helen Faucit withdrew. Her promise to play Rosalind was conditional. Juliet was her favourite part; now it had been given to a French actress, and she must content herself with comedy. Like Phelps, she retired, though unlike him she contributed to the funds of the festival. Beaten and bewildered, the committee snatched at the twelfth-hour agreement of Mrs. Hermann Vezin—not an exciting substitute—to act Rosalind. Worn out, and looking at a heavily scrawled programme, the plain men waited for their festival to open, if open it could.

v

Stratford tried very hard. Everywhere painters, plasterers, glaziers, masons and paper-hangers had set to work to get the town fresh for its crowds. These failed to come: Robert Hunter, no longer secretary, put it down to bad advertising, and certainly there was far more fuss about the festival before it opened than when it was on. When it did open, Stratford saw itself reflected in the glistening mirror of an April Saturday. Down the fortnight, sun blazed upon flags and new paint and frothing blossom; at night there were moonlit rides by the river and under the trees of the still lonely Warwick Road. No foundation-stone was laid. Stratford read with a stab that in London, on the Birthday, Samuel Phelps, watched by thousands, had planted a tercentenary oak-tree on Primrose Hill in the name of working men of England and in memory of Shakespeare. What Fechter did was not recorded.

In Stratford Shakespeare had a good opening day. Scholars from Germany and Moscow sent greetings. Seven hundred and fifty people kept up their strength in the Grand Pavilion where the purveyor of a massive and costly banquet provided "nearly all the good things necessary for the sustainment of the earthly tabernacle", with a menu that was a "rare specimen of cuisine literature": it had that coy device, mottoes for each course. In 1864 the choice included:

ROAST TURKEYS
"Why here he comes swelling like a turkey cock." (*Henry V*, v.i)
TONGUES
"Silence is only commendable in a neat's tongue dried." (*The Merchant of Venice*, I.i)

St. Mary's Church, Warwick

FRENCH RAISED PIES
"They are both baked in that pie." (*Titus Andronicus*, v, 3)
    POTTED MEATS
"Mince it sans remorse." (*Timon of Athens*, iv, 3)

The occasion lasted for some hours from mid-afternoon, garnished by more than twenty speeches. No doubt they were enjoyed by spectators who looked on from the upper galleries "with all the gratification that is to be derived from witnessing enjoyments which one is not permitted to share" (Robert Hunter). Some of the mottoes round the building had been tactlessly chosen: thus, "In such a time as this It is not meet that every nice offence should bear its comment." However, nobody grumbled. After the banquet, fireworks banged and crackled in a field by the Warwick Road. Hunter was rapturous; the fireworks, he said, were excelled by the display above, where Cynthia had risen in full majesty, and chaste stars became revealed in the dark blue canopy. Below, the full and soft Avon flowed on, paying bountiful tribute to the gentle Severn. It was a fine night, and the pavilion wine list had included champagne, hock, claret, port and sherry.

VI

The festival flowed on; its chaste stars became revealed. Even if Madame Sainton-Dolby had a "sudden indisposition" and could not sing in the *Messiah*, Madame Laura Baxter brought what *The Times* called her powerful organ. Shakespeare arrived on the fourth day, a little late: the *Twelfth Night* company from the Haymarket, with Buckstone as Sir Andrew, Chippendale as a moderate Malvolio and Louisa Angel as Viola. The audience was dubious about a brief farce called *My Aunt's Advice*, which Edward Askew (Dundreary) Sothern had adapted from the French; it was unashamedly popular, and in this first week the plain men wished to be classical. Wombwell's menagerie, which arrived that day, prepared for huge crowds; getting hardly anyone, it left at once, cursing the name of Shakespeare. A writer from *All the Year Round** travelled to Stratford. Thought once to be Dickens himself, the man was probably one of the contributors who modelled their style upon the editor's. He found

* 21st May, 1864

8

Tombs (left to right) of Richard Beauchamp and Ambrose Dudley in the Beauchamp Chapel, St. Mary's Church, Warwick

that a caravan "exhibiting waxworks and a Scotch giant" was an odd welcome; and he did not appreciate the Birthroom, where he met two huge Warwickshire policemen "blowing their noses like thunder in two great sheets of red calico". The Bust he admired: "I have here the counterfeit presentment of a face suggestive above all things of a strong vitality, freshness of spirit, and liveliness of disposition, the face of a man . . . whose head never ached." At Anne Hathaway's cottage, reached after a twilight walk across daisy-sparkling fields to Shottery, the "long expected thrill comes unbidden now . . .". After that, *Twelfth Night* enchanted him; and he was happy to go later to "a snug room in the Red Horse, there to foregather with Sir Andrew Aguecheek and Sir Toby Belch, and Malvolio, and . . . many more who were well bestowed".

The week's largest audience chose the double bill of *The Comedy of Errors*—done first, because its company had to return to London—and the tragedy of *Romeo and Juliet*. "Performed from the text of Shakespeare", a needed assurance, the farce had Henry and Charles Webb as the Dromios, bewilderingly peas-in-the-pod. Listeners were unsure about the Juliet of the French girl, Stella Colas, of whom Henry Morley would say when he saw her (for a second time) in London, after the Stratford visit:

> Artless, guileless, pouring out all the beauty of a most pure girl-hood in the newly awakened poetry of an ungrudging, unsuspecting love, Juliet is the very last character to be represented to us by the stage-artifices and ghastly grimaces of a French *ingénue,* in her stage-innocence the most self-conscious of all forms into which the front of womanhood has ever been recast.

At Stratford Robert Hunter had to regret that he could say nothing of Miss Colas as he had "so strong an aversion from hearing the sublime and beautiful language of Shakespeare read with a foreign and broken accent. . . . Mr. Nelson looked Romeo very well albeit a trifle too stout."

Friends of Helen Faucit commented acidly. On the sixth day of the festival, after a concert in the Shakespeare Rooms, with a "Merry Wives of Windsor" duet for cornet-a-pistons and euphonium, and a setting of an ode, by John Brougham, that began, "What shall his crown be? not the laurel leaf That blood-besprinkled decks the warrior's head?", the night ended, at the pavilion, with *As You Like It*. Here the sonorous William

Creswick, so Thespian in response to 'The Drama' at the inaugural banquet ("The first wailing of an infant's voice was heard in the yeoman's house in Henley Street"), now gave himself with comparable vigour to the entire Seven Ages. Mrs. Vezin was Rosalind. The week's main events were over; on the seventh day the solemnities paused so that everyone might be in form for the night's fancy ball, tickets a guinea each, the floor thick with rival Hamlets, Ophelias, Perditas, Rosalinds and Romeos. Three or four hundred, beneath sizzling gas-jets, danced quadrilles, valses and galops, until five in the morning; and twice as many, in evening costume, watched from the gallery, identifying an Hungarian Peasant, Cardinal Capucius, Edgardo of Ravenswood or Wm. Shakespeare.

VII

In the committee's short-range view, the important business had ended. The lower orders not satisfied with their "popular week"—concert, balloon ascent, plays and a ball—wanted a pageant as well. Ginnett, the "equestrian manager" and circus proprietor, heard about it in the Shakespeare Hotel. "If you get up a pageant," he said, "I'll find you horses, carriages, and all my company, to take part in it at my own expense." Next day, the people's committee got permission for the pageant to pass through the town. On 2nd and 3rd May it did so, with traditional splendours. Melpomene and her Furies, Thalia and her satyrs, St George on horseback, the Witches with cauldron and coloured fire, Romeo and Juliet in a chariot drawn by two white ponies, and Shakespeare on a grand triumphal car, were seen all over Stratford, even in such places as Bull Lane, Sanctus Street, Tyler Street and Payton Street, which the festival had not touched. People who crowded in from the villages had only one disappointment, Coxwell's balloon; he could not get enough gas to inflate it, so it was packed up and taken back to London. At the pavilion the 'popular' events ended with *Othello* and *Much Ado About Nothing*. Instead of the guinea and half-guinea prices of the first week, visitors could get into the pavilion for as little as one shilling. A few of these were not Shakespearean by temperament. The Rev. Julian Charles Young, son of Charles Mayne Young, the tragedian Macready respected, was rector of Ilmington on the northern Cotswold slopes. Having had his house full during Tercentenary week, he sent his servants to the second week's *Othello*. None of them, he noted in his diary, had been to a play before:

> The next day I asked my butler, one of the most respectable and trustworthy of men, but staid and demure withal, how he had liked what he had seen. And all I could elicit from him, and this in the most cautious and deliberate manner, was the following tribute on the merit of the actors: "Well—Sir—thank you, Sir, for the treat. The performers—performed—the performance—which they had to perform—excellent well—'specially the female performers—in the performance!"
>
> I then went to the stables and asked my coachman, an honest, simple creature, but not over-burdened with imagination, how he had been impressed with what he had seen. Grinning from ear to ear with pleasurable reminiscences, he replied with infinitely more alacrity than his predecessor—" 'Twas really beautiful, Sir. I like it onaccountable!"
>
> The cheerful face clouded over as I asked him what it was about.
>
> "I don't ezactly know, Sir!"
>
> "Do you mean to say that you saw the play of *Othello*, and can't tell me what it was about?"
>
> "Well, Sir, if you'll belave me, I don't rightly know the meaning on't; but it was very pretty—that it were!" (Then, after a moment's reflection, as if he had recalled the thread of the magic tale)—"Oh! I know, Sir, now; I know. It ran upon *sweethearting!* Aye, that it did. And there were two gennelmen, one was in white and the other was in black; and, what was more, both o' these gents was sweet on the same gal."

VIII

At Stratford the sweethearting was over. Shakespeare had been decorously garlanded, and the magistrates had almost nothing to do. If the Tercentenary had not been all its plain men had wished, it had at least honoured a townsman, and it had presented his plays in Stratford—an attention that, ninety-five years before, a short, genial figure with a mulberry wand had quite forgotten. Financially, it was not a success; it would be years before any Stratford festival could boast of its balance-sheet. At the end of May the scenery was sold. Telbin's act-drop and accompanying mechanism went for £26 to the Surrey Theatre; and a Leeds theatre manager bought, for two pounds six shillings, the great central chandelier of more than 300 jets. Presently the splendid pavilion was down, and its nails dispersed. Stratford's next excitement, on a drenching night in 1879, would be the opening of the first Memorial. From what is left of it now, behind the second theatre, already nearly forty years old, we can look over to the poplars that tell us where the chandelier once flamed, where the tragedian Creswick's oratorical thunder volleyed, Stella Colas sighed for Juliet in broken English, and Julian Charles Young's coachman reflected on the two gennelmen, one in white, one in black. A London newspaper, with the contempt some journalists reserved for Stratford, dismissed everything as a "ghastly failure".

What of Phelps and Fechter, the rivals who never came to Stratford? That born peacemaker, the actor John Coleman, managed to bring them together, a year or two afterwards, at Charles Reade's house, where Phelps, the old lion, was as grim and taciturn at first as Fechter, the middle-aged tiger, was nervous. They were friends by the time the evening ended, and Fechter confided to Reade as he left, "He is a grand old man, and I love him like a brother; but, *entre nous,* he can't play Hamlet!". Simultaneously, Phelps, as Coleman saw him out to his cab, was growling, "After all, John, he's not a bad fellow for—for—a Frenchman; but, by——! he can't act Shakespeare!" Harmony at last: it needed only Bellew and Edward Flower to complete the company.

SIX

AROUND TO THE THEATRE

I

On the evidence of 250 years, Stratford-upon-Avon was hardly theatre-minded. Odes and pageants, yes; banquets and fireworks, certainly; but the town, complacent in the lull of that mid-Victorian afternoon, could do very well without the players. Or so it seemed. Charles Edward Flower would not believe it. When he followed his father in the Flower dynasty—Stratford had its own benevolent feudal system—he saw that Shakespeare must be remembered in the theatre, that it was foolish to revere Birth-room and tomb and to leave untrodden the greater Shakespeare Country, the imperial world of the plays. Stratford, then, must have its own stage; it did not worry Flower to think that the old house in Chapel Lane had just died unmourned.

He lived at Avonbank, on the riverside between the Bancroft and Holy Trinity. From there in 1874 he bought the two-acre site on the Bancroft where Garrick's Rotunda had stood, and added a gift of 1,000 pounds. The Shakespeare Memorial Association was born, pledged, modestly, to erect

> a small theatre in which to have occasional performances of Shakes-peare's plays, and which will be available for concerts, lectures, etc., a library of dramatic literature, etc., and a gallery to contain pictures and statuary of Shakespearean subjects.

Donors of a hundred pounds or more became governors at once. In the autumn of 1875, after an appeal for designs, the judge, E. M. Barry, R.A., chose "a modern Gothic building" submitted by a firm of architects in Westminster, Dodgshun and Unsworth. Upon the Birthday in 1877 a foundation stone was laid with Masonic ritual; slowly—progress had to be slow because the land was marshy and subject to flooding—the red-brick walls, bright and staring, blushing in embarrassment at themselves, began to rise above a startled river. The block would cost £20,000, and in the long run Charles Flower gave most of this himself; Stratford contributed the rest, except for £1,000, total British response to a scheme that London took every chance to mock—"presumptuous"; "a little local effort".

Local effort it might be, but in April 1879 the theatre was complete: "a paltry and impertinent business", said the *Daily Telegraph*, "half theatre and half mechanics' institute ... respectable nobodies ... local clique ... an insult to the memory of Shakespeare". Sheridan Knowles might have called this "jolly woo-wooing": it was the common response of the day's professional critics, their horizon bounded by Leicester Square and Clare Market. Though the library and picture gallery to the north had yet to be finished, here on 23rd April 1879, was the extraordinary theatre building, a "striped sugar-stick", a djinn from a Westminster drawing-board. Built of brick with dressings of stone and some half-timbering, it had a tall, fussy central campanile; gables, turrets, an assortment of sham-Gothic decoration. The architect, it appeared, had thought clumsily in terms of the fashionable notion of Shakespeare's 'Globe'. What emerged was a motley block that looked from a distance as if it were cardboard, cut flimsily against the sky. It has never been better described than by W. Bridges-Adams, who worked in it during the last seven years of its life:

In the hard light of day it was all too clearly, all too earnestly, striving to embody everything that everyone felt about Shakespeare. According to one story, when Mr Unsworth was ragged about it by his friends, he protested that on the whole he had brought in everything pretty well. He had. The riverside site may have prompted him to borrow here and there from the castles of the Rhine or the Loire, but in all else he was faithful to his charge. Shakespeare, though drawing much from Italy, was a patriot to the core: there was a Romanesque campanile surmounted by little turrets which somehow invited one to think of English bowmen. He was an Elizabethan and he loved his Globe; a belt of Tudor half-timbering testified to this. He was believed to be Church of England, he was dead, and here was his memorial; a quantity of semi-ecclesiastical Gothic took care of that.

Inside, though it developed its own friendly atmosphere, the temple was stark at first. It held 800. Before a stage twenty-seven feet six inches in height, with an opening of twenty-six feet, hung a drop-scene of Elizabeth on progress to the new Globe. Round the dome was a sentence from *A Midsummer Night's Dream*, "The poet's pen turns them to shapes and gives to airy nothing a local habitation and a name." The opening play—and London critics hugged themselves—would be *Much Ado About Nothing*.

II

Beatrice and Benedick in *Much Ado About Nothing* were Helen Faucit, who was Lady Martin, wife of the Prince Consort's biographer—the marble pulpit in Holy Trinity is her memorial— and Barry Sullivan, a robust boomer whom Bernard Shaw, as a young man, greatly admired. Technically, Helen Faucit had left the stage. Probably remembering the trouble in 1864, she was glad to come back for a single night, and to make in Stratford her true farewell. Even if she saw (and wrote about) the heroines sentimentally in the mode of her time, she was a persuaded Shakespearean. On the Birthday morning she went across to the Bust and found

> so much of the man behind it. . . . The profile, especially on the left, speaks of the grandeur, the full face of the humour and directness. There was no seeing it until we were admitted within the altar rail. The bust looks like a living friend, whom one would wish never to part with. There is no thought of death or separation about it.

Helen Faucit would have been the person to convert a Stratford grave-digger who asked a Canon in Holy Trinity churchyard if he, as a clergyman, thought Shakespeare was safe: in other words, had he gone up or down?

He was going up on 23rd April 1879. For Charles Flower it was a peculiarly complicated day. That morning he had heard from an irate Barry Sullivan. Because Helen Faucit was there for only one night—later an actress named Ellen Wallis would play Beatrice—Flower had the greenroom fitted up for her as a personal dressing-room, and his wife sent a number of ornaments from Avonbank. Seeing this, Sullivan issued an ultimatum that unless his own room were suitably arranged, he would not appear.

Flower had to order furniture, and to make sure that the actor was provided with silver vases and candlesticks, and a lace pin-cushion.* Immediately upon this embarrassment, he replied, at a luncheon in the town hall to the tetchiness, the crane-fly irritation, of the London critics:

> They say we are a set of Respectable Nobodies. All I can say is that the Nobodies, having waited three hundred years for the Somebodies to do something, surely blame ought not to attach to us. We shall be ready to go on patiently with our work.

Stratford that day had to be patient, for from early morning the rain, Garrick weather, soaked the town as it had done two years earlier at the Masonic ritual of the stonelaying. It was a cascade when the audience began to move from Waterside to the still bare, gas-lit theatre. Once within, a Shakespearean sun blazed upon Messina. It proved to be a clear and serviceable performance, though Sullivan, to whom any part was a rite, was much less at home than Helen Faucit. Actors and audience recognized that, whatever the theatre's external aspect—and few except Londoners were teasy about it—it was intimate, friendly and bound with use to develop its own atmosphere. Nothing seemed to go wrong, even if a Birmingham newspaper was decidedly rude next day: "Mr. Sullivan played the part in a manner that no doubt would have been highly acceptable in the East End of London." He took with surprising calm this snub from his birthplace. Next night, as Stratford's first festival Hamlet, he employed his notorious reading: "I know a hawk from a heron—pshaw!" The season, which had to include *As You Like It,* as well as a one-man per-formance by an elocutionist, Samuel Brandram, who recited solidly the whole of *The Tempest,* Prospero to Ceres, lasted for two weeks, and Stratford was proud of it. London went on scoffing. "Every Englishman of education is attracted more or less to London," said a professional journal. "A new theatre in a small country town signifies nothing at all."

For a decade the Shakespeare Memorial was content to establish itself quietly as a small country-town theatre. Festivals, as a rule, occupied a fortnight in the spring—even if Sullivan's company came for three weeks in 1880 and the Bernard company for only

---

* Merely temperament. Sullivan had given a hundred guineas to the Memorial fund, and he would not accept a fee for his festival work.

one in 1884—and Stratford, which had little experience, welcomed the various directors with respect. They included, successively, such men as Edward Compton (Fay Compton's father) for two years; Eliot Galer, a provincial manager from Leicester, for one; and Charles Bernard and Miss Alleyn, with a competent touring cast, for another two. Little has remained in record from those years between 1879 and 1885. A stuffed stag, presented by the Lucys of Charlecote, began its legendary reign when Barry Sullivan's foresters carried it across the sprinkled leaves of Arden; the business became essential to any local *As You Like It* for several decades. Scenes for *Macbeth* (1883) were painted from an artist's direct observation on Charles Flower's Scottish estate. Annie Alleyn and her manager, Charles Bernard, were married at Holy Trinity in 1884; next spring they acted to unlooked-for enthusiasm in *Love's Labour's Lost*, an unkind title. Two events out of season crowned the period. One (1885) was a single sun-flashing performance of Rosalind by the new Californian actress, Mary Anderson. Her Orlando was a young man, Johnston Forbes-Robertson; the stuffed stag paraded; and a London writer dismissed the theatre as "a bare, wretched tenement, the perfection of meanness and unloveliness". Mary Anderson showed her opinion by presenting two of the terra-cotta panels—hers illustrate *Hamlet* and *As You Like It*—that we see today outside the Memorial Library, which, with the art gallery, had been finished by 1884; at the foot of Chapel Lane they face us unchanged. Another visitor out of festival—for long periods the theatre lay dark—was the American Ada Rehan; in August 1888 she came with Augustin Daly's New York Comedy Company for one night. Now, in the Royal Shakespeare Picture Gallery there hangs Eliot Gregory's formidable portrait of Katharina the Shrew, standing with upflung head and folded arms, her eyes sparkling defiance; there had never been a Kate like Ada Rehan, larger than life.

III

Nobody was prescient enough—or could have been—to see how much of the stage history of Stratford would rest upon a summer evening at the Theatre Royal in Leamington Spa. Charles Flower, wanting a company for 1886, had heard a good many tributes to F. R. (Frank) Benson, then on the road as an actor-manager. Aged 27 and son of a Hampshire squire, he had distinguished himself at Winchester and New College, Oxford, as actor and athlete. He won the three miles for Oxford; and in Baliol Hall he acted Clytemnestra in the Greek text of the *Agamemnon* of Aeschylus, a production he helped to plan. Irving gave him a few weeks as Paris in the Lyceum *Romeo and Juliet*, where he met Ellen Terry. He had had some haphazard provincial touring, with disastrous wig, before taking over suddenly a company that his manager had abandoned in Fifeshire. It was the origin of the proudest band of brothers the British stage had known.

Frank Benson was that rare personage, a vigorous intellectual. Handsome and tireless, he assembled his companies—for the Bensonians were ever renewing themselves—in what was called the first university of the theatre. If as an actor, he could vary wildly, seldom doing the same things on two consecutive nights, on his hour he could lift an audience to the skies. It was his misfortune that the event rarely occurred when a London critic was there, or anybody who could preserve the moment in print. Charles Edward Montague, one of the greatest of all drama critics, did so in Manchester during 1899, and we can take his word that Benson, when the fit was on him, could be inspired. Nobody responsible has mocked his talent as a teacher, or his influence upon the day's classical acting. A thoroughly masculine player, believing that a company should be physically fit, he insisted upon exercise and the value of games. Hence the growth of a silly legend (and many related apocryphal stories) that hockey and cricket meant more to him than Shakespeare. Though his fame has suffered in a period of inverted snobbery, no historian will deny Benson his place. We can see him as he looked in his middle years, in the Hugh Rivière portrait that hangs in the Royal Shakespeare Picture Gallery. He wears blazer and running shorts; his Roman features are set against a Shakespearean frieze; and his eyes look, as Benson's always did, into space across one's left shoulder.

Charles Edward Flower and his wife did not know what they might discover on that Leamington night at the theatre in Regent Grove. It turned out to be one of the most agonising performances of *Macbeth* in a catalogue of calamities. Everything began when George Weir (First Witch), suffering—it was said afterwards—

from the effect of nervousness and its antidotes, announced with unnatural solemnity, "The cat's mewed three times." Benson had arranged that just before the Dagger speech a tea-bell should be heard in the wings as Lady Macbeth's signal ("Go, bid thy mistress when my drink is ready, she strike upon the bell"). The bell sounded; and a fly-man, taking it as the curtain warning, lowered the curtain with the dagger speech unspoken and murder yet to do. Could this be an innovation perhaps, a daring cut, Shakespeare by one of these new young men? While the audience speculated, the curtain rose upon Benson looking skyward and using a spirited vocabulary. His Lady Macbeth was Janet Achurch. When he bore her off after she had fainted at Inverness, he banged her against an archway, whereupon she observed with crisp and audible precision, "Damn you, you clumsy fool, you've broken my back." In the banquet scene a local super, fully armoured on the steps of the throne, knocked off his helmet and played a private bat-ball game which ended when he smote the helmet, rocketing, into mid-stage, a hearty drive to cover-point who missed the catch. The gallery was ecstatic. Next, during the fourth act, Herbert Ross fastened the cauldron to Weir so that the poor man found himself chased round the stage by a bowl of fire. To Ross's joy, Weir kept asking whether he was seeing things or not. Lights failed in the wrong places; they went up in the wrong places; and, at length, glancing towards the stage-box, Benson found it empty; the Flowers had gone. That could have been the irrevocable curtain; but Benson was young and eloquent; he went across on the Sunday to luncheon at Avonbank, contrived to explain himself, and got the Stratford invitation for a single week in the following April. We dare not think what might have befallen Shakespeare in Stratford if Charles Flower had lacked a sense of humour. As it was, in *Hamlet* on Easter Monday, 26th April 1886, Benson opened thirty Stratford years—his début in the town of which he became a Freeman, and to which he would return in triumph after receiving a knighthood at Drury Lane.

IV

He and Stratford realized in the first week that they were made for each other. Down the years he was prepared to describe the town as "a yeoman centre of England, an exchange and mart for centuries of the goods and ideas of the Anglo-Celtic people", one of the sonorous sentences that Benson would drop into any conversation. Until 1919 his players were absent from this "yeoman centre" only in the years 1889, 1890 and 1895, the spring festival of 1914, the summer of 1916, and (when the theatre was closed) the last two years of the First World War. He presented every play in the canon except *Troilus and Cressida*—which William Poel did for a matinee in 1913—and *Titus Andronicus**; and he trained many of the major classical players of his period. Henry Ainley, Oscar Asche, Randle Ayrton, Matheson Lang, Lilian Braithwaite, Dorothy Green, Margaret Halstan, Nancy Price, Harcourt Williams, Lily Brayton, H. O. Nicholson, Baliol Holloway, O. B. Clarence, Walter Hampden, Leslie Faber, the comedian George Weir, Frank Rodney, Lyall Swete, Henry Caine and Arthur Whitby were all Bensonians of the prime. Young people stayed longer than they might have done because of a loyalty they could hardly have defined, to the gentle, vague, long-striding man with the classical profile, the hair flapping across his forehead, the voice like a crackling fire, the worn Norfolk jacket, the square-toed shoes, and the fingers (the hands always looked old) that were ready to grip sword-hilt or hockey-stick. He had a sunrise spirit; with Benson it was always four o'clock on a summer morning. Henry Ainley said of his persuasive gift:

Large angry men entered Benson's dressing-room to take his life for not giving them the parts of King Lear and Macbeth; but they always emerged smiling, gladly taking a pound a week less, and doubling Francisco with Rosencrantz and the Second Gravedigger. Athletically and spiritually, he not only turned men into actors, but sometimes actors into men.

His name and Stratford's are so indivisible that we forget how brief the seasons were at first: a few weeks yearly. At other times the company was out on a pilgrimage of grace. "Poor players, begging friars," he said, "we go up and down the land that the people may never go without an opportunity of seeing Shakes-

---

* Curiously, William Archer had written in 1895: "I shall certainly go to my grave without having seen anything like the full cycle of the playable plays. My ambition stops short of *Troilus and Cressida*, which is not intended for the stage, and *Titus Andronicus*, which is absurd." Archer would be a startled man today.

peare played by a company dedicated to his service." It was for Stratford, nonpareil of touring dates, that the company waited season by season: the still uncrowded market-town, the April welcome at the railway station, the friends they would encounter in High Street. They adopted Stratford as they did no other place: its bow-curved river-reach, its meadows, the Weir Brake (named after George, they said), the rosy cleft of Southern Lane, the inns that they called the 'Wagstaff', the 'Dirty Duck' and the 'Canary' ('Shakespeare', 'Black Swan', 'Falcon'). Certainly Benson himself never forgot his first *Hamlet,* a warm Easter Monday, a drift of blossom in the air, Stratford starred with early lamplight, the river chuckling in its reeds, and—beyond his dressing-room window—Holy Trinity spire rising into a misty blue behind the elms of Avonbank. To act at Stratford was obviously a romantic interlude: a country theatre, a country greeting. It meant more than the players knew. They created the Stratford theatre. At the 'Memorial' they were the first freemen of Shakespeare's own country, and they were governed by a leader born, a scholar, a seer, a man who could behave like Quixote and speak with the voice of the Shakespearean kings. To the end, even in the slow fading after he left Stratford—a progress which is not part of this narrative—he was still a man who would hold the imagination as Masefield's Lancelot had remained in Guinevere's:

> I had last seen him as a flag in air,
> A battle-banner bidding men outdare . . .
> I had not ever thought of him as old.

V

During his reign the Stratford Festival expanded from two basic spring weeks to four in spring, four in summer; once, there were eighteen plays in eighteen days. Benson kept on terms with his chairmen, Charles Edward Flower (who died in 1892), his brother Edgar—kindly, but less of a Shakespearean—and Edgar's son Archibald, though the last of these, a man of business, fretted more than once about an idealist who could not read a balance-sheet. But Frank Benson survived; few withstood his charm. Always he could coax "great leviathans to dance on sands"; get the heads of the theatre to play for him at Stratford—now Ellen

Terry, who came for Queen Katharine in 1902; now Forbes-Robertson, with his courtly Hamlet in 1908; now Lewis Waller, now Martin Harvey. London luminaries all knew Mr. Unsworth's stage, the theatre's horseshoe tiers and, outside, some steps and a few courses of ivied brick where their photographs might be taken. Besides Benson's guests there could be non-festival visitors who wanted to play at Stratford simply because it was Shakespeare's parish. Thus, some years after her Shrew, Ada Rehan returned in 1897 as Rosalind, a performance that began in the open, by the river, and moved briskly to the theatre under a deluge. Sarah Bernhardt, in 1899, acted her passionate, highly-coloured Hamlet in a jogtrot French prose version. Though the Mayor met her at the station, she drove down to Waterside in the Corelli carriage.

This was the period, too, of those fictional visitors in Q's novel, *True Tilda,* the children who had sailed along the Stratford-upon-Avon canal and its descending levels:

> The boat glided deeper and deeper into a green pastoral country, parcelled out with hedgerows and lines of elms, behind which here and there lay a village half-hidden—a grey tower and a few red-tiled roofs visible behind the trees. . . . No human folk frequented the banks of the canal, which wound its way past scented meadows edged with willow-herb, late meadow-sweet, yellow tansy and purple loose-strife, this last showing a blood-red stalk as its bloom died away. Out beyond, green arrowheads floated on the water; the *Success to Commerce* ploughed through beds of them, and they rose from under her keel and spread themselves again in her wake.

Early one morning they came into Stratford by caravan and woke to see the swans and the spire.

> "That's where Shakespeare's buried," said the Fat Lady, "and the great brick building yonder—to the right, between us and the bridge—that's the Memorial Theatre where they act his plays. There's his statue, too, beside the water, and back in the town they keep the house he was born in. You can't get away from Shakespeare here. If you buy a bottle of beer, he's on the label; and if you want a tobacco-jar, they'll sell you his head and shoulders in china, with the bald top fitted for a cover. It's a queer place, is Stratford." The boy gazed. To him it was a marvellous place.

Indeed, in many ways it was, though these chance visitors knew nothing of what happened in the great brick building, the splendour of the plays, the names of Benson or Rehan or Bern-hardt, the insulated life of the theatre, the festival talk of the town. It was a serene little world. Very occasionally the festival was ruffled. Constance Benson, better teacher than actress, continued to play leading parts she could have tactfully relinquished. Still, Corelli aside, Stratford remained generally loyal. Mrs. Benson was a kind woman and a good hostess; some things she did well; and the company could invariably summon new reserves of stamina and enthusiasm. George Weir was a definitive clown, and Benson attracted young actors who were virile and lyrical. One tentative conspiracy fizzled, like Angelo's fireworks, when in 1903 the principal guest at the first Birthday luncheon* announced unguardedly that he had been asked to conduct the festival of 1904. He was Herbert Beerbohm Tree, of His Majesty's in London, with whom a few of the governors had indulged in surreptitious negotiation. Tree, they argued, ruled the Shakes-pearean stage, and Stratford might well grow into a favoured protectorate. At this delicate hour the dear man wrecked every-thing by a bulletin that had to be disclaimed as premature; Benson, on the last night of the festival, said more forcibly than usual that he would be returning next spring. The governors were criticized, and by no one so sharply as Marie Corelli, who had been hoping for a change because she could not endure the Bensonians; doubtless Constance, who had an independent mind, had failed to defer to her. Tree, amiable fantastic, was forgiven; and when he came down to Stratford to play Hamlet at the Spring Festival of 1910, he said to Constance Benson as the carriage turned into the decorated streets, "Is this kind thought for me?"

Memorial Theatre history means such things as Benson's passionate speaking—sword upon sword—in *Antony and Cleo-patra;* the uncomplicated nobility of his Henry V, star of England; his Richard II, remembered in the picture gallery's stained glass; and the "eternity" *Hamlet* (1899), which, though it lasted for five hours, failed to give the full text because Matheson Lang, drying up, spoke only Voltimand's first and last lines. Then there were the eccentric Coleman *Pericles* of 1900; Benson's productions of the historical cycle, which anticipated those of sixty years on; and the Orestean trilogy of Aeschylus, which someone called the Acetylene Trilogy. The festivals grew in length and range. In

* Arranged by the Shakespeare Club.

Warwick Castle. The prominent tower is Caesar's;
Guy's Tower is on the right

1910, year of the first summer season, Stratford made Benson a Freeman ("You have constituted me your knight, your friend, your serving man"); the council enclosed the vellum in a casket of sixteenth-century oak, old wood from Holy Trinity, charged with the shields of Stratford, Benson and Saint George, resting upon mulberry leaves. Plays were not enough. Every summer now the town gave itself to morris-dancing, Old English games, lectures, and exhibitions. Progress (the catalogue is that of Benson's successor, W. Bridges-Adams) had not yet brought "tarmac, chars-à-bancs, cash-registers, motor-boats oiling the face of the Avon, trippers chy-iking the actors from the opposite bank, visiting hordes from every corner of the globe". In Stratford "all sang for the joy of singing", and it is apparent that acting and playgoing had a quality lost today in a world more sophisticated. I call three witnesses. First, W. B. Yeats in 1901:

One passes through quiet streets, where gabled and red-tiled houses remember the middle ages, to a theatre that has been made, not to make money, but pleasure like the market houses that set the traveller chuckling. Nor does one find it among hurrying cabs and ringing pavements but in a green garden by the riverside. Inside I have to be content with an extra chair, for I am unexpected and there is not an empty seat. Yet there is no one who has come merely because one must go somewhere after dinner. All day, too, one does not see or hear an incongruous or noisy thing, but spends the hours reading the plays and the wise and foolish things men have said of them, in the library of the theatre, with its oak-panelled walls and leaded windows of tinted glass. . . . It is certainly one's fault if one opens a newspaper, for Benson gives one a new play every night, and one need talk of nothing but the play in the inn parlour, under oak beams blackened by time, and showing the mark of the adze that shaped them.

At that time the Bensonians, in their first 'Week of Kings', were acting six of the chronicles.

Partly [said Yeats] because of a spirit in the place, and partly because of the way play supports play, the theatre moved me as it had never done before. That strange procession of kings, queens, warring nobles, insurgent crowds, and people of the gutter has been almost too visible, too audible, too full of an unearthly energy.

The second witness is Arthur Machen, writer before actor, who was a Bensonian at the time Yeats was in Stratford:

9

A Regency terrace in Leamington Spa

Rehearsals took place in queer old taverns by the waterside; in lofts and outhouses, and in fine weather, in odd corners of the garden; shouting and singing, sonorous verse, clashing swords all mingling together, and good ale not absent, and laughter ever present, the laughter of happy men who loved their craft, and were exempt for a while from the true penalty of Adam, the doing of hateful tasks for a hateful master for a living; the losing of all that is dear and good in life for the sake of being alive.

Finally, C. E. Montague, during the festival of 1904:

Wherever you look, behold it is very good! Behind you the little ordered country town in the oddly-gay mixed light of lamps early lit and of lengthening daylight. In front the fields rise and fall softly till they go out of sight, the quintessence of the contained and friendly English Midland landscape. When these things have possessed your soul with content, you go through a door and see, it may be, *As You Like It*, acted by artists on whom they are working too. At least you think so. . . . You feel a whole audience to be delightedly tasting flavours and valuing qualities in what they hear. . . .

When the play ends, outside there is white river mist and dead silence. You all go to bed like one household. Half an hour after the *Oresteia* was done, there was not a sound in the High Street. At midnight the footsteps of two belated actors and their voices at the corner as they said "Good night", rang like a sound in midnight Oxford.

Consider just two productions from the old Memorial: an odd union. One was by Benson at his most inspired; the other was a botch by John Coleman. Each, in its way, is historic. First, *Richard the Second* (1896), the only important revival in fifty years. Benson took imaginative control of Richard, at once king and no king, bred to autocracy, lord by divine right and prisoner by the right of Bolingbroke. Artist in words, incompetent in deeds, "a king, woe's slave, must kingly woes obey". With a fair wig and small beard, and the poised, shining pride of a missal-figure, Benson was quieter in method than anyone had known him. His restlessness restrained, he discovered fresh dignity, in spite of a daring moment at Westminster Hall when, flat upon the ground, he lay kicking in his despair. When he had crowned Bolingbroke, he moved—as of custom, and while staring in the glass—towards the vacant throne set against a great painted window. Then, recalling himself suddenly, he stepped aside with a gesture and a low, sad laugh. After Bolingbroke had ordered his conveyance to the Tower, Richard stood self-absorbed, his forefinger beating time vacantly to the music as the curtain fell. W. J. Lawrence took this to derive from Holinshed's relation that Richard, under his misfortunes, was "almost consumed with sorrow, and in a manner half dead". The early performance must have been inescapably poignant; the haunted artist and lost, spoilt child, surrendering his life with his crown. Montague, a few years later, applauded Benson's command of what criticism had taken pains to obscure—the capable and faithful artist in the same skin as the incapable and unfaithful king: "Every other feeling is mastered, except at a few passing moments, by a passion of interest in the exercise of his gift of exquisite responsiveness to the appeal made to his artistic sensibility by whatever life throws for the moment in his way." Visually, it was Benson's most anxiously planned revival, with a hint of medieval magnificence. It could be fussy, as in the incidental business of the lists; too explanatory, as in a rumble of thunder to point the lines, "Men judge by the complexion of the sky, The state and inclination of the day." Yet always it governed the stage. Frank Rodney, who hated to play against an audience and who loathed swans—no recommendation in Stratford—was Bolingbroke, and had to wear a helmet with the white swan crest. Angered by a double burden, he went on to act as strongly as he had ever done. Much from the revival is closely remembered, especially its interpolation at Coventry when the King's wolfhound, as in Froissart, left his master to follow Bolingbroke.

It was a thousand leagues from this to the comic *Pericles* of 1900, the most regrettable production in festival history. Acting in London at the Lyceum, and overcome by personal worries—such as the aftermath of the fire at Newcastle that had destroyed his company's possessions—Benson allowed someone he had never previously met, John Coleman, to stage *Pericles* as the Stratford 'Revival Play'. Honest John, the friendliest of men, was like an anthology of old-actor jokes, indexed and bound in leather. His voice was a cannon-ball rolling down the thunder-track. Though the theatrical quality of *Pericles* had long obsessed him, there was much in it he had to alter. In his own phrase, he expunged the first act, eradicated the banality of the second, eliminated the obscenity of the fourth, and omitted entirely the irrelevant Gower chorus. What remained, padded with a great deal of Coleman, he put on at the Memorial Theatre with such Bensonians in the company as Lilian Braithwaite, Lily Brayton, Oscar Asche, Harcourt Williams, Matheson Lang, Nancy Price, O. B. Clarence and H. O. Nicholson. Coleman, as a dramatist, was a poor relation of Sheridan Knowles and Wilson Barrett; and the Bensonians watched his performance of Pericles with incredulous joy. He was 72. As a handsome youth, shipwrecked and thrown upon the shore, he wore wrinkled green fleshings with green wool gummed here and there to represent seaweed. Gold powder, sprinkled on his shaggy eyebrows and heavy white moustache, shook off at every movement. The join of his golden wig had not been coloured to match his rouged cheeks. He had worsted stockings, also sewn about with seaweed, and boots of green satin. Because no one applauded his entrance he walked off stage, re-entered, and dried up so completely that Asche had to speak every word for him, prefaced by "You said, my lord—". Clarence and Nicholson, as fishermen, entered in front of the act-drop which had been lowered in error, and played their scene before a State procession of Queen Elizabeth outside the Globe and Bear Garden. "Come off," cried Coleman from the wings, "you're ruining my play." The Bensonians fought on—even Lily Brayton, who, as Thaisa, was supposed to love Pericles at first sight, "a case", Coleman explained, "of ocular love-making".

One of the characters told another (in a Coleman phrase*), "Thou art a stranger in these parts." Coleman was certainly a stranger; but Marie Corelli, writing in the new *Daily Express,* thought "his manner, his elocution, his art of gesture...all a revelation to Stratford". New to the town and to drama criticism, she was squabbling already with the Bensons. Happily, there would be no similar revelations again. Coleman was an anachronism, a stuffed stag, though mercifully he never recognized it.

* The young Barry Jackson, who came over from Birmingham to see *Pericles* enjoyed this line; and to the end of his life he would quote a Coleman couplet:

> In me you see the prisoner you desire,
> For I am Pericles, the Prince of Tyre.

VI

Benson's Stratford life was bound to end when it did; only the coming of the war had slightly prolonged it. In the spring of 1914 the Festival Company had a desperately discouraging tour of the United States. Canada had cheered, but in the States a dead set was made at Benson himself, apparently because a mistake by his secretary of the moment at Stratford had alienated an important and arrogant Chicago critic. In consequence, he had to meet one of the fiercest personal attacks a player had known. The Stratford governors observed this glumly. On the company's return to America in the following autumn—this was the intention— Benson would have to be superseded by one of his leading men, the handsome extrovert, Murray Carrington. No more came of it for danger loomed, the bright day faded, and the company re- opened in Stratford for the summer season of 1914 just three days before Britain declared war. Through two years the fes- tivals struggled on, into the Tercentenary spring of 1916, 300 years since Shakespeare's death. Benson had been cast as Julius Caesar in a great commemorative matinée at Drury Lane early in May and in the very trough of the war. At his London hotel that morning he received the offer of a knighthood in a letter that had followed him all round England. When the royal party entered its box, Arthur Collins, who was manager of Drury Lane, explained to the aide-de-camp. King George had no sword. Immediately Collins sent out for one to fit the occasion—it can be seen at Stratford in the Royal Shakespeare Picture Gallery— and at the end of the performance Frank Benson was knighted in the room behind the Royal Box, still wearing the bloodstained robes and with the painted white face, the sunken eyes, blue lips and lines of pain, and the half-bald wig of the dead Caesar. Benson would have wished no other setting: the first time an actor had been knighted in a theatre, an accolade for gallantry on his own field of battle. Next day Stratford welcomed the Bensons overwhelmingly.

They did not act at Stratford that summer. Instead, the Old Vic Company, under Ben Greet and with the young Sybil Thorndike, went down for a few weeks. Constance and Frank Benson ran a canteen under the French Red Cross; later he drove a French motor ambulance. Meanwhile, for two years the theatre was practically unused, and by the end of the war Stratford was no longer Benson's romantic "yeoman centre". After a makeshift Spring Festival in 1919, he knew reluctantly that he must go. The festival would pass that summer under the joint control of London's Shakespeare Memorial National Theatre Committee and the Stratford governors. They would have had Benson as director and head of a drama school, but he would not modulate to an elder statesman; he needed to continue acting, and at Stratford this would be impossible. In his place, an experienced man of half his age, W. Bridges-Adams, was appointed to the New Shakespeare Company: one unfashionably faithful to the text, with free choice of actors for its leading parts, and the power to maintain a tradition unimpaired by the coming or going of any individual. On the first night of the summer season, Bridges-Adams, with many Old Bensonians in his cast, made chivalrous acknowledgment: "Let us think, in all honour and reverence and love, of Shakespeare and Sir Frank Benson . . . to whom we say, as William Morris has said in another connection, 'Anyone can cull the flower now that you have sown the seed.'"

VII

Bridges-Adams, formerly producer at the repertory theatres of Bristol and Liverpool, was a practised Shakespearean whom the veteran Ben Greet had publicly nicknamed 'Unabridges'. His revivals, swift and fastidious, decorative without being stuffily realistic, and played from a text neither cut nor transposed, re-burnished Stratford's name. He tried to see the plays "as plays, irrespective of mutilations made to suit the whim of a star or the exigencies of stage carpentry. In short, straight Shakespeare played by a balanced cast." This continued to be the policy during an age of transition. It was also the Petrol Age. More people were hurtling through the town. Bridges-Adams knew he must keep the theatre's dignity and save it from being an exhibit in the general tourist show. The choice lay between Ye Olde Shakespeare Bunne Shoppe and Bayreuth, and the 'Memorial' must be Stratford's "unimpeachable credential". The old personal note had gone, but there was more emphasis on Shakespeare, played simply and clearly by such fine players as Dorothy Green, Florence Saunders, Baliol Holloway, Edmund Willard, John

Laurie and Frank Cellier. In 1922 partnership with the National Theatre Committee ended, and the governors became responsible for the company as well as the building; three years later came the Royal Charter, with Alderman (later Sir) Archibald Flower as chairman of the administrative council.

Stratford, in spite of alarming changes, remained at night (as Bridges-Adams said), a

> pleasant place in which to practise the gentle art of playgoing. You dine leisurely, you stroll to the theatre, you may stroll beside the river in the interval, and if you are lucky you may hear the nightingale as you stroll home. Your mind attunes itself to the play, and the play is free to talk to you without stridency.

Soon there would be an alarming change. In the early afternoon of a buffeting, gusty spring day, 6th March 1926, a man employed at the theatre was cycling down Chapel Lane when he saw ahead of him a thin spiral of smoke from the roof. He rushed to the stage door; a choking smoke-cloud thrust him back, and everywhere he heard timber crackling. There was a wild rush to Waterside. Fire brigades from Evesham, Warwick, Solihull and Kenilworth hastened to aid the hard-pressed Stratford men. Volunteers on Waterside formed a human chain to save the treasures of picture gallery and library, and thousands of books and pictures passed from hand to hand across the road to be dumped in a lecture room. Two men carried out an enormous marble bust which it took seven men to get back. In a bitter wind people worked silently until not a book or a picture remained. It was obvious now that nothing could save the building: flames had spread on both sides of the fireproof curtain; the auditorium blazed like desert-dry tinder; and, when the fire reached the roof, a wind blowing across the theatre to the Avon acted as a gigantic fan. Before five o'clock, in a tempest of sparks, the roof collapsed, and flame turned the tower into a pillar of fire. People in Stratford streets had got on with their neglected shopping. Soon after twilight the tower roof swayed and crashed in ruin, and tongues and streamers of fire shot to fifty feet. By seven o'clock it was nearly over: the theatre of Benson and Charles Flower was in smouldering chaos. By chance the wind during the afternoon had blown away from the library and picture gallery; had it slanted in the other direction, nothing could have saved the block.

Bridges-Adams, who had heard the news in London while dining at the Garrick Club, set out instantly to plan a temporary theatre while a pile of blackened bricks and twisted girders lay in the March night on Waterside.

Nobody discovered the origin of the fire; a carelessly dropped match, a cigarette stub, a vandal's premeditated act, or what Bernard Shaw, who detested the place, would have called a benefactor's happy thought. Next day the governors, with Bridges-Adams, met at the Stratford-upon-Avon Picture House in Greenhill Street, with its low, long auditorium, lush panels and ground floor gently raked. The festival had to begin in barely six weeks. Before then the depth of the stage was doubled and dressing-rooms were built for thirty persons. On the chosen date, with the chosen company and the chosen play, *Coriolanus*, Bridges-Adams opened the Spring Festival of 1926. It was ironical because, five years earlier, there had been acrimony about the winter use of the old 'Memorial' as a cinema; an experiment that started with *Pollyanna* was quietly abandoned. Now the Picture House, with Shakespeare's arms above the canopy, would house the players for six years. John Drinkwater, in his famous poem for the Memorial Theatre fund, pictured Shakespeare's people as homeless,

> They wander up and down,
> Ghosts without any home in Stratford town. . . .

It was not so. Bridges-Adams had a magical way with the Picture House stage. Several of his productions there, particularly the *Richard the Second* (George Hayes) of 1929, the *Much Ado About Nothing* of the same year—the festival's golden jubilee—and the *Othello* (Wilfrid Walter and Hayes) of 1930 vibrate in the memory; and, to this hour, when anyone says "Shakespeare in Stratford", the lights of Greenhill Street must glow again in the mind.

VIII

The tasks now were to get a new theatre and, vitally, the money for it. Americans, as ever, were lavish; they gave two-thirds of the £300,000 raised for rebuilding and endowment. During three winters of the interregnum the Festival Company travelled through Canada and the United States, making friends and influencing people, not a dire burden if Shakespeare is one's advocate. Bridges-Adams, who never pushed between audience and dramatist (and who, unlike some of his successors, knew the meaning of high comedy), had the players for the work: Walter, Hayes and Byford, and later Fabia Drake, Gyles Isham and the grand Bensonian, Randle Ayrton, with his unremitting concentration and the mannerisms of speech that somebody called Curzonian ('wăn,' 'glăss'). Ayrton scorned London, and usually took the notices when he acted in a West End theatre. He was the strongest Lear of his generation; from him Donald Wolfit learned much.

The new 'Memorial' was intended to be the ultimate in theatre design. No stage project in memory had stirred so many people. "Stratford-upon-Avon is to be congratulated on the fire," said Bernard Shaw. John Drinkwater's poem,

> Dear Sir or Madam, Up in Stratford town
> A little, famous theatre is burnt down. . . .

was spoken from stages everywhere. I heard it read, in a neo-Coleman style, all florid arabesques, by the manager of a South Devon repertory, between the intervals of *A Marriage of Convenience*. Though he was like a collectors' parody of a late-Victorian elocutionist, listeners—and few were Shakespearean—responded emotionally. So throughout the country. From Stratford the governors invited architects of Britain and North America to plan a new theatre, "simple, beautiful, convenient"; and a year later the award went to the only woman in seventy-four entrants, Elisabeth Scott, aged 29, Sir Gilbert Scott's grand-niece and daughter of a Bournemouth doctor. Her theatre was beautiful in line and wholly functional, with a fan-shaped auditorium, wide stage and river terraces. Some of the unregenerate, Bridges-Adams said, held that it was less like a theatre than a fort. He went on, in a passage written just before the opening:

> There it stands at the bridge-head, ready to turn its guns on the spiritual unloveliness which flourishes when people are content merely to make small profits out of a great reputation. There is no disparagement here of the custodians of the Birthplace, who administer their trust faithfully and well, nor of the Stratford hotel-

keepers, who supply a necessary commodity at a fair price, nor of the Stratford people generally, who have a proud regard for the amenities of their town. But the truth is that unless the theatre, as it were, takes command, the future of Stratford is one that Stratfordians least of all would care to contemplate. Because it is not enough to strew flowers on Shakespeare's grave, nor even to toast his memory at a yearly luncheon. If you really want to honour him, you must be prepared to exert yourself rather more than that. There is one way above all others, and that is the constant and worthy presentation of his plays upon the stage.

In 1929, as in 1877, but on a glittering afternoon, the foundation stone was laid with Masonic rites, a brief, stately ceremonial; swans flourished upstream to find what the excitement could be behind a rough fence that now cut across the Bancroft meadow. It was fifty years since Charles Flower had opened his theatre. The Board had disappointed collectors by shivering away from *Titus Andronicus,* much-bruited. Instead, they chose as Birthday Play—a label discarded after 1949—Stratford's favourite *Much Ado About Nothing,* staged in Bridges-Adams's high aristocratic fashion. Slowly the theatre assumed its final shape while the festivals moved on quietly in Greenhill Street before an annual audience of about 40,000. All was set for the Birthday of 1932 and a massive, unweathered building, red and silver-grey, that had been maligned as everything between a factory and a tomb. Its admirers, many and loyal, did not realize that a dragon called Doubt had been built into the power-house along with the intricate stage mechanism, the bronze and steel and marble, the Eric Kennington sculptures*, the rosewood and laurel and mahogany, poplar and walnut, sycamore and oak, burr-elm and gur-jun and a wealth of exotic timbers; the absurdly comfortable seats, the drop-curtain rayed in black, crimson, gold, silver and white velvet, and at least one door of blistered mahogany with a surround of Andaman padauk.

In Stratford streets, where every other person wore rosemary, the morning of 23rd April 1932 was windy, bright, and cold. At a marquee luncheon in New Place Garden, attended by the

* Relatively few ask now about these sculptures high on the theatre façade. The subjects are the emotions in Shakespeare's plays: Treachery, Jollity, Martial Ardour and Love, with Life Triumphing Over Death (a nude female figure kneeling above a skull) as centre-piece.

most English of Prime Ministers, Stanley Baldwin, Sir Archibald Flower, the year's mayor, asked Frank Benson to propose 'The Immortal Memory'. Benson and Flower: in Stratford no more appropriate union.

The luncheon was closely-timed; and F.R.B. at his most soaring (the little centre of yeoman England, the rhythms of the great song-maker) dangerously exceeded his measure. Soon crowds that milled by the theatre, and along the new promenade, bordered with chestnut trees, that had transformed Waterside and the Bancroft, saw the Prince of Wales's circling aircraft and the rare sight of a wigged and gowned town clerk breaking into a run. Within minutes the Prince was walking up to the dais before the theatre by which, for this one day, the flags of the nations were grouped. As soon as he had spoken, a little nervously, he unfurled the King's Flag—while others fluttered into colour—and unlocked the theatre door with a gold key. Inside, Lillah McCarthy, coming from retirement as Helen Faucit had done, spoke John Masefield's ode, with two lines that would be famous,

> The acted passion beautiful and swift,
> The spirit leaping out of flesh and bone

and immediately the curtain rose—for in those days it did—upon *Henry the Fourth, Part I*, and Randle Ayrton, each syllable stamped as by a hot iron, speaking beneath the crimson canopy of Henry's throne:

> So shaken as we are, so wan with care,
> Find we a time for frighted peace to pant. . . .

The audience remembered, respectfully, that though the proscenium might be only thirty feet wide and twenty feet high, or whatever the figures were, the stage was 120 feet in width from wall to wall and could do everything but dance a tarantella at its director's will. Not, Bridges-Adams had insisted, that he intended any mechanical orgy to be a substitute for the verse. That afternoon it all seemed rather far from the Black Forest Gothic of 1879, "the theatre that Flower built of old", the swish of the rain, the yellow gas-light, and the sonorities of Barry Sullivan.

SEVEN

BESTOWED WITH THE ACTORS

I

A few days after the fire, several newspapers—the *Birmingham Post,* the *Daily Telegraph,* the *New York Times* and *Punch* among them—had opened an appeal fund. *Punch* used a cartoon by Bernard Partridge, in his youth a Bensonian. Shakespeare's characters, the ruined theatre behind them, waited in the Memorial Gardens by the river, while Shakespeare himself was saying to Punch, in the role of Polonius, "Good my lord, will you see my players well bestowed."

The answer was Elisabeth Scott's new theatre, rightly bestowing players and audience. It could not yet be a complete reply, for time had to test it and its difficulties. They were unconsidered when Bridges-Adams, staging both parts of *Henry the Fourth,* the first in the afternoon, the second at night, conceded only one thing to the curious. Then, to achieve a processional effect at the Coronation, he employed the sliding stage, taking Henry V (Gyles Isham) through the crowd and back again, pacing ceremoniously along the packed street against the movement. Nobody wanted to be teasy or demanding. It was a time for renewal, especially on the burning Whit-Monday afternoon when Frank Benson, as Shylock, led the Old Bensonians in a commemorative performance.

He was 73. For years he had been obliged to trail through the provinces in a repetitive series of 'farewells', devised by a personage called Harold V. Neilson (born Thomas Clegg). Once a minor member of Benson's company, Neilson had had no hesitation in driving the tired old man through Hamlet and Caliban and Macbeth. Benson was weary indeed; it would be his last year in the theatre. But now for a few hours he was back with his own people. Neilson (Antonio) was in the cast instead of Henry Ainley. Still, Nigel Playfair was there, and Cedric Hardwicke, Lilian Braithwaite (once Coleman's Marina), Robert Donat, O. B. Clarence, Herbert Ross, H. R. Hignett. On Sunday the company had rehearsed until past midnight, according to the ancient Benson prompt-book which grouped the early Venetian scenes together and then a series in Belmont. Acting next afternoon was formal, though Benson's vigour and Donat's voice are remembered; nobody bothered to observe that Arragon nearly chose the leaden casket; and for once the play lost its "swan-like end, fading in music". As soon as Shylock had left the strict court of Venice, the rainbow curtain fell. When it rose, the house rose with it, cheering out its heart as Bridges-Adams advanced from the wings with a laurel chaplet. It bore one word, "Pa", and he placed it at Frank Benson's feet.

II

The summer brought another *Merchant of Venice,* wildly out of routine. Theodore Komisarjevsky, the Russian director who lived in London, examined every resource of the Stratford stage, challenging critics with a production that though it would be a normal experiment today, was endlessly bizarre in the Stratford of 1932. In a night of harlequinade colour, the capering of *commedia dell'arte* masquers, and the new emphases of a restless, exuberant imagination, Komisarjevsky put the stage through every trick. After this he would return to Stratford five times during the decade, particularly with a *Macbeth* (1933) played in scrolled aluminium screens, balefully lit, and treated as a study of various neuroses, with the supernatural element removed; a *Merry Wives of Windsor* (1935) that slipped here and there into Viennese musical, Falstaff resembling the Emperor Franz Josef; and, far better, a *Lear* (1936) saluted for Ayrton's majestic King, Wolfit's heart-of-oak Kent, the vast symbolic staircase and the ceremonial lifting of those gold convolvulus-trumpets.

During 1933 the season ran at last, without break, from late spring to early autumn. By 1939 it had audiences of 200,000. Stratford, which had long ceased to pretend that it was a quiet country town, was as dense as Assisi with tourists. Thousands who had no intention of seeing a play, went over the new theatre. One of them was James Agate, the drama critic, who got at length to the 1938 Festival, but who in September 1933 was writing in his journal: "What needs my Shakespeare for his honoured bones? Certainly not a theatre looking like a barracks-cum-roadhouse. Paid a shilling to go in. Apron stage, which for me is fatal. I get *no* illusion unless the actors are railed-off." One had by now to be a devotee of Shakespeare, or joyfully gregarious, to withstand the crowds at high summer. Bridges-Adams's hopes were disappointed, for the theatre had not taken real command. An American visitor wrote in August 1933: "I went to look for Shakespeare, but the town just keeps a tame Bard."

The theatre was full, yet actors found it troublesome. So did many spectators. Its stage was remote; one missed the clasping arms of the old horseshoe tiers, and even the intimacy of the Picture House. Dressing-rooms were meagre, and at first on the wrong side of the building. "Like a fashionable restaurant with too small a kitchen," said Baliol Holloway, who acted at Stratford frequently. Holloway said, too, that playing upon the Memorial stage was like addressing Boulogne from Folkestone, but sometimes when he came downstage on a fine June night, he could distinctly see the front row of the stalls outlined in the distance. Cheerful exaggeration, it had its truth. 'Bay' Holloway, an actor of indomitable experience, had played more major classical parts than anybody of his time. To the end he looked like the lean greyhound of a man Stratford had known at the Benson zenith. His friends regretted that from 1949, seventeen years when he could still have quickened a production into life, no director asked him back to any stage. A casualty among the theatre's changing styles, he was proud and independent, making do in radio-drama (where he was expert) and not putting up with such ignorance as that of a television director who asked him, during his last decade, if he would play the Second Senator in *Othello*. "Do you really think I could manage it?" replied Holloway ironically. "Well," said the young man uncomprehendingly ,"you could have a try." Baliol Holloway's loss to the stage was a calamity; television would not have been his world.

Bridges-Adams (who admired him) had left Stratford at the end of 1934. There was no quarrel but he believed that the theatre, assured of its tourist support whatever it did, might slide progressively into complacent parochialism.

I doubt [he said in a letter to the chairman] whether a Council which, for all its list of imposing names, often sits as a small quorum a hundred miles from London, is sufficiently in touch with the living art of today to control the policy of a theatre of national, or even international, pretensions.

Prosperous though the 'Memorial' was, Stratford Shakespeare lay in the shadow. First excitement over, few critics came down; the companies merely slogged on. Ben Iden Payne, who followed Bridges-Adams, had been a Bensonian and, in Manchester, a repertory pioneer; for three decades he had worked in America. Now he proved to be an austere Shakespearean, fond of a dull, semi-Tudor framework; season after season—Komisarjevsky aside—could be no more than greyly serviceable. Players firmest in memory are those who attacked, projected themselves across the gulf; it was this fighting quality in Donald Wolfit that caused his work during 1936–7 to spark in the mind. He played such parts as Hamlet, Kent, Petruchio, Autolycus, Iachimo and a Ulysses supremely cogent, that should have been more acknowledged than it was, especially as *Troilus and Cressida* at that time was a rarity. But Stratford acting could trail into languor. There was too little time for rehearsals; too many new productions jostled each other. Towards the end of the decade, in Stratford's Diamond Jubilee year, Irene Hentschel—the only woman director in Stratford history—put on an exciting *Twelfth Night*. That spring, early in the Birthday Play, inevitably *Much Ado,* electric power through the West Midlands failed for ninety minutes, and the cast, aided only by feeble emergency lighting, had to play in gloom on the forestage until the black-out ended. Sharply, on his cue, Borachio spoke an appropriate line: "What your wisdom could not discover, these shallow fools have brought to light."

It was the last pre-war festival; in September it had to end prematurely. People wondered whether there could be a 1940 season, with hotels commandeered, transport cut by petrol rationing, and a rumour that if London were in danger, Parliament would meet at Stratford, in the Memorial Theatre. Finally the plays did go on. They contrived until 1945 to hold their audiences, thanks principally to thousands of troops in the area, most of them American. Little could keep an ardent Shakespearean away; some were known to walk back at night to Evesham, fourteen miles distant. Iden Payne left; Milton Rosmer followed him for one year, 1943, and resigned. Robert Atkins, formidably experienced, tried hard for two years, bringing his productions forward, lessening the gap, and finding at least one performance, Claire Luce's Cleopatra, to shine over an inadequate company. Suddenly, in the year after the war, the theatre—almost, it seemed, overnight—was transformed at the bidding of Sir Barry Jackson, and Stratford, in April 1946, hoped for the realization of Masefield's couplet:

> We but begin, our story is not told:
> Friends, may this day begin an age of gold.

III

The theatre was a Never-Never-Land. For loyalists it was never what it had been. For cynics it could never be any good. Round it pressed the ghosts of the past, ahead were the fogs of the future. Now Barry Jackson, maker of the Birmingham Repertory, might save Stratford. He relied heavily upon youth. He engaged a variety of directors. He refused to crush his repertory into the first ten days of a festival; and he made actors see that six months at Stratford was not a hopeless exile, Ovid at Tomi. Several drama critics, new to Stratford—for only a few faithful newspapers had reported it regularly—began to debate every production. Visitors made for Stratford, not as travellers on enforced route-march, but in a mood of fresh adventure, looking for light upon the misty mountain-tops. In 1946, Peter Brook, then only 21, a young director matched to a young poet's comedy, produced *Love's Labour's Lost* with style and grace. Audiences at this hour of austerity needed light, colour and sound; Brook, taking Watteau for inspiration, was pictorial and unashamed. At the last he expressed piercingly that fall of frost upon the summer night. He had less gratitude in 1947 for a contentious *Romeo and Juliet,* though the production—like the Komisarjevsky revivals—would be perfectly in today's mood of experiment. Among Jackson's actors, Paul Scofield confirmed, over and over, his repertory fame at Birmingham, expecially when in 1948 he played that first profoundly moving Hamlet*, a spirit in torment no less than his father.

* *Hamlet,* in which Scofield alternated the Prince with Robert Helpmann, was staged in Victorian costume. The Festival Company's private joke that season was the supposed alarm of Queen Victoria and the Prince Consort on

Kenilworth Castle from the air

Barry Jackson's three years astonished. In absolute directorship of the theatre as well as of the festival, he put the entire Stratford house in order, its workshops, its wardrobe, its stores. Even so, his friendly chairman, Lieutenant-Colonel (later Sir) Fordham Flower, Sir Archibald's son, soon wanted to move faster. Stratford must not create its own stars; they must be already created—a policy out of key with Stratford's past—and such people as Diana Wynyard, Robert Helpmann, Godfrey Tearle, Esmond Knight and Anthony Quayle joined the company in 1948. The governors did not renew Barry Jackson's contract: ironically, though as young at heart as anybody round the theatre, he had to be, in effect, an unpublicized sacrifice to his own belief in youth. Anthony Quayle, who succeeded him (1949) was joined from 1952 by Glen Byam Shaw. In 1956 Shaw became director in his own right and remained until another, and the biggest, Stratford change four years later.

Lists of names and dates are blurring. The point is that Stratford during this period had at its command any guest-producer, any star it desired: Dame Edith Evans, Dame Peggy Ashcroft, Tearle and Gielgud and Olivier, Redgrave, Richardson, Laughton, Tyrone Guthrie, Peter Brook and a young man named Peter Hall. Productions and performances were variable; but in two senses the world now recognized Stratford as Shakespeare's country: the theatre was internationally famous. As a building it had mellowed into the town, and a new generation had ceased to talk about factories or roadhouses, or to demand why the place was not half-timbered or in snow-white marble. Inside, from 1951, 'Bay' Holloway's Folkestone-Boulogne gap was closed and the ends of the circle were curved round towards the stage. T. C. Kemp, drama critic of the *Birmingham Post* and a loyalist unafraid to be romantic, saw the theatre at twilight when the river-craft were still and the water-meadows empty:

> Look downstream [from the Tramway Bridge] and you will see the lighted theatre hanging motionless over the water, a glittering galleon; to the north the town outlines itself in ebony against the fading sky. Distant lights twinkle and burn towards Cotswold;

receiving orders to murder Rosencrantz and Guildenstern. Wisely, the director (Michael Benthall) did not allow a First English Ambassador to announce, a little peevishly, in the last scene, that "Rosencrantz and Guildenstern are dead: Where should we have our thanks?"
10

The octagonal tower on Edgehill, erected by Sanderson Miller in 1750

the stream gurgles through the arches below; and into this reserve of dusk and silence comes winging the host of those who have so often set beauty stirring in the spring at Stratford. It is a pleasant fancy to imagine that the flight is led by the Swan of Avon himself.

IV

Allowed only two productions from the years between Barry Jackson's departure and the advent of Peter Hall as director in 1960, I might well take Tyrone Guthrie's *Henry the Eighth* (1949) and Peter Brook's *Titus Andronicus* (1955). It is common form now to remember a Shakespeare revival in terms of one director or another; today they are the governing body of the stage.

Guthrie, in his *Henry the Eighth**, thrust one scene so swiftly upon another, in a long hurtle across his permanent set, that we could not fail to mark the transience of fame, to see "how soon this mightiness meets misery". Directors less theatrically aware had drawn the chronicle out slowly to the mournful note of its Fletcherian verse, lute-music rather than spirit-stirring drum. But Guthrie, working in a many-levelled permanent set, a flowing design by Tanya Moiseiwitsch (John Drinkwater's stepdaughter), gave pace and animation to the sprawling pageant; he made of the minor peers and prelates and the talkative Gentlemen people with a true root in the Tudor scene, not useful mouthpieces crying "But what follow'd?" and "You're well met once again." Occasionally he was too exuberant. Yet, for all his crowded stage, he attempted none of the new "extravagances of showmanship" (Ivor Brown's phrase) required for the first performance in June 1613, when the Globe at Bankside was burned down by the discharge of "a peal of chambers". No matter; everything was there in the peering commentary of a First Gentleman, toothily excitable; one recalls, after twenty years, his joyful little spring-heeled leap at "All the rest are Countesses."

Titus Andronicus, in a line from a better play, "flamed amazement". It was the last piece in the canon to reach Stratford: a collocation of horrors from which the governors might have flinched interminably if Peter Brook had not been at hand to warn them against rash-embraced despair. At length, on the night

* Henry VIII, Anthony Quayle; Queen Katharine, Diana Wynyard; Wolsey, Harry Andrews; Buckingham, Leon Quartermaine.

of 16th August 1955, the bloodstained thumb left its print upon the page. Brook directed the neo-Senecan melodrama with a hair-spring sensitivity. He established Rome as a remote, eerie, almost lunar world; kept the immoderate atrocities slightly out of focus; manipulated the text and its horrors so that his company need not fear derisive laughter; and intensified the atmosphere by music, his own quarter-ear *musique concrète*—not, someone said, *concrète renforcée*—that intensified a play incised by a gad of steel on a leaf of brass. With Brook's production went Laurence Olivier's Titus. Olivier had just conquered Macbeth. As Titus his terrifying quietness was the quiet at the core of a hurricane; in rage we felt the storm-wind of the equinox. Just as Lear becomes identified with the storm in his mind, so Titus does with the sea. When Olivier cried "I am the sea," it was an ocean flood; its surge beat on the world's far shore. We forgot the inadequacy of the words in the splendour of a projection that Barry Sullivan, Shaw's favourite long ago, might have recognized with awe as the real thing.

V

Within a few years Brook was one of a Stratford triumvirate headed by Peter Hall; the third was the respected Frenchman, Michel Saint-Denis. Hall in 1960, at the age of 29, became the youngest Stratford chief since Benson. Some of his Shakespeare had an oddly unselective faith in detail; but soon, in full control, he showed the ideas he could muster and the force he brought to them. He wanted continuity of method and the permanently developing cast (for which he had a list of artists under contract) that must be a director's ideal; and he hoped—there were awkward growing pains at first—to express Shakespeare's dramatic richness so that it was immediate to modern audiences, "an experience that reverberates with thoughts and feelings of today". In 1961 the 'Memorial' was re-named, wisely, the 'Royal Shakespeare', a name for a living theatre, not a summons from the dead to something that one took in with the Birthplace and Anne Hathaway's Cottage. In the previous December, Stratford, as a transitional London home, leased the Aldwych Theatre, an all-comers house that was once the stage of the Travers farces. Here the R.S.C. had among its aims "to build a strong bridge between the classical theatre and the truly popular theatre of our time". After 1963, with the Old Vic company lost and the National calling upon Shakespeare only once or twice in a year, it fell to Peter Hall and his directors to keep the plays in continuous production at Stratford, by now for nine or ten months annually. Organisation grew more complex, productions less orthodox. Some were wilful, groping for 'insights', afraid of 'well-worn texts', others were important: *Troilus and Cressida* (1960) in a shallow, sanded cockpit that represented the plains of Troy where love and chivalry were grated to dusty nothing; *As You Like It,* directed by Michael Elliott on a swelling green knoll, with Vanessa Redgrave as her age's Rosalind; a historical cycle, *The Wars of the Roses,* in a steel-ribbed setting, and with Dame Peggy Ashcroft to take Margaret of Anjou uncannily from girlhood to half-crazed queen; and, most discussed of all, Peter Brook's sternly uncompromising *King Lear* and Scofield's performance.

Peter Hall said, in general, of Stratford's contemporary way with Shakespeare: "The whole thing—stage, stage setting, costumes, speaking, creative acting, is all in a state of finding; of not expecting final solutions, but keeping open. . . . We want to be in a world of experiment." It was so in 1969 when Trevor Nunn followed Peter Hall*, and the Royal Shakespeare Company was moving on its ambitiously plotted course, with a staff of over 500 and annual audiences of more than a million. Old Coleman would have stood affrighted by a *Pericles* directed by Terry Hands, which began the 1969 season and had daunting views about neo-Platonic allegory. But it was all alert and audible, with Ian Richardson, one of the country's few remarkable verse speakers, to take Pericles on the Levantine adventure, through shipwreck and wooing, storm and loss and reunion; at the close he might have come from a mosaic in the cathedral of Torcello. At Stratford freedom will broaden from experiment to experiment. There, during the last ninety years, through a medley and a conflict of style and theory, we have watched every move in Shakespeare from the straining theatre of illusion which a worried weight-lifter might have conceived, to the speed and general

* In 1969 the directorate of the Royal Shakespeare Company consisted of Dame Peggy Ashcroft, Peter Brook, Peter Hall, Trevor Nunn (Artistic Director), with Michel Saint-Denis and Peter Daubeny as Consultants. Lord Harewood is President.

austerity of a modern revival. What we miss is any marked pleasure in the sound of the word. If acting is flexible, speech can be modishly flat. We have lost the creased backcloths, the cushioned moss, the mats of turf and the stuffed stag. Somewhere down the line we seem to have lost the sound as well, and Shakespeare's country needs both the sound and the sense.

EIGHT

OVER TO THE TOWNS

I

An honoured Royal Shakespeare production of the 1960s was *The Wars of the Roses,* basically the three parts of *Henry the Sixth,* a young dramatist's masque of kings, set in a steel-environed world. Here are both Richard Beauchamp, Earl of Warwick, and Richard Neville, Earl of Salisbury and Warwick. The first of these is also the nobleman of *Saint Joan* who has to make the feudal system intelligible. The second is the personage we know as the Kingmaker, "proud setter-up and puller-down of kings", who succeeded to the estates of the Earldom of Warwick in right of his wife Anne, Richard Beauchamp's heiress and only daughter. He was Bulwer Lytton's "last of the Barons", a man who "stood colossal among the iron images of his age, the greatest and last of the old Norman chivalry; kinglier in pride, in state, in possessions, and in renown, than the King himself." Killed at Barnet in 1471, he was buried in Bisham Abbey; but Richard Beauchamp, who died at Rouen as Lieutenant-General of France and Normandy, rests in the splendour of his chapel in the church of St Mary at Warwick.

St. Mary's pinnacled tower and gilded vanes, 174 feet above the town, beckon us on the approach from Stratford—whether by the direct road that an obscure poet called "eight miles of England in her tenderest mood, From Bridge to Gate, from town to country town" (today it is a cannon-roar of traffic), or to east and west of this, by roads where the villages lie. Presently there lifts in front, as compelling in its situation as Boston Stump or as St Matthias upon North Hill at Plymouth, the tall, spare church tower of Warwick: it tells a world, regardless now, where Richard Beauchamp lies, and upon his tomb the effigy of a warrior gazes up at the figure of the Virgin on the chapel roof.

Everybody, I suppose, must summon a different assembly as he mounts into Warwick beside the deep cavern of the West Gate and a collector's prize of a Doric pillar-box just beyond. This is the town of which Leland wrote in the *Itinerary* of 1538:

It standithe on a rokky hill, risynge from east to west. The beauty and glory of the towne is in two streets whereof the one is called Highe Strete and goith from the est gate to the west. . . . The other crossithe the midle of it, makynge Quadruvium, and goithe from northe to southe.

Warwick, ruled by castle and church, means Richard Neville and Richard Beauchamp; Fulke Greville and his epitaph, "Servant to Queen Elizabeth, Councillor to King James, Friend to Sir Philip Sidney"; Piers Gaveston, Edward the Second's favourite, beheaded on Blacklow Hill by the Black Dog of Arden, after a savage mockery of a 'trial' in Warwick Castle; the poet Walter Savage Landor, born by the East Gate, that gusty splenetic figure who could be lion, scorpion and sage; and John Masefield, who went to Warwick School, and who said once "In books may be found what our masters called Humanity, and our great-grand-fathers Civility." It can mean, too, Edward Aglionby, Recorder of Warwick, who met Queen Elizabeth I outside the town when she visited it on a progress of 1572. After promising to be "short of speech", Aglionby made a "large one", to which the Queen answered: "Come hither, little Recorder; it was told me that you would be afraid to look upon me, and to speak boldly; but you were not so afraid of me as I was of you, and I would thank you for putting me in mind of my duty." Here also is Griffyn, Master of the Leycester Hospital, who, on the same occasion, advanced humbly and offered, on his bended knees, a copy of Latin verses, graciously received, "though the Queen declined reading them at that time; if, indeed, she ever did at all*."

Warwick had a more casual visitor who, for some of us, must be permanent, Mrs. Skewton ('Cleopatra') of *Dombey and Son*:

"Don't you doat upon the Middle Ages, Mr Carker. . . . Such charming times! So full of faith! So vigorous and forcible! So picturesque! So perfectly removed from commonplace!"

And again:

* W. Field's *Warwick* (1815).

"Those darling byegone times, with their delicious fortresses, and their dear old dungeons, and their delightful places of torture, and their romantic vengeances, and their picturesque assaults and sieges, and everything that makes life truly charming! How dreadfully we have degenerated! . . . We have no faith in the dear old Barons, who were the most delightful creatures, or in the dear old Priests, who were the most warlike of men—or even in the days of that inestimable Queen Bess, upon the wall there, which were so extremely golden. Dear creature! She was all Heart! And that charming father of hers! I hope you doat on Harry the Eighth!"

"I admire him very much," said Carker.

"So bluff!" cried Mrs Skewton, "wasn't he? So burly. So truly English. Such a picture, too, he makes, with his dear little peepy eyes, and his benevolent chin."

It is agreeable to think of a friendly chat between Mrs. Skewton, Henry the Eighth and Richard Neville. Possibly Elizabeth I as well.

II

In feeling, if little else—for so much was rebuilt after its own Great Fire in 1694, just a century later than Stratford's—Warwick ("Warrewyk") today is steadfastly medieval. Though its people may not think so, to a visitor it can hardly be otherwise, established as it is beside the castle, a retainer to the castle's history, and with relatively little of its own since the Saxon Ethelfleda created it as a "burh" in 914. We can be at ease in the gentle, comely streets because tourist crowds are usually segregated in the castle, Scott's "fairest monument of ancient and chivalrous splendour which yet remains uninjured by time". The key-word, I suppose, used to be baronial, but this, full-vowelled and reverberant, has lost its impact. Though it booms, the boom is hollow. Many words must suffer thus. "Cavalcade" has never recovered since Noël Coward's adroit use of it in 1931; we have had everything down to an advertisement's "cavalcade of sideboards", no doubt with a light skirmishing force of decanters. "Thrilled", too, cannot recover the Shakespearean resonance when Juliet spoke of the faint, cold fear that thrilled through her veins, and Claudio of the thrilling region of thick-ribbèd ice. Few modern Macduffs isolate the phrase "one fell swoop" which, even if it came in fire from Shakespeare's pen, time has rubbed to commonplace. "Baronial" could have vanished in pantomime fooling—Barons Hardup and Stoneybroke—if it had not done so already in the kind of Gothick drama, all vaults and nuns, that deserved Leigh Hunt's condemnation, "a tall spouting gentleman in tinsel" far from the iron images of the medieval world.

Naturally, one would prefer to think of the spirit of Warwick Castle in Shakespeare's phrase for Hotspur, "the light by which the chivalry of England moved". Little might worry us if its centuries were stripped from the quiet town; but the castle is another world, and it was showing a dim light indeed in the years of the Black Dog of Arden, or George of Clarence, or the deplorable John Dudley, all of them in their time castellans. That aside, we cannot gainsay the sudden revelation of the view from the middle of William Eborall's wide-spanned Avon bridge, the presence—like a shout in the sky—of the immense range of buildings across the water, crowning the river-cliff. Here, as on traffic-ridden Clopton, there is usually thunder in the air, a cavalcade of lorries. For that matter, Warwick Castle seems to me to be under an anvil of thunder-cloud, however fair a morning, however bright the sun upon the ash-grey walls, and upon the great military work of Caesar's Tower, rising 147 feet from the mid-fourteenth century and the solid rock. Later, we may find that of the medieval towers, Guy's, 128 feet, at the right-hand corner of the curtain wall, is even more terrifying. Certainly they put us out of mood for sham castles, petty machicolations (gaps for boiling oil), all the variegated medieval follies that have had so long a run.

Those Warwick towers are the Middle Ages defiant; however loyal we are to Walter Scott, Mrs. Skewton, and the romantic chimera, it is hard, beneath the parapets of Warwick Castle, to purr over the dear old barons and their romantic vengeances, or, as a diarist did, to wish for an "armed knight to issue from the castle to lead us to a banquet", or, like Celia Fiennes when inside, to think mainly of "good velvet chaires in the roomes, and good pictures".

There has been a castle here since the Conquest. Now, though what we see is largely a Jacobean mansion within a massive medieval curtain wall, the thunder-towers are dominant. Warwick, in spite of pictures and furnishings, carpets and cabinets,

Florentine tables and Gibbons carvings, does linger in the fourteenth century. The towers, "brave, ancient, high towers"*, were built then, by the Beauchamps (of the crest of the bear and ragged staff) who were Earls of Warwick for about 180 years. Thomas Beauchamp, commander of a wing at Crécy and Poitiers—honour enough for a soldier of his time—built Caesar's Tower; and his son Thomas, fifty years later (1394) built Guy's Tower at a cost, nicely calculated, of £395 5s. 2d. After these came Richard Beauchamp, who entertained Henry V in 1417, who was in Rouen at the martyrdom of Joan of Arc and who lies now in his chantry chapel at St. Mary's. His only son died young. The estates went to Anne, Richard's daughter; on the death of her unscrupulous husband, Richard Neville, the Kingmaker, there was much to-do among the family trees—with such names as Clarence, "false, fleeting, perjured", and the Dudleys—before, in 1589, 'the good Earl' died, Ambrose Dudley, brother of Elizabeth's favourite, Robert, Earl of Leicester. With no one to claim it legally, the castle reverted to the Crown. Not long after his accession, when it was decaying and, by a set of curious chances, partly in use as a county gaol, King James I gave it to Sir Fulke Greville, formerly Philip Sidney's poet-friend, a local magnate who also became Baron Brooke; he was James's Chancellor of the Exchequer. His death was violent: in the bedchamber of his London house, on a September day in 1628, an old servant, after a quarrel about a delayed payment, first stabbed Fulke in the back and then, going into another room, "pierced his own bowells with a sword".

With his nephew, Robert, who succeeded him, Fulke began the present dynasty. At much expense he restored the castle's domestic block in the manner of his time. Bishop Corbet, remembered better for "Farewell, rewards and fairies", described Fulke's castle in his poem, "Iter Boreale":

> Please you walk out and see the castle? Come,
> The owner saith, it is a scholar's home;
> A place of strength and wealth; in the same fort
> You would conceive a castle and a court.
> The orchards, gardens, rivers, and the air,

* A *Relation of a Short Survey of 26 Counties* by a Captain, a Lieutenant, and an Ancient (1624).

Do with the trenches, rampires, walls, compare:
It seems not art nor force can intercept it,
As if a lover built, a soldier kept it.
Up to the tower, though it be steep and high,
We do not climb, but walk; and though the eye
Seems to be weary, yet our feet are still
In the same posture cozen'd up the hill;
And thus the workman's art deceives our sense,
Making those rounds of pleasure a defence.

The historian Dugdale said, some years later, that Warwick Castle was "a place not only once more of strength, but also of extraordinary delight; being planted with the most pleasant gardens, walks, and thickets, forming the most princely seat within the midland parts of this realm".

The earldom of Warwick, which—to make things more difficult—was held for a century and a half by the Rich family, to whom King James gave it in 1618, returned in 1759 to the castle: Francis Greville, eighth Baron and first Earl Brooke, received the Warwick earldom which has remained with the castle ever since. His successor, George, was responsible for much that we find now: pictures, floors, ceilings, chimney-pieces, wainscots, furniture; the approach to the castle through the solid rock; the kitchen and pleasure gardens; the armoury; the Warwick Vase, and so forth, facts that he enumerated in a pamphlet.

That—and there is a great deal more—is historic enough for one building. But we may think less of it than of the famous views: one from the bridge; the other, when we have walked through that rocky canyon, George Greville's entrance drive, to the outer court and found before us the embattled curtain wall of the Beauchamp Earls, gripped by its towers. On the far side of the inner bailey is the mansion upon its Avon cliff and mostly within the medieval frame. Here are the rooms so many generations have adapted, State Rooms of what Henry James called "a great hereditary dwelling"; ranges of apartments "at whose hugely recessed windows you may turn from Van Dyck and Rembrandt to glance down the clifflike pile into the Avon, washing the base like a lordly moat". Everywhere, the pictures startle us: Van Dyck's equestrian Charles the First, riding melancholy into the ages (a helmet worn by Oliver Cromwell is on view as well); Holbein's Henry VIII, square-faced and bullying, so bluff and burly, with his "dear little peepy eyes"; a portrait of Elizabeth, at the age of 25, in her Coronation robes. Works by Raphael, Rubens (St. Ignatius Loyola, vested for Mass in a scarlet chasuble), Rembrandt, Tiepolo, Lely, many others, hang in the various Drawing Rooms—Red and Green and Cedar—in the Blue Boudoir, the State Dining Room, and so forth. (At one point seascapes by Van de Velde may remind us again how remote these Warwickshire towns are from the sea; John Masefield, of all people, could not have found a place less likely for his school-days.) In the Great Hall of the castle, largely nineteenth-century now, we reflect that, probably on this site, Piers Gaveston had the barest mockery of a trial in the summer of 1312 before the Black Dog, Guy of Warwick, who had abducted him and who sent him to execution on Blacklow Hill a mile distant: there, while one soldier stabbed him, another hacked through his neck. "So vigorous and forcible", as Mrs Skewton would say, "so picturesque!"

The castle may hold too much for comfort; it blends and blurs in the mind. Outside, in its special greenhouse repository, the Warwick Vase, man-high in marble, circular and holding 163 gallons, is a charming irrelevance. It was brought home late in the eighteenth century after Sir William Hamilton, husband of Nelson's Emma, had discovered it in a lake at Hadrian's Villa at Tivoli. Now again the fourteenth-century towers take charge; the thunder swells. An ingenious writer once described the prowl-ling of two skyscrapers through the midnight snow to track and crush their victims. We can imagine the Warwick towers in a similar inescapable pursuit. Caesar's looms before us again at the bottom of the Mill Street curve outside the castle—a street, wealthy in its Tudor façades, that was once a main approach to Warwick across an old bridge, now ruined and verdant. Mill Street escaped the fire of 1694. Little enough in Warwick did. The most obvious survival is at the other end of the town, Lord Leycester's Hospital on its terrace by the West Gate, above which is the chapel of St. James, from the late fifteenth century, used by the brethren. The 'hospital', once a hall of two united guilds— we think of Stratford's—became in 1571 a home, endowed by the Earl of Leicester, for a master and twelve brethren from the towns of Warwick, Stratford and Kenilworth, and the Gloucester-shire villages of Wotton-under-Edge and Arlingham. The domestic architecture of the period is externally gay, with a fine swirl of patterned timbering. A courtyard, small, galleried and richly gabled, might serve endearingly for a cry of players.

III

Warwick's main traffic flows between the West Gate (and Leycester's Hospital) and the East Gate, above which the chapel of St. Peter dates from the reign of Henry VI. A seventeenth-century house where Walter Savage Landor was born in 1775 is on the other side of the East Gate. At first, after the West Gate, it is High Street; after the junction with Church and Castle Streets, it becomes Jury Street. All we look for is within a short arrow-flight.

The fire altered the face of Warwick. On 5th September 1694, about two in the afternoon, near the south-western extremity of High Street, not far from the Leycester Hospital, a man or boy, with a piece of lighted wood, was walking across a lane. It was a boisterous afternoon, and a spark flew from the wood to the thatch of a house close by, which went up at once in flame. Wind-driven, the flames moved in irresistible fury down both sides of High Street, which were utterly destroyed, and then some way down Jury Street as well. Here they changed direction, swept into Church Street, and, crossing from the eastern side, extended on the west as far as the market-place which was also laid in ruin. Some goods, half-burned, had been hurried for safety into the church of St. Mary: these fired the church itself, which was burned down with the exception of the chancel, the chapter house and the Beauchamp Chapel. Within six hours half the town was destroyed; damage was estimated at £120,000.

Rapidly Warwick was rebuilt, with State aid, and partly of freestone from the rock. That resolute and pleasantly artless traveller, Celia Fiennes, came in 1697 and noticed its new buildings,

> brick and coyn'd with stone and the windows the same; there still remained some few houses of the old town which are all built of stone; the streetes are very handsome and the buildings regular and fine, not very lofty, being limited by act of Parliament to such a pitch and size to build the town.

Celia Fiennes was too early to see the splendidly grave Court

House, completed about 1728 at the corner of Jury and Castle Streets, or the eighteenth-century houses and range of county and administrative buildings (including the Shire Hall) in Northgate Street beyond St. Mary's Church: a Warwick that, in spite of underlying medieval strength, seems to have the urbane harmonies of an Augustan poet. Sir Nikolaus Pevsner describes as "sombre, almost sinister" the elephant-grey stone front of what was once the county gaol. Field, the historian of Warwick (1815), enters every crevice of this "well-planned and spacious Prison . . . plentifully supplied both with hard and soft water. It is whitewashed once every year." The Male Felons' Court Yard was spacious and airy. "The man of humanity will rejoice to hear, as a happy consequence, resulting from the present secure state of the Gaol, that the use of irons, especially of the heavier kind, is now become almost unnecessary."

IV

Possibly the best view of St. Mary's tower, about which there has been much faction-fighting, is from the tiny Old Square immediately in front of it, or from the foot of Church Street, where the blue and yellow doors are friendly on a June morning. Architects are troubled about the detail of the tower, whether by Wilson or Wren, but it seems to a layman to be both strong and fastidious, commanding its town with a certain hauteur. Inside the Collegiate Church of St. Mary the Virgin the nave is spacious and uncommonly light, whatever we may feel about the cumbersome 'horse-collar' windows. There is much to see: in the perpendicular choir, the fire-damaged alabaster monument of Thomas Beauchamp, builder of Caesar's Tower, and Katherine his wife, who hand-in-hand lie together in effigy before the high altar, an unmuzzled bear at Thomas's feet, and at Katherine's a lamb; in the old chapter house, the vast monument to Fulke Greville, "Servant to Quene Elizabeth, Concellor to King James, and Frend to Sir Philip Sidney"; and, in the harsh Norman crypt (remnant of the earliest church), the ducking-stool for scolds. But the lion of St. Mary's is the Beauchamp Chapel. Richard, like other medieval noblemen—and like Browning's Bishop—was anxious about his glory after death. You did not merely lay a Beauchamp in the earth: you planned a new world for him, a chapel and a tomb, so that the living would wonder and the ghosts would gaze. The entrance to what should be known, but never is, as the Chapel of Our Lady, is at the end of the south transept. Its elaborate Gothic portal, which dates from the re-building of the church in 1704, is the work of Samuel Dunckly, a "poor mason of Warwick", who was minister of the Baptist Chapel on Castle Hill. Close by the door is the medieval brass of Thomas Beauchamp and his wife Margaret. He was the Earl who built Guy's Tower, which endures, and also rebuilt much of St. Mary's, an achievement that lasted for three centuries. Thomas and Margaret were the parents of Richard, who lies within in a "full fair vault of stone set on the bare rock". When the door of the chapel is opened, we look straight towards the gold gleam of the central tomb, and, beyond it, to the mosaic of the cast window's Flemish glass. Upon grey Purbeck marble the effigy of a medieval knight rests in copper-gilt beneath hoops that long supported a velvet pall ("hooped over with staves of copper and gilt like a chariot", said Leland). The figure is in full armour, and the long-fingered hands are outspread, raised in an attitude of adoration, but also as if they are holding something unseen. Under the head, with its curled, short hair, lies a crested tilting-helmet; a muzzled bear and a griffin are at the feet. During more than four centuries the recumbent figure has gazed up at the Virgin among the gilded bosses of the roof; round the sides of his tomb the figures of many "weepers", and also the long inscription (I have modernized it) which says:

Prayeth devoutly for the soul whom God assoil of one of the most worshipful knights, in his days of manhood and cunning, Richard Beauchamp, late Earl of Warwick, Lord Despenser of Abergavenny, and of many other great lordships; whose body resteth here under this tomb in a full fair vault of stone set on the bare rock, the which visited with long sickness in the Castle of Rouen therein deceased full Christianly the last day of April the year of our Lord God 1439. He being at that time Lieutenant-General and Governor of the Realm of France and of the Duchy of Normandy by sufficient authority of our sovereign lord the King Harry the Sixth, the which body with great deliberation and full worshipful conduct by sea and by land was brought to War-wick the third day of October the year above said and was laid with full solemn exequies in a fair chest made of stone in this Church, before the west door of this Chapel according to his last will and testament therein to rest till this Chapel by him devised in his life were made. All the which chapel founded on the rock and all the members thereof, his executors did fully make and apparel by the authority of his said will and testament, and thereafter by the same authority they did translate full worshipfully the said body into the vault above said; honoured be God therefore.*

Richard's chapel, with its Perpendicular vaulting, was begun in 1443; it took twenty years to complete and cost £2,481 4s. 7½d.—somebody was pedantically accurate—which, at a venture, might mean thirty times as much in today's coinage. The effigy is not a portrait of Richard Beauchamp: it was to be, according to the contract, an "image of a man armed". Among many people who shared in its designing, casting and its carving—a complex matter —was the Warden of the Barber Surgeons' Company in London; clearly he would have advised on the subtle veining of the hands and of the temples. It is a long, handsome face, utterly impassive, as it stares up at the pearl-crowned Madonna. We wish that it were indeed Shaw's "imposing nobleman", who says, so unpersuasively, in the epilogue to Saint Joan: "Madam: my congratulations on your rehabilitation; I feel that I owe you an apology."

Names from the fourteen 'weepers' who guard the tomb, interspersed with eighteen angels, can sound like the cast of *The Wars of the Roses*. Here, small in copper-gilt are Richard Neville, Earl of Salisbury ("That winter lion who in rage forgets aged contusions and all brush of time"); John Talbot, famous Earl of Shrewsbury ("the great Alcides of the field"); Humphrey Stafford, Duke of Buckingham ("Trust nobody for fear you be betrayed"); Edward Beaufort, Duke of Somerset ("Let him shun castles; safer shall be he upon the sandy plains"); Richard Neville, Earl of Warwick, the 'Kingmaker' ("Who durst smile when Warwick bent his brow?"); and the Kingmaker's wife, who here looks exactly as Dame Sybil Thorndike did when she played Margaret of Anjou in the Olivier *Richard the Third* of 1944. At the west end of the tomb are Henry Beauchamp and his wife. He was

* About the middle of the seventeenth century the floor of the chapel fell in, and Richard's coffin was either opened or accidentally broken. The body, though "perfect and fresh", rapidly fell to decay when exposed. Women in Warwick had rings and other ornaments made from the hair.

Looking from Edgehill over the battlefield towards the village of Radway

Richard's son, the sole Duke of Warwick. Henry VI created him Duke, and, in a moment of gay delirium, crowned him King of the Isle of Wight at Carisbrooke. He died in 1445, when he was 22.

Again I return to Celia Fiennes on her progress in 1697. St. Mary's was largely in ruin still, but the chapel stood:

There is one monument of the great Earle of Leisters and his Ladyes in stone curiously wrought with their garments, and painted and gilded; there is another in marble of the Earle of Warwick, the statue cut very finely, and the face, hands and form very lively and under his head is a roll of straw matting as you would suppose, being exceeding naturall cut in stone; in the middle stands the monument of the Earle that was Regent in France and dyed there and was brought and buried here, his statue at length in armour, but the lines of his face and hands with the veines and sinews were so finely cast and the very aire of his countenance much to the life, or like a liveing man, all cast brass and burnish'd very delicately that it looks like gold.

She says of the 'weepers':

They are in little and all in religious habits which formerly in the tymes of Popery and superstition most persons coveted to dye in, their garments are folded in differing shapes and with many wrinklings and gathers which is very exact and the more to be noted being all in such a stiff mettle as brass, and yet it looks easye and naturall.

In the profound stillness of the Beauchamp all is easy and natural. The effigies of the noble dead are ranged like sleepers. On a tomb chest is the bearded Ambrose Dudley, "good Earl" of Warwick, armoured, wearing a coronet and—for he died in his bed—pillowed upon the rolled-up rush mattress Celia Fiennes observed. Under an ostentatious wall monument are Elizabeth's favourite, Robert Dudley, Earl of Leicester, and, in ruff and gown, his third and last countess, the ambitious, beautiful and also much-married Lettice*. Up by the altar is the effigy of their son, the

* She died "on Christmas Day in the morning" 1634, aged 94, and there is a tablet to her in the Chapel, with verses by Gervase Clifton: "She that in her younger years Matcht with two great English peares; She that did supply the warrs With thunder and the court with stars . . .".

11

The Rollright Stones, just across the Oxfordshire border from Warwickshire

"noble imp", a deformed child who died in 1584 when he was 3, and whose miniature armour is preserved in Warwick Castle; "Here resteth the body of the noble Impe Robert of Dudley Baron of Denbigh ... a child of greate parentage but of far greater hope and towardness, taken from this transitory unto the everlasting life, in his tender age." Above the sleepers are the splendid dyes of the east window. Much of its glass (two shillings a square foot inclusive of carriage and fixing) was fractured but restored to its present cunning mosaic. It holds, untouched, four saints, St. Alban, St. Winifred of Shrewsbury, St. John of Bridlington and a magnificent St. Thomas of Canterbury, to whose shrines Richard Beauchamp bequeathed twenty-pound images of himself in gold.

It is odd, on leaving St. Mary's after the funerary pomp of the Beauchamp Chapel, to see framed on a pillar a matter-of-fact affidavit that a deceased person had been buried only in wool. During the reign of Charles II this was made compulsory for the sake of the woollen trade. A later statute ordered that

> no corps of any person or persons shall be buried in any Shirt, Shift, Sheet, Shroud, or anything whatsoever mingled with Flax, Hemp, Silk, Hair, Gold, or Silver, or in any Stuff or Thing, other than what is made of Sheeps wool only, or be put in any Coffin lined or faced with any sort of Cloth or Stuff or any thing whatsoever that is made of any material but Sheeps wool only.

V

Two other places in Warwick linger. One, off the top of Castle Street, is the hidden lawn of the Pageant Garden, so called because of the distinguished Warwick Pageant in 1906. It is a town for this form of display; and 1906 was at the middle of the Edwardian period when anywhere with history to speak of—and most towns would speak of it fluently—had it marshalled in episodic sequence. "Do you padge?" was a current catchphrase about which Tennyson, foe to any mispronunciation of the word 'pageant' would have growled his spectral horror. Benson was an indomitable pageant master, never short of an idea. When something at Carisbrooke had flattened the effect of Charles I's farewell, Benson said immediately, "Bring on one or two sad dogs." Today, in Warwick, one may remember the county pageant of 1930, for which

John Drinkwater, Midland patriot, wrote prologue and epilogue: "A folio of everyman, Such as our master Shakespeare drew". It was staged in the castle grounds. Midway, the body of Richard Beauchamp was borne in state past his castle to the Collegiate Church of St. Mary: "Let him be regarded as the most noble corse that ever herald did follow to his urn."

Pageants, yes; but there is no theatre in Warwick now, though Field could write in 1815 of one near the market-place:

> This building, small in extent, sufficiently affords all the accommodation required: and, though humble in its external appearance, is neatly and conveniently fitted up within. It is always opened during the week of the races; and occasionally, at other times. The character of the performers is, in general, nearly the same as those who tread the boards of a provincial theatre. But not infrequently some of the more eminent actors on the British stage have condescended to display their talents, on this humbler scene.

William Charles Macready did so in the spring of 1829, after coming on from Stratford where he had acted at the theatre in New Place Garden. Yet, even with its memory of the young Siddons as Sarah Kemble, in histrionic gales at Guy's Cliffe, Warwick has not been passionately stage-minded. Early in the present century there was nothing but a Corn Exchange with a dramatic licence and the bleak invitation, "Platform available". Considering the fame of Warwick's Men, the Elizabethan company, with Ambrose Dudley, the "good Earl", as its patron, this is what Max Beerbohm would call in blank verse, "a scandal, an incredible come-down".

Finally, the Market Place, the noisiest part of Warwick, where the omnibuses converge and cars are parked. Various buses go to Stratford. One goes to Shakespeare Avenue, one (dramatically) to 'The Cape'. People from the villages wait here. It is a great place for children and parcels and for that undefined regional accent which is at once warm and gummy. We see on a new building the arms of Warwickshire County Council, a bear and ragged staff, with the motto, *Non Sanz Droict;* Beauchamp and Shakespeare are the best of two worlds. The Market Place is versatile. It contains the local museum; another sign proclaims a 'Casino'. During most of the day the square is in a flurry of traffic, not at all the Warwick of Jago's unkind lines:

> Where Avon wider flows and gathers fame,
> A town there stands, and Warwick is its name,
> For useful arts, entitled, once, to share
> The Mercian dame Elfreda's guardian care.
> Nor less for feats of chivalry renown'd,
> When her own Guy was, with her laurels, crown'd.
> Now indolence subjects the drowsy place;
> And binds, in silken bonds, her feeble race.
> No busy artisans their fellows greet,
> No loaded cariages obstruct the street.
> Scarce here and there a sauntering band is seen,
> And pavements dread the turf's encroaching green.

Jago is a Cornish name, and Richard, born in 1715, was third son of the Cornish rector of Beaudesert near Henley-in-Arden. He became for nearly thirty years vicar of upland Snitterfield, and celebrated the county in reflective topographical verse. Luckily for Warwick pride, he did better elsewhere:

> Once gloomy Haunt
> Of solitary Monks: now beauteous Seat
> Of rural Elegance! around whose Skirts
> Parks, Meadows, Groves, their mingled graces join,
> And Avon pours his tributary Urn.

Certainly he rose to the Castle and to Francis, the first Greville Earl:

> Nor spares his generous mind
> The cost of rural work, plantation large,
> Forest or fragrant shrub, or sheltered walks,
> Or ample verdant lawns, where the rich flocks
> Sport on the brink of Avon's flood, in sight
> Of his superb abode! Magnificence
> With grace uniting, and enlarged delight
> Of Prospect fair, and Nature's smiling scenes!

I suspect mildly that Jago enjoyed *Comus*.

VI

Leamington, Warwick's decorous companion, is two miles to the north-east. Where Stratford and Warwick are Nestors, chronicles that "have so long walked hand in hand with time", Royal Leamington Spa, its full title, is in relative youth: its time of day is the mid-morning coffee-hour. It has no Ethelfleda, no Richard Beauchamp, no Birthplace or Castle. Its principal names are the late eighteenth-century William Abbotts and an early Victorian physician, Dr Henry Jephson, and there was also a friend of Abbotts, a "blameless, useful, venerable man"—thus, at least, his epitaph—named Benjamin Satchwell. He was a voluble cobbler, cheer-leader for the Leamington waters and a poet capable of this dogged quatrain:

> If Muster Abbotts had not done
> His baths of laud and praise,
> It must have been poor Leamington
> Now, as in former days.

The spa was born in the bubbling waters of a mineral spring. Originally it was Leamington Priors, a hamlet by the Leam, or elm-tree stream, just above its junction with the Avon. William Camden in 1586 had remarked upon a saline spring; but nobody for 200 years did anything about it. Speed, in the *Theatre of Great Britain* (1596) said, "At Leamington, so far from the sea, a spring of salt water boileth up." Fuller, in the *History of the Worthies of Great Britain* (1662) put it more preciously: "At Leamington there issued out, within a stride, of the womb of the earth, two twin springs, as different in taste and operation, as Jacob and Esau in disposition; the one salt, the other fresh." Dr. Rutty, in 1757, described Leamington's "salino-nitrous spring" in a work entitled temptingly *A Methodical Synopsis of Mineral Waters*. It was found to have medical virtue, and William Abbotts took the risk in 1786 of opening one hot and one cold bath for a few invalids, regular visitors. At that time even the new mail-coaches came no nearer than Warwick, and a villager on a pack-horse had to fetch letters for Leamington. Soon another venturer built more spacious baths by a new well. Leamington water recalled that of Cheltenham, then nearing its zenith, and suddenly the place was known.

> Every cottage [wrote its early historian, the inevitable Field] now made haste to furnish its lodgings; every lodging to improve its appearance; new wells were opened; new baths were constructed; new houses erected; and not only new streets were formed in the Old Town, as it now began to be called, but the plan of an entirely New Town was laid, which has since been carried into execution, including Assembly Rooms, a Pump Room, and Public Baths, built upon a scale of magnificence scarcely equalled, certainly

not exceeded, by those of any watering-place in this or any other country.

The rise from village to spa took little more than ten years, Field said in 1815, though as a Leamington man he was ripely prejudiced—especially against Cheltenham with its "serious evil of *sandy* roads". Leamington roads, of well-compacted gravel, spared valetudinarians "the inconvenience of rough or uneasy motion". Again: "In size, indeed, the Assembly Rooms of Leamington must yield, in a small degree, to those of Bath and Cheltenham; but in all other respects the latter are greatly surpassed by the former".

In spite of Field's boast, not much had happened in Leamington when the child William Charles Macready went over in 1800 with his father who had just begun to manage the Birmingham Theatre. The village, Macready wrote after nearly sixty years, in his unfinished memoir, consisted

only of a few thatched houses, not one tiled or slated, the Bowling-green Inn being the only one where very moderate accommodation could be procured. There was in progress of erection an hotel of more pretension which I fancy was to be the 'Dog' or 'Greyhound', but which had some months of work to fit it for reception of guests. We had the parlours and bedrooms of a huckster's shop, the best accommodation in the place, and used each morning to walk down to the spring across the churchyard with our little mugs in our hands for our daily draught of the Leamington waters.

The village had 543 people in 1811; but more and more springs were bubbling up, and important visitors bubbled with them: first, the Prince Regent in 1819 (presently the population rose to 2,000); then, in 1830, the 12-year-old Princess Victoria on a previously unexampled outing with her mother, the Duchess of Kent. They stayed at the Regent Hotel. When Victoria became queen she was ready to let the inhabitants—nearly 13,000—call their town Royal Leamington Spa. Much depended on the loyalty of its fashionable doctor, Henry Jephson; he stands benevolent in bronze and with a temple to himself, in the gardens named after him—nearly a century old, with lake, aviary, and amusingly obtrusive fountain. About 45,000 people live in Leamington now; nearly three times the size of Warwick, it has a double life, not merely floating on the spa waters but proud of its commerce and light industry.

It survived an awkward mid-Victorian period when inland spas and baths had to meet the competition of seaside towns and the sea. Mildly reflective in aspect, Leamington rustles with many trees; the sunlight of another age touches its gardens, its urbane stuccoed terraces, its squares and crescents and elegant Italianate villas, its Greek Doric porches and Corinthian columns, and its griefs in Victorian baroque. Unlike Bath, it is free from historical responsibility, and you will not hear a tourist say, as an American did in Bath: "I take the Waters and a dozen Tablets every morning." Nobody minds that 150 years ago, for a wager, the eccentric Jack Mytton rode into the Bedford Hotel, long vanished, and after jumping his mare over the dining-table and its guests, leapt from the balcony to the street. It is happier to recall that from Leamington the Honourable Mrs. Skewton, Mr. Dombey, Edith Granger, Major Bagstock, and Mr. Carker (with teeth) set out to Warwick Castle which was "pretty well exhausted, and the Major very much so". At Leamington, too, Carker met Edith in "a pleasant walk, where there was a deep shade of leafy trees, and where there were a few benches here and there for those who chose to rest" (Holly Walk, maybe). Keith Brace once suggested wittily in the *Birmingham Post* that Dickens, when he wrote *Dombey*, was conscious before his time of the intrusion of the glummer Victorian architecture on the Regency scene; aware, too, that the evil influence upon it was Big Business. Hence the contrast between the Regency relics, Skewton and Bagstock, and the cold-blooded calculators, Dombey and Edith.

Few other memories: Nathaniel Hawthorne, who said that "Leamington seems always to be in flower," occupied for some time a "small nest", a Regency house in Lansdowne Circus; one of Sir John Betjeman's earlier and most-quoted poems, "Death in Leamington", cannot have been the strongest publicity for a developing town. The place has had a quiet, ordered existence. For a casual visitor it has one still, with the shopping Parade—response to Bath's Milsom Street—sloping up gently from the Pump Room and the gardens that face each other, the Pump Room's own and the Jephson; the squares and terraces on either hand; and the central grace of the Regent Hotel, which when it opened in August 1819, was 'Williams's'. A former butler of the Greatheed family of Guy's Cliffe had founded it; he was glad after about three weeks to change the name to the Regent, by genial condescension of the Prince of Wales who had just visited Leamington. Naomi Royde-Smith netted the town in a few sentences when she suggested in *Pilgrim from Paddington* (1934) that the Parade runs through it, like the plot of a balanced mid-nineteenth-century novel, to Christchurch and Beauchamp Squares with their terraces and avenues. Beauchamp would be the name of the hero and several of his relatives, Clarendon possibly the family of his adored but inaccessible love. There would be a hero called Guy and a heroine Augusta, served by ancient family butlers, Binswood and Lillington; a villain, Jephson Newbold, and his sinister valet, lurking round under the name of Leam. "It all fits in most beautifully as the town opens like a book on either side of the Parade." True; even if I have generally thought of Leamington in terms of a musical play, period roughly 1850, with chorus of military men (retired) singing "Wives and daughters take the waters while we take the air."

My notes, Jingle-fashion, remember azaleas outside the Jephson; fountain-mist within; a stuccoed façade like one of Foulston's houses in Regency Plymouth; the iron web of a verandah; chestnut trees in the middle of an empty street; a sternly functional new police station, the bear and ragged staff above its door. It is of no use, as I did, to hunt for the professional stage in Leamington, though there is a good amateur theatre, 'The Loft'. Up in Regent Grove off the Parade is the building, once the theatre, where a few years after its opening Benson had that disastrous night with *Macbeth*. Later a cinema, it is shut now and looks as melancholy as most closed theatres do with no curtain to rise: just a blind-eyed brick monument. Forty years ago there was an ephemeral sensation here, a play, written by a local dramatist, that introduced the Unknown Warrior. As sensations do, it slipped beneath the obliterating files. The most dramatic thing in modern Leamington is a statue of Queen Victoria, not a particularly good one, robed in white, crowned, bearing orb and sceptre, and looking like Lady Bracknell when she observed that until yesterday she had no idea that there were any families or persons whose origin was a terminus. The people of Leamington gave the statue after the Queen's death. At first it looks like any other, fit to go with the alarmingly florid mass of the town hall behind it. Inspect it closely and you will find a neat plaque: "A

German bomb moved this statue one inch on its plinth on the 14th November 1940."

VII

Warwick and Leamington may be as starved of the professional theatre as all the Shakespeare Country is outside Stratford-upon-Avon. But from either of the towns it is a brief journey to Guy's Cliffe, north-east of Warwick and north-west of Leamington, where between 1771 and 1773 the greatest of British actresses, later Sarah Siddons, was a lady's maid in the now ruined mid-eighteenth-century mansion of the Greatheeds. It stands among the near-jungle growths on a rocky precipice above a bend of the Avon, a site described by Leland as "a place of pleasure; an howse mete for the Muses; there is silence, a praty wood ... the river rollynge with a praty voice over the stones". Here are legends of the entirely mythical Guy of Warwick, slayer of the Dun Cow, who behaved with the oddity proper to so fabulous a figure; caves for Guy or any professional hermit; and a chapel, rebuilt by Richard Beauchamp, which has a massive figure of Guy cut from the live rock. All is rather stagily exciting, like the theatre of the Siddons; Guy's Cliffe is haunted by the iambic pentameter and a host of furious fancies. Sarah Kemble was a granddaughter of John Ward, who gave Stratford's benefit performance for the Bust, and the elder sister of John Philip Kemble. From childhood she was a member of her parents' touring company. Rashly, she wanted to marry William Siddons, an indifferent actor who had joined them; and because she was only 16, and William, twelve years older, was recalcitrant, her parents dismissed him with his ears boxed, and sent Sarah, already a girl of dark, dignified beauty, into service with the widowed Lady Mary Greatheed at Guy's Cliffe. Typically, Sarah declaimed Milton to her fellow-servants. She appears to have become her mistress's confidante, and the two years she spent at Guy's Cliffe helped to form and strengthen her character. In 1773, a month after her grandfather's death, she left Guy's Cliffe, married William—for she was strong-minded—and rejoined the Kemble company upon its familiar circuit.

Sarah ought, at some time, to have played Queen Elizabeth, but having no suitable play, she never did. Elizabeth is dangerous in the theatre, though there have always been playgoers glad to be cast headlong into history, flung into chronicle. They like nothing better than to open a programme and to find most of Elizabethan England in the cast. Drake beats his drum; Burleigh nods; the Swan floats by, tossing off *Hamlet* and bantering Burbage; and Elizabeth, a dummy of the Zucchero portrait, is likely to reel off the Tilbury speech at any moment. Numberless people must have taken their history from the stage—a solemn thought. I recall a good many conscientious extension lectures and Wardour Street casualties, especially a loosely-braced anecdote on a night when the management faltered, the virginals collapsed, the cathedral organ refused to play, and Shakespeare, Frobisher, Drake and Walsingham appeared in regrettably improbable wigs. Many times in mock-Elizabethan drama we have been exposed to the kind of dialogue that would have charmed the intolerable Mr. Thwaites, who had a trick of saying in a Patrick Hamilton novel such things as "A fine morning, in Troth . . . in veritable Troth—a Beauteous Morning," or else asking unanswerably, "Didst thou dance and dally?"

It does sound a little like Scott in his own trothing mood. But he worked hard with Elizabeth, the first person we think of when Kenilworth is named. As well as a novel, it is a town, brook-threaded and straggling, not quite six miles north-west of Leamington, and with about 14,000 people; they have more than Scott to occupy them. The castle, in its overwhelming baulks of red sandstone, looms like a memorial to its own fame. The ruins are superbly grouped, even if William Gilpin, that late eighteenth-century traveller of credit and renown, failed to think so: "Magnificent as they are, they are not picturesque. Neither the towers, nor any other part, nor the whole together, unless well aided by perspective, and the introduction of trees, to hide disgusting parts, would make a *good picture*."

Kenilworth does not chill us as the towers of Warwick do. In spite of its size, in spite of that menace of stonework—fourteen feet thick in the Keep—Kenilworth's feeling is forlorn; roofless, windowless, "a tourist-show, a legend told". It has to be; and yet for those able to read the narrative in these walls, the castle must have a sad glory. Between the erection of the twelfth-century Keep and the "slighting" (destroying and dismantling) by Parliamentary forces early in the Civil War, Kenilworth knew a six months' siege after its owner, Simon de Montfort, had been slain at Evesham; Edward the Second's forced resignation of the Crown before his murder at Berkeley; a benevolent extension and restoration by John of Gaunt; and the displays of Robert Dudley, Earl of Leicester, Elizabeth's dubious favourite, who entertained the Queen so pompously, and who lies with wife and son in the Beauchamp Chapel at Warwick. Leicester spent upon his alterations to Kenilworth what was for those days the enormous sum of £60,000; and one building, his elaborate Gatehouse, remains intact.

We have to adapt ourselves to Kenilworth. These ochreous cliffs (it is the red Keuper sandstone), these spreading courts, these irregular enclosures, have to be named and rebuilt in the imagination, assigned to the majesty of John of Gaunt's Great Hall, or Caesar's Tower—another; here it is the rectangular Keep—or the Presence Chamber, Mortimer's Tower, or Leicester's Buildings. Then we must separate fact from the invention of theatre and novel: from Marlowe's play of *Edward II* for one, in which the wretched Edward cries, in the hour of abdication at "Killingworth", much as Shakespeare's Richard will do in Westminster Hall:

> But what are kings, when regiment is gone,
> But perfect shadows in a sunshine day?

and again:

> Let me be king till night,
> That I may gaze upon this glittering crown;
> So shall my eyes receive their last content,
> My head, the latest honour due to it,
> And jointly both yield up their wished right.

Later, and more popularly potent, Scott went on to make a good story about Amy Robsart, though we doubt whether she was ever at Kenilworth in her life. It may be best—as modern dramatists invite us—simply to 'experience' Kenilworth, to wander among these ancient hulks of masonry, and listen to the sound of the years. The castle is a palimpsest, Norman, medieval, Tudor, fortress merging into palace, a "lordly palace", Scott calls it, "where princes feasted and heroes fought, now in a bloody earnest of storm and siege, and now in the games of chivalry where duty dealt the prize which valour won". That is vague enough, but we should get one passage fixed from the battles, sieges, fortunes: the last visit of Elizabeth. She had given the castle to Robert Dudley, 'Sweet Robin', in 1563. She visited it on four progresses: in 1575, during the last of these, her flamboyant *cavaliere servente* entertained her for seventeen days, at a daily cost of £1,000 with an entire Kenilworth festival—a "variety of delightfull Shows" (Dugdale's term), masques, fireworks with flying dragons and fighting dogs and cats, sports, dancing, hunting, bear-baiting, Latin orations, Italian tumblers, a ferocious play from Coventry—anything fit to set before a Queen. When she arrived, a nereid called the Lady of the Lake—attended by two nymphs, "arrayed all in sylks"—approached from a torch-lit 'stand' that floated upon the vast artificial pool, and addressed the Queen with "a well-penned meeter". The lake, 111 acres of it, drained away early in the Commonwealth, environed three sides of Kenilworth: it was at once the castle's pride and defence. During the Queen's visit Leicester had upon it "a Triton riding on a Mermaid 18 foot long; as also Arion on a Dolphin, with rare Musick". Arion, forgetting his lines when face to face with the Queen, snatched off his horse's-head mask in despair and said he was honest Harry Goldingham, a good, true-born British subject. William Shakespeare, a boy of 11, must have heard of the revels and water-pageant at Kenilworth; he may even have been taken over from Stratford. Within twenty years a memory of the occasion appeared in a speech by Oberon in *A Midsummer Night's Dream**:

> Thou rememberest
> Since once I sat upon a promontory,
> And heard a mermaid on a dolphin's back,
> Uttering such dulcet and harmonious breath,
> That the rude sea grew civil at her song,
> And certain stars shot madly from their spheres,
> To hear the sea-maid's music.

Harry Goldingham might have appeared, too, in Bottom and

* Another suggestion is that Shakespeare was thinking of a water-pageant with sea-gods and fireworks, much resembling that at Kenilworth, staged when the Earl of Hertford entertained Elizabeth at Elvetham, his home in Hampshire, during 1591. A contemporary pamphlet has a woodcut of the entertainment, showing the Queen "throned in the west".

Snug the joiner. That is something to remember among the ruins of Kenilworth, just as we remember the rich tushery of Scott when Amy Robsart makes her anachronistic appearance:

> The Queen shot into the circle, her passions excited to the uttermost; and, supporting with one hand, and apparently without an effort, the pale and sinking form of his almost expiring wife, and pointing with the finger of the other to her half-dead features, demanded in a voice that sounded to the ears of the astounded statesman like the last dread trumpet-call, that is to summon body and spirit to the judgement-seat, "Knowest thou this woman?"

We cannot wonder that there were so many stage versions of the book.

During the whole of Elizabeth's visit, so one of her attendants, Laneham, recorded, "the Clok Bell sang not a note all the while her Highness waz thear." This clock, on Caesar's Tower, was stopped, the hands always pointing to the banqueting hour. Today at Kenilworth, though we may feel like one

> who treads alone
> Some banquet-hall deserted,

we can say, with Field of Leamington—differing from William Gilpin—"Where is the eye that owns not the powerful fascination, or the mind that feels not the solemn enchantment of the scene?"

VIII

Kenilworth, during its protracted siege in 1266, was governed by Henry de Hastings: Simon de Montfort the younger had got away to Guienne to seek aid after his father's death at Evesham in Worcestershire. There, in what is now the black earth of the market gardeners' vale, fourteen miles south-west of Stratford, the elder Simon fell in a hopeless fight that a monk of Gloucester called "the murder of Evesham, for battle none it was". Those few sultry August hours sealed Evesham in history; but that was in 1265, and its people are more concerned now with an annual and rewarding miracle: the coming of the fruit blossom when Michael Drayton's "fertile Gleabe" seems to be blanched, hung transiently with glistening shreds of crystal or spun-glass that might almost tinkle faintly in the morning airs. A few Shakespeareans have their own reason for remembering Evesham. When, during 1598, Richard Quiney, up in London at 'The Bell' in Carter Lane, asked that important dramatist, William Shakespeare, his "loving good friend and countryman", to lend him £30 he had also in mind a letter from his father Adrian, the Stratford mercer (spelling modernized):

> If you bargain with Mr Shakespeare or receive money therefore, bring your money home if you may. I see how knit stockings be sold, there is great buying of them at Evesham. Edward Wheat and Harry, your brother [in-law's] man, were both at Evesham this day sennight, and, as I heard, bestow £20 there in knit hosings, wherefore I think you may do good if you can have money.

Tantalisingly, that is all. We do not know what happened to the projected deal in knitwear, or whether Shakespeare was interested. Even though Malvolio was in yellow stockings, cross-gartered; though the pantaloon of the Sixth Age wore his "youthful hose well saved, a world too wide for his shrunk shank"; and Hamlet's stockings were "fouled, ungartered, and down-gyvèd to his ankle", I do not really think we can attribute it to a sudden interest in hosings at Evesham. A pity.

The town, with the Avon looped about it, looks prosperous. "There be divers pretty streets," said Leland; and it is true. The buildings, modern, Georgian, or in magpie timbering, co-exist comfortably. Smaller than Warwick or Kenilworth, it has a yeoman's pride, a market-town's responsible dignity. In occupation, it is obviously single-minded: the Vale is a vast vegetable garden and orchard, with Evesham as receiver-general; its monks were the original market-gardeners. Except in blossom, it is not a decorative landscape, but few visitors will argue. One dissentient, the dramatist Peter Terson, wrote a play called *Mooney and His Caravans* as a duologue for two refugees from Birmingham, who tried living on a caravan site.

> I taught games in the Vale of Evesham for seven years, [he said in a programme note] but it was a place that had a queer effect on me. I found it closed in, especially in blossom time, and claustrophobic and frightening. I wrote a lot of plays in the Vale, and they seemed to have this element of fear and repression in them.

Strangers to Evesham go at once to the Bell Tower, and to the parish churches of All Saints and St. Lawrence. These are side by side, the first due north of the obliterated Benedictine Abbey of St. Mary and St. Egwin, and the second, which was especially for pilgrims, near the north-west corner. The stateliness of Evesham is in the high aristocratic air of the lost abbey's remaining Bell Tower—erected some three decades before Shakespeare's birth, by the penultimate abbot, who is buried in his fan-vaulted chapel at All Saints. Standing back from the river, the tower, with its twelve tiers of arcading and the supreme assurance of its proportions, seems to have grown naturally from the ground to its coroneted vanes. This, an almonry (now a museum), a gateway, and an evocative detached arch, are all that remain of the noblest assemblage of religious buildings outside Oxford or Cambridge. At the Dissolution, when the abbey was let as a stone quarry, Evesham people joined in buying and keeping their new Bell Tower.

Two hundred and eighty years before this decision, Evesham had its most notorious day. Feudal barons had been warring against Henry III for seven years, led by that redoubtable figure in the development of our Constitution, Simon de Montfort, Earl of Leicester, who was of French birth and inherited the English title from his grandmother. After victory at Lewes in 1264, he ruled for a year in the King's name. His power did not last; many allies forsook him, and though a subtle tactician, he was trapped during the summer of 1265. At a dangerous moment his nephew, the Lord (Prince) Edward, escaped from Simon's keeping, and with his supporters, headed by the Earl of Gloucester, Gilbert de Clare, succeeded in holding the Severn's east bank, penning Simon on the west. The younger de Montfort's relieving troops should have come up in aid, but Edward annihilated them after a forced march from Worcester to a night alarm at Kenilworth. A few leaders managed to barricade themselves inside the castle and to hold out with its garrison through the siege in 1266. The elder Simon, knowing nothing of this and hastening to join his son, contrived to ferry his troops across the Severn, meaning to march by way of Pershore, Evesham and Stratford. In the belief that his enemies were still far up Severn, he encamped on the evening of 3rd August 1265, within the Evesham horseshoe round which the Avon runs. Meanwhile, the royal troops and their allies, approaching swiftly, blocked all the roads. Behind Simon, his 400 knights and his freshly recruited force of ill-trained Welshmen, was the width of the Avon, and enemy horsemen had got to the opposite bank to bar the crossing. When, on the morning of 4th August, Simon realized his position, it was too late. He had imagined that forces advancing from the north were his son's; they bore standards captured at Kenilworth. Then he saw the blood-red cross of his enemies. "By the arm of St. James," he said, "they come on wisely, but it is from me that they learned their order." Battle had to be joined. "May God have mercy on our souls," he cried, "for our bodies are the foe's." It was so in a desperate massacre. Simon's Welshmen fled and were cut down in flight. He and his picked troops fought on until at last Simon, making ruthless execution with his two-handed sword, was cornered irretrievably. One man stabbed him in the back, others closed in, and he fell, crying, "It is God's grace." The three hours' battle had been fought under a dense pall of cloud, and in summer heat that dissolved into a terrifying storm, raging and thundering above the Evesham vale. As Simon fell and was brutally dis-membered, the day was in black darkness:

> But at the end that side was beneath that feeble was
> And Sir Simon was slain and his folk all to ground.
> More murder was never before in so little stound . . .
> Such was the murder of Evesham, for battle none it was.

That was the monk, Robert of Gloucester. In this place I cannot forget the lines of Arthur Quiller-Couch: "Evesham's dedicated stones have stepp'd Down to the dust with Montfort's oriflamme."

IX

Finally, and nearer to the Shakespeare Country's central gold, three Warwickshire towns, each considerably smaller than Evesham, and all signposted by the names of Stratford-upon-Avon streets. Thus Henley Street is the road to Henley-in-Arden, 8 miles to the north-west; Alcester Road strikes westerly towards its name-town, $7\frac{1}{2}$ miles away; and Shipston-on-Stour, in the Vale of the Red Horse, is more than ten miles to the south-east, its direction marked by the Shipston Road behind the Avon water-meadows.

Alcester first. It was "the camp on the Alne": Rome lies behind

Compton Wynyates

its Tudor houses; it is close to the Icknield Way; and coins and pottery have long been dug from its soil. Red-roofed Alcester, with its pedigree, the state and ancientry of its buildings, does not parade itself: it is not an exhibition, though anyone must pause on a bright morning to enjoy the serenity of Malt Mill Lane and the overhanging upper storeys. Over the years the town has had varied luck; but it has been happy—the words are from the definitive play of Arden—to translate the stubbornness of fortune into so quiet and so sweet a style. In the rebuilt church, rather formally handsome and keeping its medieval tower, Sir Fulke Greville, the politician and poet's grandfather, and his wife lie with some magnificence in moulded and painted alabaster. The younger Fulke, Sidney's friend (who would later give to Alcester its town hall), was born in a manor, now a farmhouse, nearby; some say that the young Shakespeare could have spent a year or two as a page in such a household as this at Beauchamp Court, and seen how Tudor patricians lived and conversed.* Alcester is peaceably aware; yet always we have to wonder what lies beneath it. It is a place where, as in Daphne du Maurier's Cornish novel, *The House on the Strand,* we might not be surprised to flick in and out of the periods; doubtless the large black and white cat that followed me round when I was there was a revenant from the Roman town. Coughton Court, to the north, begun about 1500, is coeval with the oldest buildings in Alcester. Guarded by a sumptuous Tudor gatehouse, this is the home of the Catholic Throckmortons, an ancestral home with a rare sense of continuity; family tombs are in the neighbouring church. Leased by Sir Everard Digby from the Throckmorton of the moment, it was at the centre of the ring of West Midland mansions within the frame of the Gunpowder Plot's complex fiasco in the autumn of 1605. Ragley Hall, seat of the Marquess of Hertford, south-west of Alcester, is dominated indeed by its hall, huge and high, the mid-eighteenth-century work of James Gibbs: Pevsner, whom it takes a lot to astonish, agrees that "even in a house on the scale of Ragley, the effect is sensational". C. V. Hancock, the Midlands' expert topographer, applauds Ragley from a distance: "Standing high in its deer park, it presents a noble aspect, whether its porticoed east front is viewed from over the Arrow or its garden front from the Ridgeway on the west."

* See Rosemary Anne Sisson's *The Young Shakespeare* (Parrish, 1959).

12

Compton Verney

So to Another Part of the Forest: Henley-in-Arden's show-piece of a street, the long ribbon-building of the centuries; the Guildhall is medieval. North-east of Alcester, Henley has many affinities and family ties with Stratford. The slender apparition of its thirteenth-century market-cross proclaims its age—just across the Alne the rare Norman church of Beaudesert is older yet—and the lovely name and the town's oaken timbering proclaim its former site among the woodlands. Shakespeare's forbears were from Arden. In listening to *As You Like It* we can blot out Thomas Lodge and *Rosalynde*—if anybody but specialists ever turn to them—and think only of a Warwickshire pastoral, full of oak, hawthorn, sheep, and deer, with bonuses of a palm-tree, a green and gilded snake and the occasional lioness:

> A lioness, with udders all drawn dry,
> Lay crouching, head on ground, with catlike watch,
> When that the sleeping man should stir.

One night in Stratford, during the early nineteen-forties, a Memorial Theatre Oliver, losing his bearings, and to the horror of Rosalind and Celia, substituted "baroness" for "lioness", one of the occupational risks of acting, and here hardly noticed by the audience: practically anything can be said in blank verse if it is uttered with conviction. Henley, like Stratford, was strict about the drama: oddly, Daniel Baker, the feared Puritan bailiff of Stratford, was Henley-born. In 1609 and 1610 they were enacting that "neither Master Bailiff nor other inhabitant shall license or give leave to any players to play within the Town Hall, upon pain to forfeit for every default, 40s". There was an exception in 1615, probably an edifying piece. I have not observed at Henley any of the "loose life" that created comment at the Quarter Sessions of 1655, scarcely a liberal period:

> Usually heretofore there have been at Henley-in-Arden several unlawful meetings of idle and vain persons about this time of year for erecting May Poles and May Bushes, and the using of Morris Dances and other heathenish and unlawful customs, the observation whereof tendeth to draw together a great concourse of loose people.

Good sentences, well pronounced, and entirely out of date, unless an attachment to immoderately-sized ice-creams is loose living.

These, years ago, much impressed the Director of the National Theatre of Greece on his way to Birmingham to see the modern-dress *Timon of Athens* at the Repertory Theatre. That startled him equally, and he assured us that neither Timon nor Apemantus was a plausible modern Athenian.

A third small town moves us from Arden to Feldon, to Shipston-on-Stour, right away beyond Stratford by the Cotswold rim. Warwickshire's now, it was once a piece of Worcestershire isolated in Gloucestershire. We feel that the map-makers must always have had Shipston left over; on shuffling the pieces, there the town was, waiting patiently for its fate. Undeniably a patient town, endearingly modest, it never seems to me to have a very strong identity, yet as the centre of sixteen villages it must have identity enough for shoppers. The 'Tramway', so-called,used to run to it from Stratford; Lady Bracknell would find here many families and persons whose origin was a terminus. Originally, Shipston was the "sheep's town", with a renowned and vanished market—like Stratford it has its Sheep Street—and its coil of buildings, soberly mellow, contains some good Georgian houses from the woollen industry's ripe period. Obviously Shipston has had history enough, but the drums and trumpets have sounded in the distance: its life has been a "chronicle of day by day", and it is not a chronicle richly decipherable, in spite of the loyalty of its historians. There is a strong medieval church tower in brown-stone. Far back the place was a settlement of Offa, King of Mercia. Close to the town, the blade of the Roman Fosse Way cuts sharply and diagonally across the green, undulating land heavy with elms. With its layers of record Shipston should be firm-rooted, yet inexplicably I am always surprised to find it there, just as everyone was surprised to see Pistol on that summer evening in the Cotswold orchard. "Sweet knight," he cried, "thou art now one of the greatest men in the realm." Whereupon Silence, who had been half detached from the proceedings—he might almost symbolize Shipston—exclaimed judiciously, "By'r lady, I think a' be—but Goodman Puff of Barson." Barcheston, 'Barson', is a hamlet at Shipston's side; and for all its other, and unexpected, fame—English tapestry weaving began there under William Sheldon's influence in the mid-sixteenth century—it must live with us for the massive and, I hope, not mythical Goodman Puff.

NINE

INTO THE COUNTRY

I

The Fosse Way is old, but the Rollright Stones are much older. This, eighteen miles south-east of Stratford, is our farthest limit of the Shakespeare Country: a prehistoric circle 700 feet up on the borders of two shires, Warwick and Oxford, planted there before water-drops had worn the stones of Troy. "You mean the quarry," said an Irish roadman when we asked him the way on a spring afternoon outside Long Compton. "No," we said firmly; "not the quarry." And another man approached to say with a note both reverent and reproving, "They mean the Stones." He whispered his instructions; one does not talk lightly of these things on a borderland where folk-memories are long, witch-craft is not a broomstick-fable, and half-defined superstition loiters. The stones are in a rough grass-plot entered from a ridge-road past a notice incongruously official: you cannot cage pre-history. Under a westering sun the pocked and pitted stones, incredibly ancient, more than sixty of them, resemble a round of grey, lichened oak stumps, enormous, irregular fossilized sponges, or a sequence of sculptured objects by a primitive Henry Moore. Some lean; some are harshly bent. One looks like a petrified dwarf. The tallest is about seven feet high, and the smallest is four feet. For a second I was thinking absurdly of a theatre in the round, or a model of a setting for *King Lear*. They are probably from the Early Bronze Age. Camden said of them: "The common people usually call them rollrich stones and dreameth that they were sometimes men, by a wonderful metamorphosis turned into hard stones."

The circle is in Oxfordshire; but across the road, seventy yards or more distant and in Warwickshire, is an outlier, the King's

Stone, an isolated monolith nine feet high, with a strange back-ward thrust. It may have some burial significance. Naturally, all manner of stories cluster about the Rollright. One is that a king marching upon his way to conquer the country, encountered a witch who cried to him, "Seven long strides shalt thou take," and

> If Long Compton thou canst see,
> King of England thou shalt be.

Whereupon, properly encouraged and calling:

> Stick, stock, stone
> As King of England I shall be known

he took his seven-foot stride. Instead he saw only the earthen mound—once thought to be a Long Barrow—now in front of the King's Stone. The witch answered him triumphantly:

> As Long Compton thou canst not see
> King of England thou shall not be.
> Rise up, stick, and stand still, stone,
> For King of England thou shalt be none;
> Thou and thy men hoar stones shall be,
> And I myself an eldern-tree.

Promptly the king turned to a single stone, and his men became the main circle of the Rollright. Presumably the witch became an elder-tree, though how this could have helped her is obscure. At a little distance there are also five upright slabs, the 'Whispering Knights', said to be traitors, who were plotting against the king when the witch turned them to stone. Or they may be praying. On an upland afternoon we can choose any version that sounds plausible. It is by no means a rendezvous for winter darkness if one is at all impressionable and realizes that at midnight the King's Stone and the Whisperers go down to the spring to drink, while the stones of the circle, men again, join hands and dance in the air.

By the circle, with Shakespeare's Country, all south Warwick, in a distant haze of hedge and hawthorn and elm, we are not far off the road to Stratford that runs down through Long Compton village, by the southern end of the battered diamond that is Warwickshire. The road, plunging on to Shipston and the Vale of the Red Horse, arrives at length by the bottleneck of Clopton

Bridge. Outwardly, Long Compton suggests that nothing has happened there since the witch and the king: a processional line of solid, enviable cottages in brownish stone; a church's thirteenth-century tower; a lych-gate with a thatched two-roomed dwelling house over it, as if a lower storey had been knocked away. The vicar in 1740 built it for his verger. This is the village of a lyric by that forgotten poet, Norman Gale, "There as a dreaming child it lay And took the evening light." Maybe: there can be a shiver in the sun. Beyond Long Compton we move towards Stratford among the waves of the sheep-country, the corduroy ploughland and feathered elms. In the arras of Warwickshire landscape we can understand why Sheldon set up his looms at Barcheston: looms for "tapestry, arras, moccadoes, carolles, plonketts, grograynes, sayes, and sarges". Over to the west of Long Compton is Barton-on-the-Heath where Christopher Sly roared into life, "old Sly's son of Burton-heath, by birth a pedlar, by education a card-maker, by transmutation a bear-herd, and now by present profession a tinker". The main road takes in Tredington, which still has Civil War bullets in the church door; Ettington (or Eatington's) distant ruined church in the park; and the curve of Alderminster. Westward, and 2 miles south of Stratford, Clifford Chambers, as green and gracious as any Warwickshire village (it used to be in Gloucestershire), is at peace among its history, its late-Elizabethan brasses, manor and timbered rectory. We can say, as Michael Drayton wrote of the manor which he would visit during Sir Henry Rainsford's day, that it is still

> the place of health and sport,
> Which many a time hath been the Muse's quiet port.

There were Shakespeares at Clifford; and its villagers, though they are forgiving, shake their heads in private about that alleged birthroom in Henley Street. Pictorially and atmospherically, Clifford Chambers can cast itself as "the Muse's quiet port", the home of the Sweet Swan of Stour.

II

Nearer to Stratford than the Rollright Stones—the distance is fourteen miles to the south-east—the mansion of Compton

Wynyates waits to be found, not minding very much whether it is found or not. I remember coming upon it first through a mesh of road and lane from Lower Brailes, close to the south-eastern edge of the Warwickshire diamond. Brailes has a church, dedicated to St. George, which is called popularly "the Cathedral of the Feldon"—the old fieldland "more tractable to be stirrede for corne" than the woodlands of Arden. Labels can be troublesome; but this church keeps a cathedral's authority. Its fifteenth-century embattled tower, lofty above the stone cottages, is like a judgement from which there can be no frivolous appeal. It was there in the Middle Ages, 120 feet high, ruling a town of between 2,000 and 3,000, the third largest in the county: Birmingham, or Bremicham, was an insignificant settlement. The church endures, though the village itself has no idea of its dead splendour. Outside, on the external parapet of the south aisle, St. George's has a burst of sculpture: relics, probably, of a mason indulging himself with grotesque gargoyles and two faces that remind me of Quince and Old Siward. Within, though much adapted through the centuries, the church retains its tower's strength of purpose. Historians may wonder at the date "Brayles 1659" on chalice and paten, for this was during the nine-month Protectorate of Richard Cromwell, one of the less recognized heads of state, and hardly a time when churches would be likely to replace their altar vessels.

That evening we could not stay long in Brailes; it was ten minutes later, after a sinuous course, that we emerged upon a ridge-road, deserted between its banked trees and long-shadowed by a declining sun. Then, unwarned, we saw of a sudden, through a gap in the right-hand foliage, a sight as romantic as the lost manor to Alain-Fournier's Meaulnes. This was infinitely grander: the magic of a Tudor mansion in rosy brick—was there a hint of violet in the rose?—a vast house with twisted chimney-stacks, set in a hollow that might have been planned to receive it. Above its gardens climbed the green slopes: Compton Wynyates, John Russell has said, is seen "as in the bowl of an enormous spoon". Owned by the Marquess of Northampton, this must always be a captain-jewel in the carcanet of Warwickshire houses. Its bricks, partly diapered, its courtyard, its gables in black timbering, its external felicities, have been observed again and again. The excitement is still that unprepared discovery, that disclosure in the combe. The glowing feminine beauty of Compton Wynyates occupied all our minds as we drove on through the Tysoe villages, and down at last to Ettington and Stratford.

Compton's particular quality is for strangers to the Midlands—more so, I think, if they have been bred in a bare seaboard world, its colour only in rock and wave, and a manor probably nothing more than a large slated farm among stunted elms. Allusion and analogy cluster at Compton Wynyates. Thus the house is Tennysonian:

> Roof-haunting martins warm their eggs:
>   In these, in those the life is stay'd.
> The mantles from the golden pegs
>   Droop sleepily: no sound is made,
> Not even of a gnat that sings.
>   More like a picture seemeth all
> Than those old portraits of old kings,
>   That watch the sleepers from the wall.

Or it is amiable to assume that here the players acted their comedy of *The Taming of the Shrew* before the translated Sly, old Sly's son of Barton-Heath: "It is a kind of history."—"Well, we'll see't. Come madam wife, sit by my side and let the world slip: we shall ne'er be younger."

Royalty—of course, Elizabeth, and others—stayed in this house which was built by Edmund Compton and his son, William, and finished about 1520. James I created the earldom of Northampton; the first Compton Earl and his three sons fought at Edgehill. Later, in June 1644, soldiers of the Parliament took the place after a three days' siege. "The rebels," said Dugdale, "with four hundred foot and three hundred horse, forced Compton House, drove the park and killed all the deer, and defaced the monuments in the church." The Northampton family got it back for a fine of £20,000 and a promise to dismantle the fortifications; and there were various other twists of fate before the house could rest in its roseate tranquillity. Its name can be 'vineyard', or 'wind-gate', a hill-gap through which the wind blows. In London we find Wynyatt Street on the Northampton estate in Islington; and searchers in N.1. will come upon such family-associated names as Compton, Spencer, Ashby, Northampton and Bingham Streets, and Marquess Road.

Except at its siege, Compton Wynyates was free from fighting. The "blast of war" sounds much more clearly up on Edgehill, Drayton's "loftie Edge", from which, if the weather is fair, we can look right across the plain to the March of Wales. This is a height of 700 feet; beneath it, said a seventeenth-century writer, "the Meadowing Pastures therein, with their green Mantle, are so embroidered with Flowers, that from Edge Hill we may see it as the Garden of God". Now, as for 200 years, a thick screen of beeches hides the summit. In imagining the battlefield of Edgehill as it was on a Sunday afternoon in October 1642, we must think only of bare, hedgeless grassland, dipping steeply from the escarpment. The battlefield is overlooked by a comic 'folly', the Radway Tower (part of a conspicuously situated inn), which was built by Sanderson Miller, wealthy amateur architect and forerunner of the Gothick revival, who lived in Radway Grange below the ridge; this is the house in which—irrelevantly— Fielding read the manuscript of *Tom Jones* to the elder Pitt. Miller, in 1750, put up his tower—its toothy battlements look like the fangs of an old garden rake—to show where King Charles stood before the battle. Horace Walpole believed that the building and its neighbours, set there to give an idea that all were strongly fortified, had about them "the true rust of the Barons' wars". If you say that of Miller's Folly, what can be left for Warwick Castle? But there it is; and Richard Jago, who was Miller's friend, and often wrote like it, said that the tower "crowned with graceful pomp the shaggy hill", and that its broken arch and mouldering wall were "well taught to counterfeit the waste of Time". It is indubitably a landmark, a shrine to the kind of Romantick taste still fashionable when 'Monk' Lewis wrote *The Castle Spectre,* drama of the large, vague gesture, the resonant platitude. In a prized scene, Earl Osmond, who has been "lost in thought and traversing the room with disordered steps", says to Angela, "Romantic enthusiast! These thoughts did well for the village maid, but disgrace the daughter of Sir Malcolm Mowbray. Hear me, Angela. An English baron loves you; a nobleman, than whom our island boasts few more potent." She observes, reasonably, that her heart is Edwy's, whereupon there is the courteous exchange:

Osmond: Edwy's? A peasant . . . Girl, girl! you drive me to distraction.

Angela: You alarm me, my lord! Permit me to retire.
All of it would go very well with the Radway Tower; and one summer there should be an open-air performance.

Still, we must visualize a towerless, stripped, and desolate Edgehill on the day, with the harvest scarcely in, that Kipling wrote of:

> Naked and grey the Cotswolds stand
> Beneath the autumn sun,
> And the stubble fields on either hand
> Where Stour and Avon run.

Here the armies of King and Parliament confronted each other in the south of Warwickshire, two months after Charles had raised the Royal Standard at Nottingham on a stormy evening. Robert Devereux, third Earl of Essex ('Old Robin'), at the head of the Parliamentary forces—they called him, ambiguously, "Lord General for King and Parliament"—had hoped, after marching through the friendly county of Warwickshire, to cut between the King's army and the way to Oxford and London; Charles had got first to the strategic Edgehill ridge. The forces were fairly matched, each of between 12,000 and 13,000 men, the Parliament with a very slight advantage. Essex was without John Hampden, commanding the artillery and two regiments, who was at Stratford-upon-Avon, a day's march behind.

Upon that Sunday morning, when the Parliament's horse and foot formed up across the plain, the left end of Essex's line—facing the ridge—reached to a point marked by a stumpy commemorative pillar on the road between Edgehill and Kineton village. On the ground between this pillar and the hamlet of Radway, the main battle was fought. Essex based the right wing of his cavalry upon Radway; in the centre he led his foot, armed with pikes and muskets; and the other cavalry, with foot regiments, held the most exposed position on the left. Against them were Prince Rupert, the King's valiant and hot-tempered nephew —son of the Electress Palatine—with four cavalry regiments and the King's Lifeguards on the Royal right; the infantry, under Sir Jacob Astley, in the centre; and Lord Wilmot, with five regiments of horse, on the left. Before battle that afternoon, King Charles addressed the officers in his tent: "Your King is both your cause, your quarrel, and your captain. Come life or death, your King will bear you company, and ever keep this field, this place, and this day's service in his grateful remembrance." Later he rode along the lines, armoured in steel and wearing his Star and George on a black velvet mantle.

At Radway village, where the parson, Jeremiah Hill, went staunchly through with the service, church bells were ringing when Essex opened fire. According to one tradition, service had started in the church of Middle Tysoe. Hearing gunfire, the clerk exclaimed to his parson, "Dam'em, they're at it," and rushed from the church, followed by parson and congregation. It is like the Cornish story of a wreck signalled on a Sunday morning, the congregation's tumultuous dash to the doors, and an anxious voice from the pulpit, "Now brethren, let's all start fair." At Edgehill, as soon as those first shots echoed over the battlefield, Sir Jacob Astley (in words often wrongly attributed) uttered a brief prayer: "O Lord, Thou knowest how busy I must be this day. If I forget Thee, do not Thou forget me. . . . March on, boys." Almost at once the unsuitably-named renegade, Sir Faithful Fortescue, and his men deserted the Parliament, discharging their pistols into the ground, but this availed them little as they still wore the orange scarves of Essex and were a target for their new and unknowing friends.

Rupert, aged 23 and as impatient as the wind, led an immediate cavalry charge on the right, moving fiercely and obliquely, and cutting down the Parliament's cavalry and some of the infantry opposed to him. It was a rout. Confusedly, the Puritans broke and fled, racing as far as Kineton three miles away; Rupert's men did not draw rein until John Hampden and his Buckinghamshire Green Coats, hastening from Stratford, met the fugitives a mile beyond Kineton and planted across the road a battery to halt the pursuit. Back at Edgehill the Royalists were in doubt. Unwisely their cavalry reserve on the right had followed Rupert's lead, so that upon one side the King's centre was exposed. There, where the Royal Standard flew, Essex attacked heavily. Moreover, on the Royalist left, where Lord Wilmot's cavalry, charging when Rupert's did, had driven the enemy before them, the Puritan Sir William Balfour, with his troop of horse, had kept warily apart. Wilmot gone, Balfour's men worked stealthily across to join the assault upon the Royalist centre. Round this the guns were silenced, Sir Edmund Verney, the King's Standard-bearer, was killed and the Standard taken, and Lord Lindsey was captured—gravely wounded, he died next day. Rupert's men at this time were down in Kineton, looting the Puritan baggage wagons.

For a while it seemed that the Parliament had triumphed, but Captain John Smith of Skilts, near Studley-in-Arden—whom the King knighted after the battle—gathered some of Rupert's returning cavalry, fell upon the Parliamentary flank, and regained the Standard. After a mêlée in the dusk the Parliament drew back, exhausted; their adversaries were just as weary, and though in the bitter, frosty night the armies remained encamped upon the field, they did not engage again next day. Essex retreated to Warwick, claiming a victory; and the King paused at welcoming Oxford, without pressing on towards London. The issue, as history-books say, was indecisive. Losses, especially the Parliament's, were heavy, though estimates differ. But in one sense it was a deferred Puritan victory; from the contemplation of this muddled fight came Captain Oliver Cromwell's vision of the Ironsides and the New Model Army.

Bulstrode Whitelock, the historian, said: "Upon the news of this battle, all countries were alarmed and frightened, being a strange thing in England." Since the autumn Sunday, there have been many stories of haunting at Edgehill. A few months after the battle a pamphlet appeared, giving evidence—attested by a Justice of the Peace and a minister—that on Christmas Eve, 1642, between twelve and one in the morning, shepherds, travellers and countrymen had heard

first the sound of drummes afar off, and the noyse of souldiers, as it were, giving out their last groanes; at which they were much amazed, and amazed stood still, till it seemed, by the neerenesse of the noyse, to approach them; at which too much affrighted, they sought to withdraw as fast as possibly they could; but then, on the sudden, whilest they were in these cogitations, appeared in the ayre the same incorporeall souldiers that made those clamours, and immediately, with Ensignes display'd, Drummes beating, Musquets going off, Cannons discharged, Horses neyghing, which also to these men were visible, the alarum or entrance to this game of death was strucke up, one Army, which gave the first charge, having the Kings colours, and the other the Parliaments, in their head or front of the battells, and so pell mell to it they went; the battell that appeared to the Kings forces seeming at first to have the best but afterwards to be put into apparent rout; but till two or three in the morning in equall scale continued this dreadfull fight, the clattering of Armes, noyse of Cannons, cries of souldiers, so amazing and terrifying the poore men, that they could not believe they were mortall, or give credit to the eares and eyes; runne away they durst not, for feare of being made a prey to these infernall souldiers, and so they, with much feare and affright, stayed to behold the successe of the businesse, which at last suited to this effect: after some three houres fight, that Army which carryed the Kings colours withdrew, or rather appeared to flie; the other remaining, as it were, masters of the field, stayed a good space triumphing, and expressing all the signes of joy and conquest, and then, with all their Drummes, Trumpets, Ordnance, and Souldiers, vanished.

When, at last, the spectacle and the sustained paragraph were over, the watchers hurried to Kineton to knock up a Justice of the Peace and a minister and to relate the whole story—one that, if Justice and minister knew the First Folio, which we doubt, might have reminded them of Calpurnia's terror:

> There is one within,
> Besides the things that we have heard and seen,
> Recounts most horrid sights seen by the watch . . .
> Fierce fiery warriors fought upon the clouds
> In ranks and squadrons and right form of war . . .
> The noise of battle hurtled in the air,
> Horses did neigh, and dying men did groan,
> And ghosts did shriek and squeal about the streets.

On the following night William Wood, Justice for the Peace, and Samuel Marshall, Preacher of God's Word in Kineton, went up to Edgehill with the same men and several people from neighbouring parishes. There, in the open field, the spectacle was repeated, "the two adverse Armies, fighting with as much spite and spleen as formerly". On the Saturdays and Sundays of two successive weeks the "hellish and prodigious" sights were observed. King Charles, hearing the news, despatched three named officers from Oxford, and three other "gentlemen of credit", who returned with their confirmation, "distinctly knowing divers of the apparitions or incorporeall substances by their faces, as that of Sir Edmund Verney, and others that were slaine; of which upon oath they made testimony to his Majestie". To this day, we are told, Edgehill is refought, though the spectres take no account of Aubrey's charming gossip. According to this, Sir William

Harvey, discoverer of the circulation of the blood, was sitting during the fight beneath a hedge at Knowle End, studying Virgil with his pupils, the young Prince of Wales and the Duke of York. He took from his pocket a book to read, but it was not long before "a bullet of a great gun grazed on the ground near him, which made him remove his station".

Down the hill from the beech-crested escarpment, whence (John Speed had said, long before the battle) "we may behold another Eden, as Lot did the plain of Sodom before that Sodom fell", modern Kineton is the most pacific of large villages. It has a market square and an ornate, pinnacled church tower, burnished buff in the sun. Within, the church is bleak; it is happier outside where rows of old tombstones, carved and scrolled, lie in the grass. The War Department has taken over much land here; the Kineton road is intersected by various level crossings for military railways—the only rail transport left in the area.

After two miles the road back to Stratford reaches Compton Verney. There, where the stately Palladian mansion, partly by Adam and as masculine as ComptonWynyates is feminine, stands in Capability Brown's landscaped park, Peter Hall used house, park and lakes as the film setting of *A Midsummer Night's Dream*: the Wood near Athens, "a league without the town"; the bank of wild thyme; the oxlips and violets; the woodbine, eglantine and musk-roses; "thorough bush, thorough brier, over park, over pale": Athens-by-Arden. Compton Verney is accessible and friendly, if a little sad. Jago, naturally, delighted in the verdant grass and variegated grove, the bubbling rills in sweeter notes displaying their liquid stores, and the chequered lawn rich as th'embroidered floor from Persia's gaudy looms. Briefly, we gather, a very pleasant park.

III

That is in the country south-east of Stratford. We can reach the town by various ways from the north-east, beginning at Warwick, Jago's "rocky hill . . . for Health and Pleasure form'd". A direct road, elm-crested, touching no villages at all, used to be among the quietest on earth, inviting a slow amble between the hedgerows, an unvisited republic of hawthorn and cow-parsley. Today there is a steady thunder of wheels, a hurtle of traffic improbable when I used to stay in a cottage more than two miles from Stratford; behind it cornfields, vast in the twilight, rolled up towards Snitterfield, and in front of it, over the Warwick Road, we could get to Hampton Lucy through lanes so hushed that we might have walked on felt soles across a trench of feather mattresses. Closer to Stratford is The Hill where the Flowers lived; up its drive *The Time's* drama critic, Victor Cookman, walked in the daybreak after a night's discussion at a Stratford hotel in 1934, and dropped Bridges-Adams's resignation through the letter-box. Behind the Warwick Road are the gentle, embroidered Welcombe Hills, with a conspicuous granite obelisk (a small boy called it an odalisque) the same height, 120 feet, as Brailes church-tower: it is in memory of Mark Philips and his brother who built Welcombe House a century ago. Welcombe has a Shakespearean ring: the dramatist, who owned land and tithes round here, was involved in a dragging parochial dispute eighteen months before his death. John Jordan, long after the Garrick Jubilee, was determined to be the laureate of Welcombe and the ravine named the Dingles:

> On Welcombe Hills I tune my willing verse,
> Point out their beauties and their fame rehearse,
> Their ancient fame shall elevate my lays,
> A subject worthy of the Muse's praise.
> Upon these Hills one pleasing morn I stray'd
> To see what art and nature there display'd
> The DINGLES first attract my wond'ring sight;
> Their grandure gave astonishing delight.

It was practically impossible to stop Jordan when he began to tune his willing verse*. I prefer the 'grandure' of Jago.

A second way from Warwick also descends from the West Gate by a slope between what Phillpotts's Thirza Tapper called villa residences. Soon the road, traffic-thudding, bears south to arrive at Barford in a twist of the Avon. An inn, the 'Joseph Arch', with a bearded, hard-hatted yeoman on its sign, reminds us of the Victorian leader of the agricultural labourers. Bred at Barford where he died in 1919, aged 93, he worked in the fields from boyhood, encouraged the county Agricultural Labourers'

---

* Joseph Greene rewrote, embellished, and greatly augmented the poem: "Welcombe Hills, near Stratford-upon-Avon, A Poem Historical and Descriptive". See Levi Fox's *The Correspondence of the Rev. Joseph Greene*.

Union and then a national body, and represented a Norfolk division in Parliament. A crusted encyclopaedia begins its entry: "Joseph Arch, agitator . . .". Beyond the village, a matter-of-fact place—though its church has marks of Civil War gunfire—it is lazy, claustrophobic country, intensely green: against it glares the hot scarlet of double-decker motor-buses, and brick cottages by the roadside are a dusty red. When the road slants towards Stratford, we see the tall, distant nave of Hampton Lucy riding beside the Avon and looking, among the meadows, as big as an East Anglian wool church. Closer to us is Charlecote of the Lucys, a mansion begun in 1558, year of Elizabeth's accession, and shaped like a letter E; though much altered in the nineteenth century, it is grand enough for any layman. Through 800 years Charlecote has been the seat of the Lucys, the "renowned ancient family" (Camden). Here are the Elizabethan gatehouse's rosy, octagonal towers:

> Your search pursue to Charlecote's antient Lodge
> And Gothic turrets picturesque and light;
> Where Avon's stream with many a sportive turn
> Exhilarates the meads. . . . .

(Jago, obviously.) Here, too, are family portraits, panelling and marble, and books that include a quarto of *The Merry Wives of Windsor*. Outside are venerable elms (the "civilized trees" of Nathaniel Hawthorne), acres of brocaded park, flocks of Spanish piebald sheep and a herd of fallow deer: a most courtly estate, Ivor Brown's "true piece of the seigneurial English Midlands". Queen Elizabeth stayed there—a monarch who, in somebody's alarming phrase for a later Queen, "literally belted out the royal mystique", an operation it is worth pausing to consider. Formerly, Charlecote had to be pulled into a Shakespeare-poaching story; but the poet's depredations among the Lucy deer, the wrath of Sir Thomas and the revengeful creation of Justice Shallow belong, I hope, to the apocrypha. We do better to recall Sir Thomas Lucy of Charlecote for the epitaph—it is in the church—that he wrote for his wife Joyce who died a few years before him:

Here entombed lyeth the Lady Joyce Lucy wife of Sir Thomas of Charlecote in the county of Warwick, Knight, Daughter and heir of Thomas Acton of Sutton in the county of Worcester Esquire

Charlecote: the Tudor gatehouse

who departed out of this wretched world to her heavenly kingdom the 10 day of February in the yeare of our Lord God 1595 and of her age 60 and three. All the tyme of her lyfe a true and faythful servant of her good God, never detected of any cryme or vice. In religion most sounde, in love to her husband most faythful and true. In friendship most constant: to what in trust was committed unto her most secret. In wisdom excelling. In governing of her house, bringing up of youth in the feer of God that did converse with her most rare and singular. A great mayntayner of hospitality. Greatly esteemed of her betters; misliked of none unless the envyous. When all is spoken that can be said a woman so garnished with virtue as not to be bettered and hardly to be equalled by any. As shee lived most virtuously so shee died most Godly. Set downe by him that best did knowe what hath byn written to be true.—THOMAS LUCYE.

That has never sounded to me like the meagrely-sketched Shallow of *The Merry Wives*. For that matter, Shakespeare need not have been commemorating a Charlecote figure when, in the fourth act of *Henry VI, Part I*, he sketched the briefly commanding part for a Sir William Lucy.

A sign, on the way to Stratford, points to Kissing Tree Lane: it reminds us that J. B. Priestley, English man of letters, lives near Alveston, at Kissing Tree House. Critics who write little but criticism have a peevish way of calling him 'prolific', as if this were a demerit: we need more professionals with Priestley's bounty and good sense. An essay of forty years ago* describes his first visit to Stratford. Museums exasperated him, but New Place Garden seemed to be an exact setting for the outdoor scenes of *Twelfth Night,* Olivia coming down the paved path like a great white peacock, and Maria flitting like a starling against the bank of flowers. For years now Priestley has been Stratfordian by adoption. I hope it cheers him to remember—the ubiquitous Field speaking—that "Alveston is so much noted for the salubrity of its air that the late Dr. Perry scrupled not to call it the Montpelier of England". On the way into Stratford we look across to the spiky pinnacles of the new church (1839). Was it round Alveston that I once noticed a direction to a private residential estate called Verona?

After Tiddington—where John Jordan was born—we end this journey by the Stratford riverside. Another way from Warwick

* "Seeing Stratford" in *Apes and Angels* (1928)

13

The church of Hampton Lucy seen across the Avon from Charlecote

is by river only: the authority is Sir John Squire in his discursively autobiographical *Water-Music*. J. C. Squire, out of fashion now, wisely influenced literature between the wars; there was no richer review than *The London Mercury*, a title that may have derived from the Plymouth Liberal newspaper, the *Western Daily Mercury*, on which he worked as a young man; he was already a legend in West Country journalism when I knew his editor, R. A. J. Walling. Squire valued friendship and laughter. Few, have remarked on his constant awareness of the brevity of life, a note, recurrent through his prose and poetry, that we find in the only book, *Shakespeare as a Dramatist*, of his proposed Shakespeare sequence:

> Mayflies, ephemerides, atomies of a moment: that is what we are, and these lines as they are now written though they live for a hundred years, are, in the light of astronomic time as though they had never been written, like the season's leaves that fell from the poplars in Paradise, or the scales that were shed by the fish that lived in the moon's sea, now immemorially dry.

So also in the poem at the end of *Water-Music*:

> And stars gleamed through the darkling air,
> Before there was a human heart
> To solace, but they did not care
> And will not care when men depart.

This is not the prevailing mood of *Water-Music*. Ostensibly the fortnight's record of a canoeing holiday, it flashes back and forth over the years. At one point Squire and his friend, with paddling and portages, got from Warwick to Stratford by way of Barford and Hampton Lucy, penetrating those curiously remote reaches among the dappled pools, the shoals and rapids and runnels, and the trees that might have come from a water-colour by de Wint. Struck by its height and mass, they stopped at Hampton Lucy to see the nineteenth-century Gothic church. "Somewhere about 1820", said Squire, "some Lucy must have spared no expense on this little cathedral." So it proved: underneath the east window was an inscription saying that the Reverend Thomas Lucy had spent *magnum pecuniam* on it. Thence to Alveston and various difficulties before Squire did by car the final stage to "a comfortable hour before bed in the lounge of a Stratford hotel".

If, yet again, we go back to Warwick and start the Stratford journey, we should take a higher road that works round at length to upland Snitterfield, home of Shakespeare's father and a village where Shakespeare's mother owned the property her husband had to sell during his troubles. For nearly three decades Richard Jago, author of *Edge-Hill; or, The Rural Prospect Delineated and Moralised,* was vicar of the church with its sturdy tower and its woodwork of Arden oak; there he was buried in 1781. Reserved among strangers, Jago was always relaxed, "sprightly and entertaining", among friends. Twice married, he had by his first wife (*elegantissima puella,* said Shenstone) three daughters who were remembered by three silver birches in the vicarage garden. Not many devotees of Jago, a select band, get to Snitterfield. There are more Shakespeareans, for this was the parish, equidistant from Stratford and Wilmcote, where the poet's grandfather leased his holding from the father of Mary Arden. We must always see places as one first knew them. That is why Snitterfield, for me, stays withdrawn in pale sunlight under a grey scarf of February sky. Few villages can be more reticent.

IV

We are accustomed to the far from reticent John Jordan, wheelwright and mock-poet, whom John Mair, in *The Fourth Forger* (a name for William Ireland) described as a man with "a dark, heavy face, fuzzy black hair, and ploughman's physique, who gave a deceptive impression of honest stupidity". He was, indeed, an alert and agile Shakespeare quack, responsible for the later growth of a story fabricated elsewhere about 1762. Jordan enlarged it to celebrate a group of villages approached conveniently from Stratford. On his dubious word, Shakespeare was fond of "drinking hearty draughts of English Ale", a habit that stamped him as a sociable and human personage, like Prince Hal seen through the eyes of the 'Boar's Head' tapsters:

> They . . . tell me flatly . . . I am a Corinthian, a lad of mettle, a good boy,—by the Lord, so they call me,—and when I am king of England, I shall command all the good lads in Eastcheap. They call drinking deep dyeing scarlet, and when you breathe in your watering, they cry 'hem!' and bid you play it off.

Two sets of drinkers at Bidford, a village seven miles down the Avon from Stratford, boasted of their skill with the tankard, and challenged Shakespeare and his Stratford friends to a trial. Apparently only the Sippers were in business when Shakespeare's men arrived, the Topers having gone discreetly to Evesham fair. However, the rival drinkers engaged; and, said Jordan, "our Bard and his companions got so intollerable intoxicated that they were not able to contend any longer." After half a mile on the journey home to Stratford, they lay down at the side of the road; next morning, when his friends roused Shakespeare, urging him to return to Bidford and renew the fight, he refused, saying merely that he had drunk with

> Piping Pebworth, Dancing Marston,
> Haunted Hillborough, Hungry Grafton,
> Dodging Exhall, Papist Wixford,
> Beggarly Broom, and Drunken Bidford.

Jordan had a ready winner. The crab-tree became as profitable and as unfailing as the mulberry; it even appeared on maps of the district. The whole rhyme, as I have said, is as ludicrously persistent as "Punch, brothers, punch"; once you are caught, Marston will dance and Exhall dodge until the sun goes down. These villages, or hamlets, all matter for a hot summer's day, are from a world, pastoral, sylvan, or soothingly river-lulled, that Shakespeare would recognize. The last six are grouped to the west and south-west of Stratford; the first two stand apart. Knights Hospitallers once had a preceptory at Temple Grafton ('hungry' Grafton because of its poor soil, or for some lost topical reason), but it counts infinitely more that in this mild village, west of Shottery, William Shakespeare and Anne Hathaway could have been married. It was clear in November 1582 that Anne was pregnant. When William applied to the Bishop of Worcester for a special licence that would mean only one asking of the banns, the clerk made an error, recording a licence for William Shakespeare and "Annam Whateley de Temple Grafton". It was understandable: in the Consistory Court on the same day a man called William Whateley had been involved in a tithe suit, and the clerk's concentration must have wavered. William and Anne were soon married, and maybe—these qualifications are tiresome—at Temple Grafton: here John Jordan dropped a simple catch. A Puritan report of 1586 says that the Temple Grafton priest who seems to have been a bit of a Martext, was "unsound in religion, he can neither preach nor read well; his chiefest trade is to cure hawks that are hurt and diseased, for which purpose many do usually repair to him".*

Elsewhere the village of Exhall has a church unimproved by restoration ("The refurbishing contained elements of discomfiture," as an Ambassador observed in another context). 'Papist' Wixford, which was owned by Evesham Abbey, is popular with anglers on the river Arrow, and with willow-fanciers and sheep. In its church on an altar-tomb, is a superb early fifteenth-century brass of Thomas de Cruwe, an attorney, and his wife. Trussed in plate armour, he seems to have a worried lion as a footstool; a small dog crouches in the folds of his wife's drapery. A Tudor manor-house at Hillborough owns a fat circular dovecote for 900 pigeons. Long Marston prizes a story of Charles II, disguised after the battle of Worcester as Mistress Jane Lane's servant and being bullied by a cook, in front of ignorant Roundhead troopers, for his clumsiness with a meat-jack. Bidford, best of Jordan's children, never needed his rubbish about the Society of Sippers. A powerful stone building of many mutations was once an inn; but the joys of the winding village are its church beyond the lime avenue and the fifteenth-century, heavy-buttressed, monk-built bridge of eight arches across the Avon. Bidford was a Saxon settlement. Lorry-battered now, it can play no longer the unassuming prima donna of the Shakespeare villages. I have wondered why Jordan omitted Welford-on-Avon off the Bidford road: a fresh-faced, thatch-and-timber village with a tall maypole.

Bidford makes a delighted claim on me; it was there, during the early nineteen-hundreds, that Barry Jackson, who loved the rough-and-tumble pomping folk, saw in a tent performances of *Sweeney Todd,* ever durable; *The Battle of Evesham* ("as most localities can produce a battlefield, I have a notion that the same work served anywhere"); and *The Campden Wonder,* which had nothing to do with Masefield's play. This was playgoing we have lost: a walk across Bidford Bridge to a booth in a field, and a seat with white antimacassar; scenery of unchangeable 'wings', with a few drop-cloths; and a leading lady—who also officiated at the paybox—ready to explain the plot, as a countess to her

* Quoted by A. L. Rowse in *William Shakespeare* (1963)

maid. Barry Jackson used to recite an exposition along these lines:
"Well, Jinny, I am afeared that some ill may 'ave befallen 'im,
for by this time 'e should be returned 'ome. And yer know,
Jinny, I should be sorry if anything 'ad 'appened to 'im, for I
trusted 'im and there are wicked robbers who may 'ave *mis*laid
'im. And, yer know, Jinny, when a man 'as a bag of gold, it is a
great temptation to wicked men, and, yer know, Jinny, etc. etc.,"
as long as the countess could find words. Later, the big scene was
the trial; here, unfortunately, the delicate young hero declared
to a huge and solemn judge, with a wad of cotton-wool on his
head, "Though you bring in a verdict of hinnocent against me, I
shall go to my death guiltless." Nobody noticed, for the actor
spoke with immense conviction, and with that (as Jackson observed more than once) a captive theatre audience is unlikely to
question anything material.

Two other villages, each to the north-west of Stratford and in
the valley of the Alne, are Wootton Wawen and Aston Cantlow,
each of which should be announced by a major-domo at an
important reception. They are between Henley and Alcester.
Wootton Wawen ('Wawn'), among the trees, has a spectacular
church, high and isolated, with intricate crocketing on the tower
pinnacles. There is Saxon work; but, in general, it is like having
the Middle Ages at one's door. Carved oak abounds. An armoured man has lain on his tomb, in alabaster, since 1428.
Another man, probably a descendant from nearly eighty years
on, also in armour and with his wife and large family, is in brass
upon a grey marble slab. Aston Cantlow (the Cantelupes owned
the manor) is between Alcester and Bearley. Its boldly forthright
church of St. John Baptist was the parish church of Wilmcote,
the village where Mary Arden lived among the oak and painted-
cloths, the copper pans and brass candlesticks, the poultry and
bees. Probably Mary and John Shakespeare were married at
Aston Cantlow, but this, unluckily, was in 1557, and the local
registers begin in 1561—one of the near misses of history.

V

From Aston Cantlow we can come back into Wilmcote, home
of Mary Arden's girlhood. On my earliest visit to Stratford I
found a crevice by the gasworks in the Birmingham Road, and

walked up to Wilmcote by the canal—then like an untended ornamental water—solitary on the towing-path above the weed and sedges and suspicious swans; and past the bridges and the black lock gates. At Wilmcote, little more than three miles from Stratford, is the house from which Mary would have ridden along the lanes to her wedding; since 1930 it has been owned by the Trustees and Guardians of the Birthplace. Cottage is an understatement for this substantial timbered farmhouse, buff and white and russet behind its wall and its box hedges; yet that used to be the easy diminutive. Shakespeare had to be an affable drunkard; his mother had to live in a cottage. The word seemed to be humanizing. In these days it is just Mary Arden's House, gabled and dormered; the stone foundation for its walls brought from Wilmcote itself; its oak beams the stoutest of Arden timbers; old agricultural implements in farm buildings behind; and a large rectangular stone dovecote for more than 2,000 doves (possibly a recount in progress). It is a pleasant cote, if less pictorial than the bulge at Hillborough or, far away, that nonpareil by Dirleton Castle in East Lothian. I wonder where the fat ale-wife, Marian Hacket, lived in Christopher Sly's "Wincot", if that is indeed Wilmcote village. We can hope so, though some influential opinion favours a Wincot four miles south of Stratford, between Clifford Chambers and Quinton. If this is right there is no point in wondering how Marian would receive the news that fossil remains of the ichthyosaurus have been found in the blue lias at Wilmcote. It has always sounded to me like a promising tap-room subject for Sly, old John Naps of Greece, John Turph and Henry Pimpernell, over their hearty draughts of English ale.

We are almost back at Stratford and the scene of Mary Arden's wedded life—nobody less like a Marian Hacket. If I make a brief deviation, it is simply because Anne Treneer, gentlest of Cornish poets, lived during the 1930s at Bearley, coming over to it from Loxley, east of the Avon, which she also wrote about in *A Stranger in the Midlands*. Anne taught English at King Edward the Sixth's High School for Girls in Birmingham. She dearly loved the hamlet of Loxley, discovered on a quiet autumn day: "The only sounds were here a bird note, there a stick breaking under my feet, and a soft sound of wind in the thorns." But she stayed longer in Bearley where she knew Oliver Baker, the local historian; and it is for her, philosophically adaptable but with

Cornwall in her heart, her prose and her verse, that I think of this unpretentious village. Two notes from her Midland book are essential Anne: "With some of the Science people it was like reading Herrick to the Rollright Stones." "It is surprising how many poets since the fourteenth century have had to be mad. Fourteenth century poets were not mad."

Down towards Stratford, and a mile and a half to its north, is Clopton House, coolly peaceful and much rebuilt and enlarged since the town's early benefactor, Hugh of the bridge. Ambrose Rookwood, a wealthy young Catholic, leased the house in 1605 as part of the Gunpowder Plot's Midland plan. After the discovery "massing reliques" were seized at Clopton, among them "a vestmente of white stuff like Tishue with a pall and armelettes belonginge to the same and a piece of redd sarsenette to wrapp up the same", a black vestemente of damaske with a pall and armelettes", "ffive Latine bookes" and "a paire of prayinge beades of bone". From what John Coleman in 1900 insisted, craggily, upon calling Hopperton Hall, we go at last, over to the west of Stratford, to the village of Shottery. Though nobody could be churlish about its ancient black-and-white, Shottery (or "Shottri" as it is called in a letter of 1598) is a thoroughfare to a single house owned since 1892 by the Birthplace Trustees. Described still as a cottage—a name gummed too firmly for change—not many people expect a one-up, one-down affair, and in fact it has twelve rooms. A naturally beautiful building which has done its affectionate best to imitate the postcards, it stands below its orchard at the end of the village. When we have crossed Shottery brook, there it is, the long façade, timbered, tall-chimneyed, with its flaps of thatch, spreading east and west behind its flowers and clipped box, its roses and jasmine—the appropriate air is "Greensleeves". Resembling two houses, one higher than the other, it is the double messuage of Hewlands Farm, once on the edge of Arden, in "the purlieus of the forest", and, if we wish, the goal of Celia's direction to Oliver (he sought "a sheep-cote, fenced about with olive-trees"):

> West of this place, down in the neighbour bottom,
> The rank of osiers, by the murmuring stream,
> Left on your right hand, brings you to the place.

(A bottom is a valley with a stream in it.) Part of the house dates from the fifteenth century. There at Hewlands, the tale goes,

Anne Hathaway, nearly eight years before the birth at Stratford of her future husband, was born in August 1556. Rapture at Shottery is a stock response. Only one in 50,000 can have the professional detachment of a Pevsner: keeping to architecture, he was able to dispose of the place in four lines. This was before the damaging fire in late November 1969 which affected one-third of the building, though a rapid reconstruction was promised; it seemed likely that by the next spring we could appreciate again the amiable sedateness, the chimney-corner and open hearth, and murmur appropriately at the baking-oven with its wooden door, the four-poster Tudor bedstead of carved oak, the mattress of plaited rushes, and the intoning of "linsey-woolsey". Frequently I have tried to imagine William and Anne upon that immoderately comfortless, straight-backed, narrow settle by the parlour hearth. A similar struggle inspired another visitor:

William: Here on this seat we sat—
                All the guides have it pat—
                Nightly in loving chat,
                Woman to man.
Anne: Lover to lass, you mean?
William: Lord, what a sober scene;
                Would I had never been
                On lover's mission:
                Here, cold and stiff, we sit
                Waiting a chance to flit,
                Achingly tired of it
                And our tradition.

This, written, heretically, in what is now the Shakespeare Institute, I last quoted at Balatonfüred to a Hungarian connoisseur of the Shakespeare romance that is so anxiously grafted upon William's early life. Though I daresay he and Anne were happy—there is nothing to say they were not—I have never warmed to the wooing and presumably enforced marriage*. It is simpler to

---

* After her father's death in the autumn of 1581, Anne—but there is no evidence at all for this—could have stayed with relatives at Temple Grafton: hence the Worcester clerk's place-name. Some writers, including the best and most realistic of modern Shakespeareans, Ivor Brown, suggest that an Anne Whateley could have existed. If not a clerk's error, she might have been a probably younger rival of Anne Hathaway, beaten at the post. But all is agreeably conjectural, and here we must stick to the William and Anne we know.

applaud the cottage for its domestic graces. Dixon Scott, in 1911, put it in a few lines:

> Out of the least promising materials there has gradually flowered this perfect embodiment of a popular idea. Anne Hathaway may have lived somewhere else—but this is just the kind of cottage the world would like Anne Hathaway to dwell in; and so it has beautifully ripened in response to that desire. It is a pretty sentiment come true.

After responding to the sentiment, it is only right to walk back along the Stratford field-path to Evesham Place, and at length round to Avonbank gardens between church and theatre, and out beside the theatre itself and that other Shakespeare country:

> His legs bestrid the ocean: his rear'd arm
> Crested the world; his voice was propertied
> As all the tuned spheres. . . .
>   For his bounty,
> There was no winter in 't; an autumn 'twas
> That grew the more by reaping; his delights
> Were dolphin-like; they show'd his back above
> The element they liv'd in: in his livery
> Walk'd crowns and crownets; realms and islands were
> As plates dropp'd from his pocket.

That is more to the point, I think, than Anne Hathaway's settle.

TEN

RETURN TO THE CENTRE

I

Usually, within half an hour of any return to Stratford, I loiter towards the Gild Chapel: not to enter it, for this is disappointing, but to stand outside and regard its pale dignity, a sight Shakespeare, from New Place, would have seen daily during his retirement. The Gild Tower is like a cliff that fights an invisible tide. It is wave-washed, slowly wave-worn, as the years break over it, hollowing and channelling.

Looking back, we can map the Shakespeare country in its towers: the Gild, for one; St. Mary's above Warwick, where Richard Beauchamp's fame lives registered upon his brazen tomb; Guy's Tower, which chills as much as the naïveté of Sanderson Miller's Edgehill folly exasperates; the church of Brailes, majestic on its borderland; the sovereign pride of the Bell Tower of Evesham; the tower added to a farmhouse near Alcester because the Prince Regent thought the view from Ragley Hall would be "improved by a castle"; church upon church in Arden and Feldon, some with towers as dark and burly as a medieval keep; others, strong as a tower in hope, that seem always to have the sun upon their thrusting pinnacles.

A few we have missed: the very early tower of Ilmington in its church of Norman origin on the south-western edge of Warwickshire's rough diamond, where the Cotswolds loom; and, beyond the border, the splendour in the sky that is Chipping Campden tower as we come into a street like the background to a medieval illumination. Nothing disturbs either the town's grave harmony in stone—it is its own Campden Wonder—or the woolstaplers' fifteenth-century church: there, behind the marble tomb of Sir Baptist Hicks and his wife, are the figures of their daughter and her husband, Lord Edward Noel—later Viscount

Campden—swathed shiveringly in grave-clothes as they rise from their tomb at the general resurrection. The Grevels, wool-merchants, were Campden men, and William, whose grand bay-windowed house remains, is called on his memorial brass *"flos mercatorum Angliae"*. Here, by the Cotswold tower, are these ancestors-in-chief of Fulke Greville, who lies in St. Mary's at Warwick, and whom Walter Savage Landor (a Warwick man) brought back in the Imaginary Conversation with Sir Philip Sidney at Penshurst: "A solitude is the audience-chamber of God." Fulke Greville said once that, in poetry, he found his "creeping genius more fixed upon images of life than images of wit". A likeable figure*, but we look only for his forbears in Campden.

Over the Warwickshire border are the villages of Ilmington and, more northerly, Quinton. The first of these was the home of Sam Bennett, the fiddler, who died in 1951. He was the spirit of the folk-music and folk-dance of an older England that at one period so occupied Frank Benson. A more macabre memory haunts the calm of Lower Quinton—under Meon Hill—where a hedge-cutter was found dead in the early spring of 1945, his own hay-fork pinning him to the ground: the crime remains un-solved, but there has been talk of ritual murder and of witchcraft, shadows that have hung about this borderland. Shakespeareans, avoiding the Weird Sisters, prefer to think of it as the edge of "Cotsall", where Master Page's fallow greyhound was outrun; where Shallow and Silence, country justices, live in their deep autumn; where Falstaff comes recruiting; where Davy urges Shallow to countenance William Visor of Woncot against Clement Perkes o'th' hill; where all gather in the orchard after supper, with their wine and a dish of leather-coats; and Pistol, riding in from London, discharges his news of "lucky joys and golden times". In these miraculous Cotswold scenes Falstaff must yield to Shallow. On the modern stage there has been no Shallow like Laurence Olivier's in 1945, prating of the mad days he knew

---

* Celia Fiennes saw Fulke Greville's tomb when she visited Warwick: "One thing is noted of him there that he thought it his greatest character to be esteem'd a great Friend and Companion of Sir Philip Sidney's which is but of poor availe to him now dead, if he was not the friend of the great Jehovah, but such is the folly and vanity of the most of the world to be in esteeme with the wise and great men of this world."

when all the world was young, and Jack Falstaff, as "a crack not thus high" and page to Thomas Mowbray, Duke of Norfolk, broke Skogan's head at the court gate. No actor has given so clear a gleam from Shallow's inch of taper, and none has had beside him Miles Malleson's Silence, jetting into song.

Historians, always looking for sources, have supposed that the names of Visor and Perkes take us deeply into Gloucestershire: they presume so on the ground that in 1612 a Vizard was living at Dursley, of which Woodmancote (or Woncote) is a suburb, and that in the sixteenth century a family named Purchase or Perkis lived quite close, at Stinchcombe Hill. But Dover Wilson, in his edition of *Henry IV: Part II*, prefers Malone's earlier identification of Woncot with Wilmcote ("equally, if not more likely", Wilson says); there is also a 'Hill' in Stratford. Oxfordians have had mild fun with Visor:

> The dialogue . . . appears to resolve itself into an appeal by Davy, on behalf of one William who, with a concealed identity, and dwelling at Woncot (Wilmcote), is an arrant knave, and the subject of complaints; but who, being debarred, by reason of his knavery, from speaking effectively for himself, must remain 'silent.' Shallow, himself standing for justice, and associated, in this play, with another Justice, significantly named '*Silence*,' advises Davy to 'look about,' and assures him that his protégé shall have no wrong.' Very mysterious, is it not?*

II

I cannot recall an important Shallow among the Royal Shakespeare pictures at Stratford-upon-Avon. No more planetary cast has been assembled than these actors and actresses from three centuries, all playing with relish to the gallery. There used to be another tower above them, the sugar-stick of the old Memorial Theatre. When, on that disastrous March day in 1926, it flared in a pillar of fire seen far over the Avon valley, a quick shift of wind saved the library and picture gallery, connected with the

---

* Percy Allen's *The Life Story of Edward de Vere as "William Shakespeare,"* 1932. The author was the most courteous and civilised of men, and nobody could put forward the Oxford conjectures with so much disarming gentleness.

theatre by a bridge. We have photographs of Bridges-Adams and some of his company—the season's young Puck (Joan Duan) is beside him—standing, a week or so later, upon the bare rim of the theatre and peering into its blackened round. The rest of the Memorial block behind them stood in its Tudor Revival manner as it had through more than forty years, and as it does now, content, externally, to rest like good cousin Capulet, an onlooker at the ball. Not so within, where the gallery is a fanfare of the theatre theatrical: Harlow's Trial of Queen Katharine, with the Kemble family, and Sarah Siddons traffic-directing in the middle; rugged Samuel Phelps as the Hamlet he could not bring to Stratford (there is no Fechter in the collection); Ada Rehan's Shrew in her rose-coloured flaunt; Priscilla Horton as the Ariel she acted in Macready's textually-restored revival of 1838 (only *John Bull* complained of Ariel's wires and cog-wheel); Frank Benson in repose, the portrait in which Hugh Rivière caught his eager idealism; Fabia Drake, painted by Walter Sickert, washing her hands in that nerve-straining Komisarjevsky revival; Anthony Quayle's Falstaff, here an angry eruption of a man, with claw-like hands; Ruskin Spear's livid impression of Laurence Olivier as Macbeth on the edge of doom; Edith Evans as Volumnia in a portrait, Robert Buhler's, that is tragedy in repose; Peggy Ashcroft's Imogen, in soft yellow and brown, reminding us of a production, set between huge oaks cast from Stratford trees, that was like meeting a fairy-tale on its own terms; and, a loved theatre picture of its day, Laura Knight's impression, from the wings, of Paul Scofield as the young Clown of *The Winter's Tale*: a shining simpleton, from the sheep-cotes of Arden, whom Autolycus tricks, and who later becomes "a gentleman born . . . any time these four hours". The gallery contains so much: preposterous, as in Garrick's soaring to Parnassus by angelic glider; exciting, as in Fuseli's Weird Sisters, each an ancient damnation; odd, as in a portrait of Michael Redgrave's Hamlet, a tortured soul without Redgrave's inherent nobility; unexpected, as in a scene from *Titus Andronicus* by Samuel Woodforde, brother of the Norfolk diarist; expert in pen-and-ink line, as in those *Punch* drawings by the master of his art, Ronald Searle.

Everyone seems to be here: Barry Sullivan and Helen Faucit; Geneviève Ward; and, when I was last in the gallery, Cecil Beaton's 'Actor' (David Warner), of a school of young Shakespeareans admired especially by its own generation*. Elders are less sure. Still, there was a similar pattern with the younger Bensonians. The picture gallery's Bensonian windows must move all with a sense of theatre history: Frank Benson himself appears in one as Richard II. His son, Eric, killed during the First World War, is in another window as Saint George.

Helen Faucit has both a portrait and the marble relief her husband, Sir Theodore Martin, gave to the gallery after an officious Marie Corelli had stopped it from going to Holy Trinity Church. That year Sir Theodore presented to the church its marble pulpit; Lord Ronald Sutherland Gower worried in his journal (18th October 1900) about the dedication of "what I regret to think a most incongruous piece of church furniture". Holy Trinity (with the later spire?) is in the background of one of the gallery's curiosities, a picture by Henry Wallis of "A Sculptor's Workshop at Stratford-upon-Avon, 1617". Work has just finished on the new and gleaming Bust, and some Victorian-looking children play about the door, or peer round it, finger in mouth.

The gallery has its Shakespeares, including the 'Flower', thought once to be the source of the Droeshout engraving. Angelica Kauffman's romanticism—her portrait might be of any Elizabethan aristocrat—offers the kind of hopeful make-up many actors must have tried. In London the most debated stage Shakespeare—always excepting Shaw's, with notebook and National Theatre propaganda—was Clemence Dane's *Will Shakespeare* (1923). Though it failed to keep the West End stage, admirers have been constant. True, the plot, an 'invention', can test us. Christopher Marlowe is at a Deptford inn with Mary Fitton, the Dark Lady, who, in male disguise, has borrowed the name of Francis Archer. Shakespeare swoops in upon them, over the window-sill. Marlowe (says the direction) darts at Shakespeare "and is thrown off. He staggers against the table, knocking over the candle. As he strikes the second time his arm is knocked up, striking his own forehead. He falls across the bed. There is an

---

* Major acting is analysed today less closely than it used to be; Stratford-upon-Avon is fortunate in having an uncommon critic and analyst in Gareth Lloyd Evans, whose essay on the speech and technique of Gielgud, Olivier, Scofield and Ian Richardson in *Shakespeare Survey 21* (1968) is a model of what this kind of writing should be and seldom is.

instant's pause, then Shakespeare rushes to him, slipping an arm under his shoulder". A few seconds later, Marlowe is dead. The play with its ghosts and its calling voices, its players, who, from the Shottery window, are "a black, fantastic frieze upon the yellow winter sky", its hot, bold verse and its packed prose, does reach us from the late Tudor world; some of it is lustreless now, but it can be valued for Elizabeth's sake, a lonely queen married to her land and knowing what she has lost. In one passage Henslowe tries to describe Shakespeare to her:

> Madam, if ever you saw him, you would not forget—
> A small, a proud head like an Arab Christ,
> And noble, madman's fingers, never still—
> The face still though, mouth hid, the nostril wide,
> And eyes like voices calling, shrill and sad. . . .

Certainly a challenge to the Shakespeare, Philip Merivale. Before the production the players went down to Stratford-upon-Avon to be photographed. They acted away dutifully in the Birthplace, upon Clopton Bridge and on the settle at Shottery; but the visit was not the luck-bringer it should have been. Hard though it is to restore Shakespeare in his own period, H. F. Rubinstein continues to do it in a rare sequence of short plays that add up to a dramatic biography. The most alarming effort in memory was by an American writer of proved intelligence; for no apparent cause his Shakespeare was a glum tease dumped in the middle of a farcical Stratford, with a good deal of clodhopping and one clod called Dim Wit Ben. I prefer Scott's game in *Kenilworth*. Shakespeare, who in 1575 would have been 11, speaks (as a seasoned dramatist) to the Earl of Leicester in an anteroom of the Court. "Ha," says the Earl, "Will Shakespeare—wild Will!— thou hast given my nephew, Philip Sidney, love-powder—he cannot sleep without thy Venus and Adonis under his pillow. We will have thee hanged for the veriest wizard in Europe. Hark thee, mad wag, I have not forgotten the matter of the patent, and of the bears." And, after this surge of tushery, Scott continues: "The *player* bowed, and the Earl nodded and passed on— so that age would have told the tale—in ours, perhaps, we might say the immortal had done homage to the mortal."

This is not the last of Shakespeare. The keeper of the royal bears complains to the Queen that "amidst the extreme delight

Evesham: the Bell Tower, from the Avon

with which men haunt the playhouses, and in especial their eager desire for seeing the exhibitions of one Will Shakespeare, the manly amusement of bear-baiting is falling into comparative neglect". The Earl of Sussex, asked for his opinion, says that, even if a bear-baiting man himself, he wishes Will Shakespeare no harm: "A stout man at quarter-staff and single falchion, though, as I am told, a halting fellow; and he stood, they say, a tough fight with the rangers of old Sir Thomas Lucy of Charlecot, when he broke his deer-park and kissed his keeper's daughter."* Here the Queen interposes to say that the business was heard in council, there was no kissing in it, and Shakespeare had put his denial on record. The debate proceeds until Leicester, tactfully, recalls a speech in which "Shakespeare hath touched some incidents of your Majesty's happy government. There are some lines, for example—I would my nephew, Philip Sidney, were here, they are scarce ever out of his mouth—they are spoken in a mad tale of fairies, love-charms, and I wot not what besides; but beautiful they are, however short they may and must fall of the subject to which they bear a bold relation." Whereupon Walter Raleigh repeats, "with accent and manner which even added to their especial delicacy of tact and beauty of description, the celebrated vision of Oberon", which ends:

> And the imperial votaress passed on
> In maiden meditation fancy free.

We do not wonder that Elizabeth, delighted with matter and manner, kept time to every cadence, murmured the last lines as if hardly conscious she was overheard, and then "dropped into the Thames the supplication of the keeper of the royal bears to find more favourable acceptance at Sheerness, or wherever the tide might waft it".

Having got so far, Scott allows Wayland Smith, in the garden of Cumnor Place, to call on " 'Will Shakespeare, my friend in need! I will give them a taste of Autolycus.' He then sang, with a good voice, and becoming audacity, the popular playhouse ditty, 'Lawn as white as driven snow, Cyprus black as e'er was

---

* *Shallow:* Knight, you have beaten my men, killed my deer, and broke open my lodge.
 Falstaff: But not kiss'd your keeper's daughter?
The Merry Wives of Windsor, I.i.

14

The Hathaway dwelling ("Anne Hathaway's Cottage"), Shottery, before the fire

crow'." Audacious, certainly. The year was 1575. *The Winter's Tale* appeared in 1611.

Seven years after writing *Kenilworth,* Scott returned to Warwickshire with his daughter Anne, and had a glimpse of the castle in the rain: "The last time I was here, in 1815, these trophies of time were quite neglected. Now . . . they are preserved and protected. So much for the novels." They lunched at Warwick Castle, "still the noblest sight in England", visited in St. Mary's the monuments of the Nevilles and Beauchamps, "names which make the heart thrill", and ended the day at Stratford. Next morning, 8th April: "We visited the tomb of the mighty wizard. It is in the bad taste of James the First's reign; but what magic does the locality possess! There are stately monuments of forgotten families, but when you have seen Shakespeare's, what care we for the rest. All around is Shakespeare's exclusive property." They lunched at Charlecote, "the abode of ease and opulence"—more talk, inevitably, about the deer-stealing—and, at length, taking their road by Edgehill, "looked over the splendid richness of the fine prospect from a sort of gazeebo or modern antique tower, the place of a Mr. Miller". *Gazeebo:* for the Radway Tower that is the perfect word.

III

Over the square tower of the Royal Shakespeare Theatre flies the ceremonial flag, Shakespeare's amber and black. When I was there on an early summer afternoon, it was half-masted in Sir Lewis Casson's memory; but as a rule it is at the peak: the dramatist at home. In effect, his flag is Stratford's. Though it is a market-town; though in its day it has declared such other industries as brewing—the brewery* was opened in 1832—canning and light engineering, Shakespeare must govern; it is a long time since somebody's unkind summary, "ale, agriculture, antiques, and aluminium".

That strange period as an inland port is now little more than a folk-memory. It began when William Sandys, between 1636 and 1639, opened up the river from the Avon's junction with the Severn at Tewkesbury. After the Commonwealth Andrew Yarranton was the leading member of a syndicate that carried out

---

* The brewery was closed in March 1969.

work between Evesham bridge and Stratford. One of Yarranton's plans*, never fulfilled, but described in his book, called amply *England's Improvement by Sea and Land,* was for the creation of a pair of towns: New Brunswick, actually begun, at Bridge Town on the east bank from Stratford, would be a centre for granaries, linen, manufacture and brewing; and New Haarlem at Milcote, a granary and linen-weaving centre where the Avon meets the Stour. For a long time a barge trade flourished on the Avon: Defoe, in the early eighteenth century, said that the navigation enabled Bristol "to drive a very great trade for sugar, oil, wine, tobacco, iron, lead, and in a word, all hcavy goods, which arc carried by water almost as far as Warwick". In return, cargoes of corn, and especially of cheese, were taken down to Bristol by water, on the river that uncoiled itself like a gentle, lazy grass-snake between the drowsy meadows and beside the mills. Half a century later, Jago could write briskly, if hyperbolically:

> On Avon's bank, for inland commerce form'd,
> Stratford her spacious magazines unfolds,
> And hails the freighted barge from Western shores,
> Rich with the tribute of a thousand climes;
> By her, in husky grain or native arts,
> Wise industry's blest produce, well repaid.

At the beginning of the nineteenth century Wheler could still speak of "the appearance of a small sea-port town"; and in George IV's reign, with river, canal and tramway at its command, Stratford seemed to be a capital of industrial transport. Then the economic story grew complex. With the arrival of what Edward Fordham Flower called "these railway years"—in Stratford now a wistful phrase—traffic on the river waned quickly; it was forgotten too soon that during the 1830s 10,000 tons of coal were shipped yearly from Stratford down towards Evesham.

The canal from King's Norton to Stratford had been opened in 1816; and, at Queen Victoria's accession, the Bancroft must have looked startlingly industrial, with its two canal basins (one today an ornamental lake) and the flicker of tramway lines round to its wharves. The industrial years live in the commemorative wagon at the top of the Bancroft Gardens, and in the name of the Tramway Bridge. Though the horse-drawn tramway never got

---

* See Charles Hadfield and John Norris's admirable *Waterways to Stratford* (1962).

farther than Shipston and Moreton-in-Marsh—the two tracks diverged near Ilmington—there had been great ideas for it: again the railway killed them. The tramway, used during roughly the hours of daylight, carried more coal than anything; but holders of a prescribed licence could take passengers. *London Society,* a magazine published in 1864 soon after the Shakespeare Tercentenary, contained an article by a visitor who had travelled some years before—there is no date—up from Moreton-in-Marsh to Stratford:

> The journey was performed outside an ordinary railway carriage which had been adapted to the necessities of horse traction. Attached to the carriage in front was a platform, on which the sagacious horse (the only locomotive used on the Stratford and Moreton railway) mounted when it had drawn our carriage to the top of an incline, thus escaping being tripped up as we descended at a rattling good speed. The inspectors of the Board of Trade not having found this tramway, the occurrence or non-occurrence of accidents was left chiefly to the goodness of Providence. When we came to the foot of the incline, the guard applied his brake as tightly as he could; we all, to the best of our individual capacities, held on to our seats, and, if we had taken firm hold, we thus managed to avoid being pitched off head foremost. When the carriage came to a stand, the horse dismounted, and drew us along as before. . . .
>
> At what pace we went, or whether that pace would be most appropriately calculated in miles to the hour or hours to the mile, we hardly know. It was all so very pleasant and seemed to last so long—we are of opinion that, except on the breakneck inclines, no great despatch was either sought after or obtained, and it would generally have been quite safe to get down and walk a little.

When this article was written, the tramway, though "meriting the attention of all archaeologists", existed only as "a superseded idea".

IV

Today, the canal, by no means a superseded idea, has been affectionately restored; like the river it has to be one of Stratford's fringe benefits. Stratford is Shakespeare's town: birthplace, school, grave, theatre, Centre, Institute. True, something may happen now and again without Shakespeare in it. There may be a concert at Charlecote, Purcell and Vivaldi in the programme. The Royal

Ballet or the D'Oyly Carte will come to the theatre during the off-season (which means simply that no Shakespeare is on). Early in October there is the Statute Fair, the 600-year-old Mop, with street stalls and side-shows and the odd theatrical feeling inseparable from this kind of event; it would hardly surprise us to meet Bernard Miles's old countryman as he leans across his wheel and erupts the laugh that is like tearing out an oak-tree by its roots. The calendar has its other domestic events; but unless we row up river, through what Henry James called a "liquid slowness", into one of the remoter reaches, silver and green, we are never very far from Shakespeare. Even then we shall probably be remembering actors who took a boat upstream—the Bensonians were as much on the river as off it—or we shall be trying to repeat what Shakespeare said about his Avon, though he put it into the mouth of a Renaissance Italian in Verona. Riverscapes round Stratford have that youthful lyric quality. Somebody—he never elaborated it—held once that most of the Shakespeare country could be considered in terms of the plays, and I daresay that is so. Warwick speaks for the chronicles; Snitterfield has a note of astringency, *All's Well* perhaps; the country near Henley is, with reason, Arden; it can be wistfully autumnal beneath Edgehill, say the last act of *The Winter's Tale*; the upland by the Rollright has a touch of *Lear;* Charlecote is the patrician *Much Ado*; Shipston is a single line, "It seems to me that yet we sleep, we dream."

Analogy can be pressed too far. Still, Stratford-upon-Avon, as it should be, is a blend of many plays and moods, from the elegiac "Fear no more" in Holy Trinity, to the "sweaty haste" by the omnibus station, which by day can be a dire place for the imperfectly social. Late at night, and especially on a winter night, even that ugliness is transformed, after the last buses have gone out to Evesham or Warwick, or the furthest steep of India, and Stratford is as quiet as Hermione on her pedestal. Often I think of the town as we do of those speeches in *Troilus and Cressida,* which can seem harsh when dissected, phrase by phrase, with such words as "monstruosity", "constringed", "deceptious", "propugnation", "oppugnancy". When spoken, they can fuse into eloquence. We forget the stones on the plain; ahead is Troy.

We are back where we began, in midmost England, in Shakespeare's town which is the heart of heart, and his theatre which is at the core of his own world. Round it is the land of grave content; tree and tower and "open pastures where you scarcely tell white daisies from white dew". It is a land between the towns of Arden and the scarp of Edgehill; a land that, from the steep descent of Sunrising, looks momentarily like a Ruisdael panorama; a land between the distant trumpets of Kenilworth and the lost battle of Evesham; a land between the assured massiveness of Stoneleigh, the Ionic portico of Ragley, the two-storeyed oriel of Coughton gatehouse, the cottage at Shottery; a land between the Grevels at Campden and Greville at Warwick; between Brailes and Bidford; between the Rollright and the palimpsest of Alcester: a land of chestnut, ash, and elm, oak and beech, willow and poplar, the musk-rose, the bold oxlip and the crown-imperial; sheep-cropped turf on Cotswold, red soil in Arden, grass silky-tough by the river. It is a country "branchy between towers", an England within England. Through it there curves and loops the middle-English river to which Landor turned:

> I bend
> My knees upon thy bank, and call thy name,
> And hear, or think I hear, thy voice reply.

All of us hear the voice, though it must speak as differently to every listener as Shakespeare's country to every wanderer; as differently as Shakespeare himself, who lies in the chancel outside which the Avon flows, must speak to every man and woman, now and in the years to be.

SOME BOOKS

Oliver Baker, *In Shakespeare's Warwickshire*, Simpkin Marshall (1937)

F. R. Banks, *Warwickshire*, Penguin Books (1960)

John H. Bird, *Sam Bennett, The Ilmington Fiddler*, John H. Bird (Stratford-upon-Avon 1952)

Ivor Brown, *Shakespeare*, Collins (1949)

——*The Women in Shakespeare's Life*, Bodley Head (1968)

Alan Burgess, *Warwickshire*, Robert Hale (1950)

Oscar James Campbell and Edward Quinn (Editors), *The Reader's Encyclopaedia of Shakespeare*, Thomas Y. Crowell Company (New York, 1966)

M. C. Day and J. C. Trewin, *The Shakespeare Memorial Theatre*, Dent (1932)

Christian Deelman, *The Great Shakespeare Jubilee*, Michael Joseph (1964)

John Drinkwater, *John Hampden's England*, Thornton Butterworth (1933)

Ruth Ellis, *The Shakespeare Memorial Theatre*, Winchester Publications (1948)

Alice Fairfax-Lucy, *Charlecote and the Lucys*, Oxford University Press (1958)

Celia Fiennes, *The Journeys of Celia Fiennes* (edited by Christopher Morris), The Cresset Press (1947)

W. Field, *A Historical and Descriptive Account of the Town and Castle of Warwick and of the Neighbouring Spa of Leamington* (Warwick, 1815)

H. E. Forrest, *The Old Houses of Stratford-upon-Avon*, Methuen (1925)

Levi Fox, *Stratford-upon-Avon*, The Garland Press (Bristol, 1949)

——*Official Guide to Stratford-upon-Avon*, Stratford (current)

——(Editor) *Correspondence of the Reverend Joseph Greene, Parson, Schoolmaster, and Antiquary (1712–1790)*, Her Majesty's Stationery Office (London, 1965)

Edgar I. Fripp, *Shakespeare's Stratford*, Oxford University Press (1928)

——*Shakespeare's Haunts Near Stratford*, Oxford University Press (1929)

(Lord) Ronald Sutherland Gower, *Old Diaries, 1881–1901*, John Murray (1902)

Charles Hadfield and John Norris, *Waterways to Stratford*, David and Charles (Newton Abbot) and Phoenix House (London, 1962)

C. V. Hancock, *East and West of Severn*, Faber (1956)

W. H. Hutton, *Highways and Byways in Shakespeare's Country*, Macmillan (1926 edition)

(Sir) Barry Jackson, *Barnstorming Days* in *Studies in English Theatre History*, edited by M. St Clare Byrne, Society for Theatre Research (London, 1952)

Gerald Jaggard, *Stratford Mosaic*, Christopher Johnson (1960)

F. E. Halliday, *The Life of Shakespeare*, Duckworth (1961)

——*A Shakespeare Companion 1564–1964*, Penguin Books (1964)

Robert E. Hunter, *Shakespeare and Stratford-upon-Avon . . . Together with a Full Record of the Tercentenary Celebration*, London (Whittaker) and Stratford-upon-Avon (Edward Adams) (1864)

Richard Jago, *Edge-Hill, or The Rural Prospect Delineated and Moralised*, Dodsley (London, 1767)

M. R. James, *Abbeys*, Great Western Railway (1926)

T. C. Kemp and J. C. Trewin, *The Stratford Festival*, Cornish (Birmingham, 1953)

Louis Marder, *His Exits and His Entrances*, John Murray (1963)

Arthur Mee (revised by E. T. Long), *Warwickshire*, Hodder and Stoughton (1966)

(Sir) Charles Oman, *Castles*, Great Western Railway (1926)

(Sir) Nikolaus Pevsner and Alexandra Wedgwood, *Warwickshire* (The Buildings of England), Penguin Books (1966)

Peter Quennell, *Shakespeare, The Poet and His Background*, Weidenfeld and Nicolson (1963)

A. L. Rowse, *William Shakespeare*, Macmillan (1963)

John Russell, *Shakespeare's Country*, Batsford (1942)

J. Dixon Scott, *Stratford-upon-Avon, with Leamington and Warwick*, Black (1923)

William Stuart Scott, *Marie Corelli: The Story of a Friendship*, Hutchinson (1955)

Rosemary Anne Sisson, *The Young Shakespeare*, Max Parrish (1959)

T. J. B. Spencer (Editor), *Shakespeare: A Celebration*, Penguin Books (1964)

Caroline Spurgeon, *Shakespeare's Imagery*, Cambridge University Press (1935)

(Sir) John Squire (J. C. Squire), *Water-Music*, Heinemann (1939)

Anne Treneer, *A Stranger in the Midlands*, Jonathan Cape (1952)

J. C. Trewin, *The Night Has Been Unruly*, Robert Hale (1956)

——*Benson and the Bensonians*, Barrie and Rockliff (1960)

——*Shakespeare on the English State: 1900–1964*, Barrie and Rockliff (1964)

(Dame) C. V. Wedgwood, *The King's War: 1641–1647*, Collins (1958)

R. B. Wheler, *History and Antiquities of Stratford-upon-Avon*, Stratford (1805)

Francis Brett Young, *The Island*, Heinemann (1944)

ALSO BY J. C. TREWIN

THEATRE HISTORY AND CRITICISM
The English Theatre
We'll Hear a Play
The Theatre Since 1900
A Play Tonight
The Stratford Festival (with T. C. Kemp)
Dramatists of Today
Mr Macready: A Nineteenth-Century Tragedian and his Theatre
The Night Has Been Unruly
Benson and the Bensonians
The Gay Twenties (with Raymond Mander and Joe Mitchenson)
The Turbulent Thirties (with Mander and Mitchenson)
The Birmingham Repertory Theatre: 1913–1963
Shakespeare on the English Stage: 1900–1964
The Journal of William Charles Macready (Editor)
The Drama Bedside Book (with H. F. Rubinstein)
The Pomping Folk: In the Nineteenth-Century Theatre
Robert Donat: A Biography

AUTOBIOGRAPHY
Up From The Lizard
Down to the Lion

THEATRE MONOGRAPHS
Edith Evans; Sybil Thorndike; Paul Scofield; Alec Clunes; John Neville

PLAYS
A Sword for a Prince: Plays for a Young Company
Plays of the Year (36 vols. Editor)

HISTORY
Printer to the House (with E. M. King)

ALSO EDITED
The West Country Book
A Year in the Country (Beach Thomas)
Theatre Programme
Sir Walter Scott: A Prose Anthology
Lamb's Tales (completed. Nonesuch edition)